The ONLINE PROFESSOR'S PRACTICAL GUIDE TO Starting an Internet Business

Danielle Babb, Ph.D.

Foreword by Dr. John Rutledge
Leading Economist and Presidential Advisor

EP
Entrepreneur. Press

Editorial Director: Jere L. Calmes
Cover Design: Desktop Miracles
Production and Composition: Eliot House Productions

Library of Congress Cataloging-in-Publication Data

Babb, Danielle.

The online professor's practical guide to starting an internet business/by Danielle Babb.

p. cm.

ISBN-10: 1-59918-345-5 (alk. paper)

ISBN-13: 978-1-59918-345-9 (alk. paper)

1. New business enterprises. 2. Electronic commerce. 3. Internet. I. Title.

HD62.5.B335 2009

658.8'72—dc22 2009002687

Printed in Canada

13 12 11 10 09 10 9 8 7 6 5 4 3 2 1

Dedication

This book is dedicated to those serving in our armed forces—present, past, and future. Without you, we would not enjoy the freedoms or the security we do. Your service and dedication to this country are tremendous and often underrecognized. It is my hope that those of you returning from overseas will be able to use this book to start your own business—you inspired this book. Thank you for all you do for our nation, for keeping us free, and for putting yourself in harm's way on behalf of the rest of our country. Starting businesses would be the last things on our minds were it not for your sacrifice and the sacrifice of your families. It is my greatest hope that you can take the knowledge contained within these pages and apply it in your pursuit to create a financially free life for both you and your loved ones. May God bless you and enrich your lives in all ways possible.

TABLE OF CONTENTS

PART III

A ROAD MAP TO SUCCESS

FOREWORD

Reader, you are in for a treat. But I advise you to clear your calendar for the rest of the day. Once you start reading this book you are not going to be able to stop until you see the back cover. Dani Babb is an extraordinary person. In 30 years and 15 million miles of traveling the world of business and finance I have never met anyone who comes close to Dani in creative energy, in integrity, in depth of experience building online businesses, or in

the pure, raw passion to help people take charge of their lives by starting and growing companies of their own. Anyone who gets to the end of this book without their juices flowing should check their pulse—they don't need a book; they need a doctor.

I should disclose from the start that I am an entrepreneur. I have started, grown, harvested, and on occasion buried, dozens of companies in my life in every sector of the economy. I decided long ago when I saw the look on my dad's face when he came home with a pink slip from the factory where he worked that I would never work for anyone else. I don't want anyone telling me when to show up, how hard to work, what to wear, or when to go home. I don't want anyone deciding to lay me off or downsize my job. And I want to keep the value of the work I do for my family. Even more, I want to have the freedom to decide what to build and which dreams to chase. Running your own business, on your own terms, is the only way to do that.

Lots of people today have reached the same conclusion. They have learned from the recent economic crisis they can't count on big institutions to give them a stable place to earn a living, take care of their families, and save enough to retire. They want to be their own boss.

Today, these future entrepreneur have two secret weapons, the internet and Dani Babb.

The internet allows people to live, work, and build businesses anywhere they want. Dani Babb will show them how to do it. Not the theory of how to build an online business—how to actually make it happen. She has successfully started dozens of online businesses of her own. And she is a gifted educator who knows how to explain to you the things you will have to do to succeed.

I believe this book is important. The world needs all the entrepreneurs it can get to provide jobs and paychecks. And it needs the optimism of an army of entrepreneurs to make people believe in the future. But an army of entrepreneurs means build one business at a time. Dani can help you be one of them. Now start reading.

—Dr. John Rutledge, Chairman of Rutledge Capital,
and the author of *Lessons from a Road Warrior*

ACKNOWLEDGMENTS

I'd like to acknowledge Matt Spica for his satisfaction with our unconventional way of doing things in the face of critique, and for the pride he takes in my work. Thanks, as always, to Bob Diforio, literary agent—he is incredible, dedicated, and kicks butt for his clients. Thanks, Bob, for helping to make writing such a joy! To Jere Calmes, Jillian McTigue, and Leanne Harvey for believing in this book and for their insight and advice. To

John Rutledge for providing inspirational insight into what it takes to be successful–and for being a sounding board for the relentless thoughts that race through my linear head. To Alex Lazo for his unique perspective and fresh insight, all based on friendship, and to Arlene Blix for always being there no matter how many days pass or how much time elapses. To Shane Hill for his amazing committment, trust, and friendship throughout the past two years. In loving memory of my grandfather William Keller, who proudly served his nation, and my husband's grandmother Pat, who proudly served her family and her community. You are all an inspiration and continue to be in life and in the afterlife.

WHY AN ONLINE BUSINESS, AND WHY NOW?

The demand for online businesses has never been greater! More than 70 percent of individuals are worried about the economy, and that number has steadily grown throughout 2008 (Fox News, 2008). The economy and oil prices topped the list of issues for the 2008 presidential election. Families feel as though they aren't saving as much as they need to (CNN, 2007). College education costs are rising (U.S. Department of Education,

2007); the dollar is falling (Fox News, 2008). Working parents are finding themselves in the midst of a difficult decision–should one of them stay at home with the children, or should both of them work and have a nanny raise the kids (MSNBC, 2007). What if one or both of them could work at home?

In this book you will find everything you need to begin an online business–from starting the business to creating a website that is Web 2.0 based, to advertising and promoting your work to overseas sales, and growing and expanding your business. Dr. Danielle (Dani) Babb, your Online Professor, walks you through all aspects of creating a successful online business through real life, practical advice, surveys from the trenches, and skilled expert insight.

You may find yourself a retiring boomer not quite ready to leave the work force and having many unmet career challenges and passions. You may find yourself a military spouse wanting something to do regardless of how many times in two years you move. You may be entering or leaving college and wanting your own career online instead of jumping into corporate America. You may be a corporate-America soldier sick of trying to climb the ladder to make someone else richer, or you may just have an idea you are passionate about and want to see where it can get you.

In addition to the insights in this book, we have a supporting website that lets you hold virtual office hours with Your Online Professor! Visit YourOnlineProfessor.com for tools, tips, forums, questions and answers, and more. Let it be your virtual partner in the world of online business–from startup to high growth.

Regardless of your reason, if you want to run and own your own online business, then you are reading the right book! Through experience and surveys, insights and information, we will tap into your passion, find creative ways to profit in an online business, and explore ideas, opportunities, and experiences!

DIFFICULT CHOICES

Many people struggle with this decision: Should I go to work for someone else, or should I work for myself and take big risks? If they are self-employed, they feel they will not have access to health care or promotional opportunities or 401(k)s, but resources are out there that many of us who have already taken the big step towards financial freedom say are even better. These facts, coupled with numerous bits of information about the online world, make the decision not so difficult to make anymore. The answer is becoming increasingly clear, yet people are having a hard time navigating the system that may very well be the answer to their prayers.

VIABILITY RESOLVED

Online businesses—from bookkeeping to selling on eBay to teaching online—are all viable alternatives that allow an individual flexibility, freedom from corporate America, and the ability to pursue his own dreams *and* keep the fruits of his labor for himself. Many people dream of being the founder of an eBay or an Amazon—a multibillionaire without a financial care in the world. It seems that all the good ideas are taken, then another one pops up. Why can't that next great idea be yours?

Whether you want to make supplemental income, leave corporate America behind for good, pay for your kids' college education, or fund your retirement, now is the time to start your own online business, and in this book I will walk you step by step through how it's done, what to do, how to find your passion and turn it into profits, how to promote and advertise in a socially driven online world, and how to make a living for yourself online! The possibilities are literally endless and the income potential has no boundaries, beyond those that you set for yourself.

The Online Professor's Practical Guide to Starting an Internet Business is a fundamental tool for individuals looking to survive economic turbulence, increase earning potential for single-income households, and create work-life balance. Everyone from college students needing to earn some side money to stay-at-home parents trying to make tough decisions about who will raise their children (and how) to corporate employees who are sick of the rat race or employees who want to supplement their income by living out their dreams can find enjoyment and money in an online business. Even young adults still in high school can take the knowledge within this book and apply it to their lives, creating an early start on a life of financial freedom, even to the point of setting themselves up for an early retirement!

Do you feel stuck between earning more money at work and showing the boss that you're committed and spending time with your kids before they grow up and leave to pursue their own careers and lives? Are you tired of paying astronomical gas prices and clothing costs just to get by? Are you sick of an automated system paging you at 2 A.M., expecting you to answer and be available at all hours of the day, tied to your PDA like a leash? You are not alone.

FACTS ABOUT ONLINE WORK

I repeat: you aren't alone in your quest for flexibility in the workplace or desire to have work-family balance. Here are some interesting facts:

The number of parents who stayed at home with their children in the United States in 2006 was an estimated 5.5 million—yes, million—5.4 million moms and 98,000 dads, according to a report released in 2006 by the U.S. Census Bureau. This report, by the way, was the first ever analysis of stay-at-home parents. These 5.5 million people could be working from home, not sacrificing time with their kids, and making extra money on the side in an online business.

Another fact: According to the United States Department of Labor, Bureau of Labor Statistics, of the 136,602,000 workers over the age of 16 in the United States in 2004, a whopping 15.1 percent of them, or 20,673,000 people, worked at home for a company. This was five years ago! While new numbers aren't being released yet, given greater access to the internet, the current numbers are bound to be higher. If you are one of these individuals, would you rather keep the money you make and work so hard for, or would you rather give it over to corporate greed?

Did you know that the number of online students in the United States is nearly 4 million, and that more than 80 percent of students take at least one online course in their program? This was during the fall 2006 term—a nearly 10 percent increase over the number reported the previous year; and these are the most recent numbers available. The 9.7 percent growth rate for online enrollments far exceeds the 1.5 percent growth of the overall higher education student population. What does this mean? This is yet another untapped sector of incredible job growth for online workers. Nearly 20 percent of all U.S.

higher education students were taking at least one online course in the fall of 2006. Why is this relevant? Online teachers are conducting these courses—accounting for hundreds of thousands of workers.

Incredibly, the number of people in the United States working from their homes in the fields of bookkeeping, accounting, and auditing exceeds 2.1 million, according to the U.S. Department of Labor, Bureau of Labor Statistics (2007). This shows the huge potential—and viability—of online work in a job as simple as bookkeeping. It also shows how acceptable it is to work from home, and just how much companies trust online workers. Everywhere we look we see a trend towards online everything. We are ordering groceries and office supplies, custom dog food containers and magazine subscriptions online. The market is endless with the internet—the entire world can be your customer base!

One of the factors fueling this incredible growth is the number of people who have internet access, particularly broadband access, from their homes. As of March 18, 2004, Nielsen/NetRatings—the global standard for internet audience measurement and analysis—reports that nearly 75 percent, or 204.3 million Americans, had access to the internet from home. More current reports, though not as thoroughly vetted, show that number to be closer to 80 percent, with 90 percent having some sort of access. Not only that, but developing nations are adding broadband access at record rates, making the economy truly global. The internet is so broad reaching now that it is no longer an obstacle to working at home. More nations are coming online with broadband access at home, which means if you are running a business you had better be prepared to take it global, and quick!

To add to these astounding figures, the number of people who telecommute is more than 10.6 million—11 percent of the workforce—according to the 2005-2006 National Technology Readiness Survey. This has undoubtedly increased, but again we must wait for more current numbers. People want to work online and many want to work from home. Online businesses save companies money, save people personal time, and have high retention rates for employees and contractors. Flexibility is a key to this excitement and buzz.

If you have been interested in creating your own online business, you've probably been reluctant at some point because of the number of internet- and infomercial-based scams designed to take your $99 and provide you with little to no substance—and none of the step-by-step guidance that new entrepreneurs need. In this book I demystify online businesses, and there's an entire chapter devoted to avoiding those online scams that sucker you in for $99 while you're watching late-night insomniac TV.

Perhaps you already have an online business and want to expand it, or perhaps you have a bricks-and-mortar store and recognize that an online business would be a great supplement to your fine establishment. Whatever the reason, this book is for you. I will give you real content, real stories from the trenches, and realistic advice.

GENERATIONAL GAPS

Interestingly, the Gen Yers have a strong desire to work in groups and find that online businesses and working in partnerships allows them this flexibility. Gen Xers have a strong desire to run with their small business but still want to maintain a corporate feel—and overall structure, in general. Web-based businesses can provide all of this and more. Baby boomers need to create extra income to retire in comfort. With boomers living longer than any previous generation, many have second or even third careers instead of sitting on the rocker. They want to start their retirement with a new career and a second chance at doing what they love.

With energy costs rising, commutes getting longer, and people feeling more stress than ever, web-based businesses are a fabulous alternative that can provide the kind of life for yourself that you want, *not just one that you feel you have no choice but to select.*

KNOWING YOU HAVE WHAT IT TAKES

So how do you know if you have what it takes to be an online entrepreneur? Here is a quick checklist:

- ❑ Do you have high-speed internet access at home or at your new office and experience with browsing and searching the web? And do you keep finding interesting websites that are doing what you feel you could do more efficiently . . . if only you knew how to conduct business online?

- ❑ Are you bored with your job, do you have some funds, and are you looking for a fruitful way to invest online and spend your time productively?
- ❑ Are you just graduating college or high school, but a corporate job doesn't feel right for you?
- ❑ Does your current job require extensive driving? Are you not prepared to spend an exorbitant amount of money on gas because you want to hold down more than one job, all in opposite directions, just to make ends meet? Are you tired of feeling like you're going nowhere in corporate America?
- ❑ Are you tired of trying to move those Mary Kay or Avon products? Have you had enough of multilevel marketing schemes and stuffing envelopes? Are psychic hotlines and telemarketing jobs simply not working out in your favor, and do you want something that is real—something that you control?
- ❑ Are your children growing up fast? Did you perhaps quit your job to take care of them, or did you begin your adult life as a stay-at-home parent? Are you wondering what you'll do with kids leaving for college or entering school, and do you want to contribute financially to their futures?
- ❑ Do you have an idea or multiple ideas that you are passionate about? Whether or not you have limited startup funds, do you know if you got the opportunity that you could realize those ideas until they reached fruition and beyond?
- ❑ Do you think, "I would love to do XYZ, but I just don't know how to start. I wonder if others have done the same thing? Are they making money at it? Why does it seem I'm the only one working so hard?"

Chances are, one of these descriptions fits you. Even if none of these descriptions fits you exactly, don't fear. Visit YourOnlineProfessor.com and take quizzes to see what types of careers work best for you! Anyone can be a successful online entrepreneur and business owner.

■ ■ ■

Still want to know you can DO THIS? Keep reading

HOW TO USE THE UNIQUENESS OF THIS BOOK

This book is different than others you can find on the bookstore shelves. As a professor, I know that interactivity with your "professor" is essential. I also know that connecting you with other brilliant entrepreneurs as well as linking you with those of us who have made mistakes and learned from them is essential. I know that not feeling alone in the trials and tribulations of online businesses and entrepreneurship is a critical success factor. I also know that resources and support on the internet that are reliable and consistent are few and far between.

Your *Online Professor's Guide* is interactive. Every chapter has resources online at YourOnlineProfessor.com website. Do you want to know what business might best suit you? Take the quiz. Do you want to network with others using Amazon's affiliate program? Go to the forums. Do you want to chat directly with me? That is what I am here for—feel free to contact me. Everything is brought together on YourOnlineProfessor.com for all of you who have decided to take the first step and get this book. As you work through the book, take advantage of the online forums and prompts that appear at the end of each chapter.

Another great benefit of the web? It is always current. Think of the website as being a giant, up-to-date, easy-to-use, and functional (avatars included) version of an appendix. The site contains many experts who share their ideas with you as well as tools, tools, tools, which are always up to date. You get the real deal. You also get forums, blogs, networking, affiliate links, sites, many ideas for your own business, links to people with great knowledge, quizzes to test yourself, personality tests, Q&A from me on major topics—and it's all relevant, all fresh, all current.

Take a look at the site, and make it an integral part of your day to network with others, learn from them, share stories, get tools, and find opportunities. It is all about us and our ability to help one another. Go make it happen.

PART

I

DREAMS TO DOLLARS

CHAPTER

1

WHAT KIND OF ONLINE BUSINESS IS FOR ME?

The Brainstorming Challenge

The key to a successful online business is turning your passions into opportunities and your opportunities into profits. If you don't love what you do, you will quickly grow tired of it, procrastinate, or see it through to nothing! Remember, anything is possible, every single passion you have can be turned into profit—and even better, residual income, too.

Let's imagine something, although it may sound all too familiar as a day-to-day occurrence. You are sitting in traffic, it's 6 P.M., and you're no closer to home than you were 15 minutes ago. Your family is calling, warning of the impending coolness of your home-cooked meal and the kids' rapidly approaching bedtimes. Your boss is e-mailing you on your BlackBerry about a 7:30 meeting that you feel no more like going to than you did the business dinner last night that kept you from the nightly bedtime-story routine. Gas is more expensive; the $100 per week you spend going to your routine job is getting on your nerves—and emptying your wallet. You and your wife have contemplated her return to work, but then the kids would be taken care of by a nanny, so you're willing to sacrifice. The thought of a part-time job enters your mind, but who has time for that when you can't find time to take a walk around the block after the dinners you miss now? You've had some ideas; there are things you love doing. But you don't see a way out of the rat race. You are tired, you're fed up with corporate America, and you dream of doing your own thing.

Or perhaps this is you: You have been a stay-at-home mother for years; you left a job to raise your children. Your kids, a toddler and an elementary-school student, need you there consistently. You want your children raised with your values and your ethics, not a caretaker's judgments and morals. You have contemplated part-time work, but after you pay for day care, you'll barely make enough to offset your new costs, if you make any profit at all. You're going a bit stir-crazy at home, too; you contemplate perhaps going back to

The Decision to Go Online

What do others say about the decision to go online? In a survey of hundreds of online business owners that I conducted for this book, an overwhelming 82 percent said it was not a difficult decision to go online, but 17 percent said it was too difficult and decided not to. Of these, some indicated in the survey that being a single parent had influenced their decision, while others hesitated to give up the perks of the day job, such as the social benefits and health care.

school or starting a business, but that takes time and money—two things you are limited on these days. You have passions and hobbies, but having them and having *time* for them are two different things.

Every single one of your passions, regardless of your life and personal situation, can be turned into dollars. The passions you have, whether unique or common, are profit centers if you tap into them. Turning passions into opportunities, and not being afraid to take a step forward, is paramount to success.

Everyone who reads this book may have an entirely different goal, from supplementary income to a full-time, full-scale entrepreneurial business with hundreds or thousands of employees—running your own online empire! Right now the ideas seem frightening and overwhelming, but the internet has made doing business online easy and very inexpensive to start! We have to begin by brainstorming, and through knowing that you can achieve what you are setting out to do. We have incredible opportunities in today's market to create new, unique businesses and earn money using the web. That is what this book is all about: learning what the opportunities are and how to capitalize on them.

There are many opportunities available to help online entrepreneurs explore ideas they are passionate about and to accomplish success. But first you need to understand how the web works, how to navigate the web, and how to fine-tune yourself to online cultures, from which you will eventually extract your target audiences, in order to fully grasp how you can make the web work for you. We will talk about all of these things, from finding your passions to advertising online! One of the great benefits of conducting business online is the flexibility of having a virtual business place that is accessible from anywhere in the world where online access is available.

Of course, one major benefit to doing business online is that you do not have to leave the comfort of your home in order to go to work (even if you have to ship items to customers)—all operations can be managed right there in your living room if that is your choice. Another attractive benefit is that it offers significant savings; there is no dress code so there is no maintaining a suitable wardrobe; there is no renting office space; and a definite plus given the current energy crisis, you will also save on gas. Let's not forget either: You will save time. The time that you would have taken simply to get dressed, and to drive to work and back, you can use to work at your online business out of the comfort of your own home, even if only for an hour or two.

But it gets better than this: some online businesses run themselves and the most you really have to do is manage the money that is being deposited into your bank account at the end of the business day. The possibilities for conducting business online are endless. And yes, instead of working for the web, you can actually make the web work for you.

DETERMINING IF ONLINE WORK IS RIGHT FOR YOU

First, you need to determine what your goals are. Is income supplementation enough? Do you want to start slowly, adding to your income, but eventually, if everything works out, take it full time? Do you want to begin full time from day one? Each of these scenarios is possible on the internet. You don't need to be a web specialist to accomplish all of the options I discuss, but you should be familiar with the basic operations and principles of the web, visit online sites and see what you like and don't like, what draws you into a site and what keeps you from ever visiting again.

You need to decide, too, if the timing is right. Do you already work 18 hours a day at your day job? Perhaps you will need to cut this back before beginning your online business. Take an accurate assessment of what you have time to do, and find an hour or two per day to invest in your new business. The level of flexibility you currently have, the amount of time you have to dedicate (and are willing to dedicate), and how much risk you are comfortable taking are all aspects that you need to take into account as you move toward making a decision.

TURNING YOUR PASSIONS INTO DOLLARS: THE BRAINSTORM

The key to any successful online business is turning your passions into dollars. To do this you must analyze the opportunities surrounding your passions, and this requires brainstorming. This sounds like work, but once you get into something you love, it is a blast! It might sound complicated, but with some alone time and a pen or whiteboard and dry-erase marker, you will find it engaging, and perhaps for the first time, you'll feel like "Wow, I can do this." Yes, you can do this. Ask yourself these questions to get started:

1. When I go through my day, what do I dread? (Stay away from these items as business ideas!)
2. When I go through my day, what do I enjoy? (Write these items down!)
3. What would I do if I had two hours to spare? How would I spend it?
4. What limitations do I have right now on my time?
5. What do I do to unwind?
6. What do people come to me for to get my expertise on? Is it because I enjoy it so much that I know a lot about it? Or did some experience (like a health condition) force me to learn about it?

Now let's take each question individually and I'll provide an example:

1. When I go through my day, what do I dread?

If you hate grocery shopping and picking up the dry cleaning, you won't want a business as a personal assistant. If you hate managing money, you won't want to be a bookkeeper. Knowing what you don't like is perhaps more important than knowing what you do like! It is easy to come up with a list of things you would rather not do unless forced to, so this is where most people start. Once you have detailed everything you dislike, coming up with a list of what you do enjoy is relatively simple.

2. When I go through my day, what do I enjoy?

Do you love the one hour you get at the coffee shop catching up with friends? Do you love taking the dogs or kids for a walk? Do you love to shop? Why not set up interest groups for busy professionals? Be a dog walker, or take children to the park? Schedule online and advertise on the web! Consider becoming a professional eBayer, selling something you love, like designer clothes, thimbles, you name it—there's profit in them all!

3. What would I do if I had two hours to spare? How would I spend it?

Identifying what you'd do if you had the opportunity is great insight. Would you hit the gym? Why not create personal training plans for people online and monitor their progress through your site, offering advice and encouragement? Would you spend it at the mall? Create a store that rents out high-end clothing! Taking an avocation (hobby) and turning it into a vocation creates a business that you not only will enjoy, but also will inherently be dedicated to.

4. What limitations do I have right now on my time?

Knowing what you don't like is important, but so is realizing your true limitations, in regard to both time and resources. If your children are very young and you really need to work inside the home, you won't want to be a personal assistant that has to run errands or a shopper for your eBay store. If you know you need to get out of the house because you haven't had a reason to do your hair or shave that beard in a week, perhaps it's time to find a job that gets you out of the house!

You must analyze other limitations as well. Are you a person with a disability that you need to work around? Let's work that into the plan. Do you have time constraints and other duties you must perform, or perhaps even a full-time day job that you need to work around (or through) until your business takes off? We'll work that into the business plan, too.

5. What do I do to unwind?

If you enjoy something enough, you might even find it relaxing–and it will hardly feel like work. Better yet, you might be able to help others enjoy it, too. Are you a connoisseur of fine bath salts, which help you relax at night? What about a store that sells the salts and provides expertise and forums for people to share their ideas and favorites?

6. What do people come to me for to get my expertise on? Is it because I enjoy it so much that I know a lot about it? Or did some experience, like a health condition, force me to learn about it?

This is a great springboard into something new! Do people come to you for medical advice about fibromyalgia? Why not start a paid help site with the latest in research and forums for people to share information? Do they come to you for your knowledge about computers and the latest gadgets? Why not offer a review site that just happens to sell products too and allows others to share their experiences?

Here are some other ways to equate your passions and interests with work:

- I like shopping = consider opening an eBay store.
- I like buying and selling on eBay but I don't want to go shopping = become an eBay trading assistant.
- I like designing and being creative/drawing = opportunities exist in web development for small businesses and individual proprietors.
- I like teaching others = maybe a job teaching online is for you.
- I enjoy handling finances = lots of opportunities exist for bookkeepers for small-business owners.
- I enjoy handling business and multitasking = consider becoming a personal assistant for a busy professional.
- I am a real estate agent in my day job and need some work for nighttime = consider being a property manager or landlord.

Following are a couple of examples of how to turn a passion into an online business.

Haven for Music Lovers

Let's say you love music and your hobby is not only listening to music but also networking with other musicians who play, collect, and listen to music. You can venture into the music culture online and learn how other music lovers interact there and how they find what they are looking for through their network of resources online. You source out your target audience and what they need or make demands for. You then take your ideas to the web and conceptualize how you want to reach the specific audience that is looking for the exact music products and services that you, of course, have to offer. Then you start to move through your off-line and online networks

> No matter what you decide and find your passion to be, a job will suit you. Later in this book I'll provide you with numerous examples and references to find a job that matches your goals, personality, and interests. Sometimes, though, the best ideas come from the heart, so you need to do whatever gets you thinking clearly and start analyzing your own interests. Take a long walk or a hot bath, and begin thinking, "If I could do something all day for fun, what would it be?" We can start there with your business!

of music-loving friends and promote your site accordingly, and infect them with your passion for music and all that is of music and because of music. Ultimately you merge networks together using your website as the glue and you find that you have gathered a rather diverse group of people with one main common interest. You offer them your products and services and they buy them. You meet and exceed their expectations and they spread the word and you become a valuable resource online for music products and services, if not for networking, and then you start selling advertising space to sponsors who are looking to your network for their target audience. At that point you sell targeted advertising because you can justify the cost respectively—costs can vary drastically though.

You can probably begin to see this unfolding. It is exciting and it is lucrative.

Primed for Online Shopping

If your passion has anything to do with selling items that you happen to know a lot about, you are in luck because the internet is primed and ready for online shopping! There are more internet-savvy people browsing and searching the web than ever, perhaps even looking for the same products and services that you want to sell. The online business market is now bigger and growing by the hour. The demand from other nations is huge as well. Web 2.0 applications like social networking communities (MySpace), social blogging (Blogger), social broadcasting (YouTube), social messaging (Twitter), social bookmarking, social commerce, and social multimedia sharing have given many people online comfort zones where they feel safe participating in a virtual environment. It is almost second nature for people to assume a lifestyle online—even an identity online. It is where they socialize, collaborate, participate, communicate, and most importantly conduct business. The online community is already primed for online shopping and is always open to new ideas and opportunities when it comes to products and services. So buyers are already out there looking for you. All you have to do beyond positioning yourself to be found by them, or finding them before they find you, is learn how to conceptualize your ideas so that when you implement them online, you will be able to meet and exceed your customers' expectations in terms of the products and services they are looking for.

When you have captured the attention of your target audience, suggestive-selling and cross-selling techniques are very easy to employ. And the remarkable thing is that consumers want to be guided and seek education on your products and services, so it is only fitting that you give them what they ultimately want. There is so much to do online that buyers really won't mind saving time and getting everything they need from one comfortable online virtual business. Web design and programming has evolved to the point that it is not uncommon for website owners to deliver to their viewing audiences a rich, interactive, and dynamic experience that resembles the same type of experience of brick-and-mortar stores so that ultimately they can connect with their audiences and encourage impulse buying. The online community is ready, and though there is a multitude of options out there, they still yearn for others and are still looking for more. This is where you and your ideas come in!

EARNING RESIDUAL INCOME

Who doesn't want residual income? Residual or passive income is income that comes in even if you aren't actively working for it or are working very little for it.

Online businesses are a great way to create residual income. Memberships, for instance, to existing data are sources of residual income. Check out ezinearticles.com/?Residual-Income--What-It-Is-and-Why-You-Need-It&id=45885 for a great article on residual income. Basically defined, you create a single sale and receive regular payments. This may be monthly, annually, or some other interval, but no further selling activity is generally required. Sometimes in the online world you may need to create a newsletter or something that will keep

Endless Ways to Make Money Online

There are literally endless ways to make big money online. The key is to find something you will want to wake up doing every day, without that, you may as well stay in your corporate job. Finding your passion is key to success.

people from leaving your site or cancelling their membership, but residual income is the great major income generator online.

Following are some great residual income opportunities according to the article; I've adapted them for online businesses.

- Telephone calls and line rental (advertise your services online)
- Mobile phone supply, line rental, and calls
- Web hosting supply (offer space online)
- Autoresponder supply (monthly rental)
- Any software that is supplied on a rental basis
- Property rental (yes, you can do this online)

What are some other ways? Run affiliate websites and earn commission dollars. You could have a whole host of sites that do nothing but generate residual income.

- Online game rentals, game auctions, game classifieds (big money in the game industry)
- Online calling card sales with PIN delivery by e-mail or by SMS (short message service)
- Selling ring tones and music by SMS
- Reseller, web hosting
- Resell website templates
- Online classified ads (which would include property rentals and so on)
- Online customer service (through live chat applications so you can literally handle customer service issues for online businesses that don't have the time or resources)
- Online waiter

With genuine residual income, the automated reorder process means that you don't have to spend time servicing and supporting your existing customers. You can focus your energies on finding new customers and/or recruiting new distributors or affiliates, thereby continually growing your business at the fastest possible rate. You may want to stay actively involved and may not want a passive or residual income business, but it is certainly something to consider. Repeat agreements or subscriptions keep you from having to consistently sell, too, which is something many of us just don't enjoy doing.

Doing business online is most likely the ideal way to earn not just residual income but a decent living. It is therefore important that you determine exactly what your goals are for exploring online business options. If your intention is to make residual income and you can allocate only a set number of hours for working online, then you may need to choose an approach that will accommodate those particular constraints. If, on the other hand, you intend to make your online business a full-time career and there are no significant time constraints, then the opportunities are almost limitless. In each case, the main objectives should be to target the right audience for the business ideas that you propose to implement and to make sure you can deliver the products and services that your target audience is actually seeking online.

TO WORK OR NOT TO WORK: ADDITIONAL IDEAS TO KEEP IN MIND

Too often people get carried away with the notion that just any business idea will work online. Perhaps this misconception brews because it really is not necessary to create a business plan in order to start a business online nor to formally register the business with a governmental agency (given that the internet is not regulated). Some people enter the online business world without a business strategy when they actually should have one. (Although if you do choose to use one, I highly recommend visiting the site myownbusiness.org/plans/doc/all.doc for great resources.)

Any business idea, if strategically implemented, can be successful online. Business online is still business. This does not change. It is still the same people, looking for the same products and services, though in a different location (that is, of course, more accessible to them) and using a slightly modified process for conducting business. All this has to be taken into consideration when exploring business ventures online. Still you cannot beat the fact that you, as the online entrepreneur, simply will get more reach online than you would have off-line. If you want, your target audience can be anywhere in the whole wide world, once they have access to the web.

So what are some good online residual income opportunities to explore? We will go through them in depth throughout this book, but here is a sample to whet your appetite. It depends on how hard you are prepared to work online, of course, how many hours you want to put in, and what your ultimate goals are, but the sky is the limit here. If you want to do minimal work online with businesses that typically run themselves and just watch the money roll in, then the following may tickle your fancy, though they each require at least maintaining your own website:

- Online multilevel marketing
- Online affiliate marketing networks
- Advertising networks
- Anti-spam services
- Autoreminder services
- File delivery services
- File download services

We are going to get into all of these later (particularly in Chapters 8 and 15), but let's touch on a few valid ideas to get you thinking. If you are prepared to get a little more involved you may be interested in exploring some of the following types of online ventures where you are being funded by another entity to promote its products and services for it:

- Reseller website hosting
- Reseller domain names
- Reseller website design
- Reseller online bookkeeping
- Affiliate bookstore (like Amazon and Barnes and Noble, for example)
- Reseller software store
- Reading e-mails
- Mailing newsletters

Of course there are lots and lots of options we will discuss beyond residual income ideas, from bookkeeping to eBay assisting. But now that you've whetted your appetite and you feel thoroughly ready to work the web until it works for you, you may want to explore the following:

- Online auctions
- Online tag words

- Online classifieds
- Online portals
- Online memberships
- Online product stores (tangible and intangible)
- Online service centers

SELLING AD SPACE

If you want to become rich on the internet you will do more than work hard; you will work smart and sell advertising space. While some may disagree, it is a valid and very lucrative business model no matter what your passions create! It's just not an easy market to tap into in that grand capacity, unless your website has a lot of traffic or you are significantly connected or socially networked online. So you will want to read through this entire book on how to use social networking and web 2.0 sites to build your brand.

Your new site may acquire a lot of traffic only if you are yourself heavily investing in both advertising and marketing coupled with a lot of networking. So it's something of a double-edged sword. In order to make money advertising, you first have to achieve some level of success online in terms of popularity, if not financially. But it could actually become the epitome of doing business online. It's that jackpot at the casino that you kept playing and playing and playing for until you finally won it. Still, you can benefit from advertising without hitting the jackpot. It is always a good idea to include advertising methods in your website projects as preparation for that potential jackpot.

WORKING FOR SOMEONE ELSE BUT REAPING THE REWARDS

Many people struggle with the decision of embarking on the journey to work for themselves over working for someone else. One important reality that should not be overlooked in this decision is the fact that even working for yourself, you are working for someone else: your customer or your client.

There are many great differences when you contrast the two paths, but the one vital constant is that you are serving someone no matter what. Within corporate America, you are serving your direct supervisor, and everyone else up the intercompany ladder of success, in addition to other outside forces like the company's shareholders and customer base. When you go to work for yourself, you are serving your customers or clients, your staff, your vendors, your suppliers, and your investors if you have them.

Now granted, going to work for yourself does open up a world of opportunities and freedoms that would otherwise be completely out of reach if you stayed within your cubicle, including the choice of whom to work with or for—meaning you now have the opportunity to decide whom you hire, with whom you do business, whom your target market is or will become, which vendors you contract with, and so on. In the end, though, you are working with and for all of these groups. The more clients you attract, the more vendors you form relationships with, the more advertising media outlets you contract with, the more people you are working with and for.

My final thought on this topic is this: All the people with whom you come into contact, whether they are your first customer, your fifth investor, a potential supplier, or a vendor, share one thing in common. They are vital to your success and the success of your newly launched idea and business. Never forget this, as doing so could burn a vitally important bridge that led to great success in the first place. And remember—there is *no* such thing as a "small" business. Every business can become whatever you want.

TREAT EVERYONE WELL!

You never know where business will lead you or where you will stumble across a potential investor or a potential client. In many ways you have to make your own luck, which includes taking every opportunity to get to know everyone! You never know who your next client or investor will be or where your next strategic partnership will come from.

If you are looking for or need investors (although not everyone does or will), realize that investors are just like you and me. They do the same things that we do—grocery shop, visit the local gym, and so on. If you happen to strike up a conversation with someone, and the topic is your business or idea for a business, let your passion come through. You never know if the person you are looking at is the angel investor you have been hoping for or the person who will put you in contact with an angel investor (someone who provides capital for a startup). And yes—there are stil dollars out there.

YourOnlineProfessor.com

One of the most difficult things about starting a business is figuring out what is best for you. YourOnlineProfessor.com, your online professor's virtual office, has many forums and tools for you to explore and begin figuring out what excites you and where your passions are. Network with others and share your dreams.

Residual income is everyone's dream right? Many have been there done that. Network with them today! Visit YourOnlineProfessor.com for help in learning what residual income means, and how to get it right.

Do you want to sell ad space but aren't sure what to do to make it work for you? Visit YourOnlineProfessor.com's virtual site to get help and many links and ideas on where to go to get ads that make you money.

As you can see, there is a wealth of information and help waiting for you at YourOnlineProfessor.com.

CHAPTER

2

AN ONLINE BUSINESS

The Answer to Life Balance?

Everyone decides to go into business for himself for a different reason. For some, it is work-life balance and the profound opportunity to be in charge of your own destiny! This is an essential part of owning a business, particularly one online. Online businesses afford a work-life balance that is unprecedented in history.

If you have a family, you may be all too familiar with the feeling of being torn between work and family. Many parents make

difficult decisions to increase their family's income or to stay at home with the children, and there is often the concern that increasing your dedication to one equates to a lack of dedication to the other. This doesn't need to be a concern anymore. More than 75 percent of the individuals I have personally helped transition to a full-time online job have families and most cited this as a reason to move to such a job—staying home with the kids and earning a living while doing it. Talk about having your cake and eating it, too!

Whether you are single and want a social life or married with five children, you most likely want and need to find work-life balance. That can be difficult in the constantly connected age of the internet and BlackBerries, iPhones, and Palm Treos. You are probably tired of others telling you what to do to be the best, and you know your business. You may be just out of college and the thought of going to work for "the man" is more daunting than getting that A in chemistry. That's OK, you don't need to.

As of yet, corporate America has been slow to respond to individuals who need and crave work-life balance in their careers, yet individuals are empowered to take this need into their own hands and make it happen for themselves by having their own online business. Remember that all of your experiences and work in your corporate job have led you to the expertise and understanding that you have today—all of which can be applied to your work online.

Besides the mounting frustration with gas prices and long commutes, a feeling of wasted time and lost money, perhaps you feel like you have little or no time for yourself. You may find yourself unable or unwilling to juggle work-life balance anymore and you may feel torn going to work each day, which feels like prioritizing work over family or having a life.

As a result of these frustrations, more and more workers are choosing online businesses to earn their primary or supplementary sources of income, or even looking at online businesses for residual income, something we will discuss in more detail later.

Many of my colleagues have done as I have: left corporate America behind for good and pursued their own businesses.

After battling severe primary insomnia for years and having relentless bosses that really liked 7 A.M. meetings (which often left me with less than an hour of sleep per night), and sick of the lack of stability and being held back by someone else's opinion of my capabilities, I decided I'd take action, becoming a full-time entrepreneur and doing it in the new era—on the internet. This decision was difficult because I felt corporate America provided stability and health care, among other things. Two consecutive layoffs in the world of information technology quickly falsified belief number one, and finding that health care wasn't all that expensive to buy on my own quickly did the same for myth number two. I had somes experience as an entrepreneur running computer businesses in the '90s.

Like many others, I started by adding part-time work to my day job, working nights online from home. Eventually my part-time income closely matched my day-job income, and I left the corporate world behind for good. Within two years I had quadrupled the salary I was getting as an information technology director for a Fortune 500 company. I have coached hundreds of people who have successfully done the same; many were motivated by not wanting to feel forced to choose between their work life and their children or spouse.

You have many options here—an online business can be run from literally anywhere. In my survey, I asked what drove individuals to make the decision

Reasons to Choose an Online Business

Survey respondents could choose multiple reasons for their decision to create an online business. The answers may surprise you. More than 84 percent cited flexible hours, an overwhelming number. Higher earning potential ranked second at 38 percent; the cost of commuting, 30 percent; the time of commuting, 25 percent; wanting to be at home with younger children, 21 percent; and wanting to be at home with older children, 5 percent.

to take their business online instead of using more traditional business means. Some of the comments received included: Needing day care while working, wanting flexible hours, time to see the kids/grandkids, and being your own boss. Additional comments were the desire to slow down a bit, spend more time doing something new and in a more relaxed environment, or taking time out to handle a personal issue that came up or required time to grieve. Freedom and autonomy was another listed response, as was staying home with pets.

YourOnlineProfessor.com

Life balance—ahh isn't it so sweet? Get some balance on your thinking and where to go from here at YourOnlineProfessor.com. Dr. Dani and other entrepreneurs are there to answer your questions and help you make the right decision for you.

CHAPTER

3

GETTING STARTED

How Do I Get Started?

We have discussed at some length how to figure out which types of jobs are right for you, and then how to evaluate them (and potential clients) based on what is most important to you as an individual and what you need and want from your online career. Once you figure out what you are interested in, it is time to get started!

When you start your own online business (or any business for that matter), it is natural to want to take on any work you can get, but it is important to go through the necessary legal steps to make your business legitimate before you begin. You should also be thinking about how you want to build the brand and image you want, which means turning down work on occasion—or even often.

This might seem counterintuitive when you are also simultaneously trying to build your capital and wealth.

LIBRARY OF CONGRESS RESOURCES FOR ONLINE BUSINESSES

Let me introduce you right away to some excellent resources that are run by the government. Take a look at the Library of Congress site for doing business on the internet (loc.gov/rr/business/ecommerce/). This site contains everything from how to write newsletters to how to measure site traffic. You should keep it handy throughout the development phase.

DECIDING WHAT TO SELL

First you need to determine what kind of business you want to establish on the web. What kind of business is worth doing in terms of feasibility? There are many brilliant ways to conduct business online. Selling products is one of them. Selling memberships and other services is another. But choosing the best possible mix of products and services must be carefully mapped out.

Let's look at selling products. The first things you have to think of are from whom you are going to get your inventory; where you are going to store it; if you are going to keep an inventory; and how you are going to deliver your products to your customers in a timely fashion so that they reach your customers in the condition they expect the products to be in—whether new or used. If you do not want to invest in an inventory of products, you may want to explore establishing relationships with vendors who may drop-ship to your customers with your shipping label on each package; it would then be your responsibility to make your vendor invisible to your clients. What does this mean? That if your vendor messes up, you mess up. There's no passing the buck here. You then have to suffer whatever it costs to make things right between you and your customer or lose the customer.

The alternative would be to keep an inventory, whether small or large, and take on the responsibilities of shipping and customer service, which is traditionally how it is done. You should explore drop-shipping methods if you have a good relationship with the product vendor and, better yet, if this vendor is local to you so if any problems arise you can go and see the vendor, personally. If your customers are not satisfied with your products, their storefront experience, or your customer service, they will simply do what is second nature to them and move on to your competitor; with more than 18 million businesses online, and counting, your competitors are not just many, but also just a few mouse clicks away.

Services worth selling include time, memberships, digital downloads, and advertising. If you sell physical products like clothes or cars, try to not have inventory if at all possible; this keeps storage costs low and keeps you from paying shipping twice (once from the manufacturer and once to your client). If your product is software, consider online downloads only or requiring the customer to pay more for a CD. Drop-ship as much as possible.

If you are considering a service business like online bookkeeping or being a personal assistant or web designer, you will need a service-based model. You obviously cannot maintain someone's car from California if the car is in New York. But you can be a virtual personal assistant or web developer quite easily remotely. For the most streamlined business, try to avoid those that require you to meet people face-to-face often; conduct virtual meetings instead.

What Should You Sell or Market?

About now, you've got to decide upon exactly what you plan to sell and from there work your way into the most appropriate electronic commerce options. Let your business drive your e-commerce, not the other way around.

If you are selling digital products like art or music, it is very easy to sell online. Many people create web templates or logos and sell them online. Even if you have an information-only nonpaid site, you can earn residual income by affiliating yourself with companies that pay royalties and affiliate money or by getting paid for ad click-throughs.

You can also pull the content into the application that you are using and set up as many niche sites as possible, considering yourself a one-person online mall. Look at buildanichestore.com: you can build your own eBay-driven niche site for only $97. Now look at NicheSiteScript.com; this costs $199, but you can make multiple niche sites specific to search engines that are of course, connected to your affiliate memberships with Amazon (10 percent commission) or Revver (20 percent commission) coupled with revenue from pay-per-click programs like Google AdSense, Yahoo! Publisher Network, AdBrite. Sound exciting? It is! Create as many AdSense search portal niche sites as you want for just $69.95. See Chapter 8 for more about advertising, and Chapter 13 for a myriad of ideas for online jobs.

CHOOSING THE RIGHT TYPE OF ONLINE BUSINESS

Decide what type of business you want to have online:

- E-commerce (business exists online only)
- Non-e-commerce (a traditional or brick-and-mortar store that is not an online-based company)

If e-commerce, what are you going to sell?

- Products
- Services
- Both

If you are going to sell products, what are they going to be?

- Tangible
- Digital

If you're going to sell tangible products, ask yourself these questions:

- Do I intend to keep an inventory or not? (This will determine how you will handle freight)
- Do I intend to sell in bulk or not?
- Do I intend to sell in the United States, internationally, or both?

We'll return to these issues later in the chapter.

STREAMLINING YOUR BUSINESS

To streamline your business, you need to keep your costs as low as possible. Think about the essentials. Try to carry no inventory if at all possible; ship direct from the manufacturer if you are selling a product. Try not to take on any employees unless your business is really growing faster than you can handle or you need customer service people or salespeople. Remember employees cost a lot of money. You can always bring on contractors in the beginning. Keep maintenance to a minimum and outsource your web development if you can, freeing up your time to build your business. If you are creating a truly web-based business, it doesn't need a physical location. You want a business that is self-running if at all possible, or one that runs with as few contractors or employees as possible.

The process for commerce enabling a website is succinct especially if you're prepared to carefully assess your online business needs in terms of what you are offering for products or services (or both) and how you can best meet the needs of your target audience online in terms of electronic commerce.

EMPLOYEE'S OR CONTRACTOR'S

What did my survey participants say about whether they had to or wanted to bring on team members or contractors? Sixty-eight percent worked alone, as the only person in their small business. Twenty-one percent had 1 or 2 staff members, 5 percent had 5 to 10 staff members, and 4 percent had 31 to 100 members in their not-so-small business.

Inventory Considerations

If you plan to keep an inventory, this means that you have to assume the responsibility of shipping the products to your clients. In this instance you will then need to establish relationships with the freighters that best suit your delivery needs. There are air, land, and sea freight carriers available; the ones you'll use depend on where you are having your products delivered and the quantity being delivered. If you plan to deliver locally or nationwide (in the United States), you may want to consider relationships with UPS, USPS, DHL, and FedEx since you may use them as needed; these freighters would most likely deliver mainly by air (by plane) and land (by truck) and can also be used for international deliveries, though this will prove extremely costly in most instances.

If you plan to deliver in bulk internationally, you may be interested in researching local sea freighters and forming relationships accordingly. In most instances, they offer packing services as well as shipping services, and though their prices are more affordable, the time for delivery is increased.

If you are not planning to keep an inventory and aim to deliver locally, you will need to establish a relationship with your vendor so that it will drop-ship to your customers using your branded labels on the packing slip, making the vendor completely transparent to your customers. If you are delivering outside of the United States, your relationship with a sea freighter would be equally beneficial to you; you will then have your vendors drop-ship to your shipper, who then ships directly to your client.

MAKING YOUR BUSINESS LEGAL

Just because your business is online doesn't mean you don't have to go through traditional steps to making it a business in the eyes of the law. You may think this will stifle your creativity, but you can generally accomplish the legal tasks in a day or so and just get them out of the way.

Choosing a Name

What's in a name? Just about everything! You must be sure the name you select for your business is not already taken. You can do a search online for your potential business name and also check sites like NameSecure.com to see if the name you want for your site is taken or not. Try to stick with *.com* if possible; it is still the industry standard. After you find a domain name, do some searching online and make sure others aren't using it already. For more on this, see "Which Comes First—the Domain Name or the Business Name?" on page 130. A company name is the official name of your business—the domain name is your website address. If you plan to run a conglomerate as I have, you might want something simple that covers them all as an "umbrella" company—like mine—the Babb Group (thebabbgroup.com).

Determining the Company Structure and Filing Requirements

Now you need to figure out what your company structure will be. Do you want to run your business as a sole proprietorship? A corporation? A limited liability corporation? A partnership? Here are some pros and cons for each.

A sole proprietorship or partnership is relatively easy to set up. You simply need to get a business license from the county you do business in and then file a fictitious business name statement with your county or state. The income is passing-through and is reported on a Schedule C for tax purposes. This is by far the easiest type of company to set up, but discuss with a qualified accountant the financial pros and cons for you given your specific needs.

Corporations are a bit more difficult to set up and have yearly or quarterly fees. You also have to file quarterly tax returns, which is cumbersome for many, particularly while profits are low, zero, or negative. You can always change your sole proprietorship to a corporation later on down the line if you wish to. You must file the paperwork (usually available online) with your secretary of state to set up a corporation. An accountant can help you, as can a corporate attorney. Be prepared for some upfront fees and more hassles as well as separate taxation for you personally and for your business. The benefit here is that if your business is sued, it is considered an entirely separate entity from you, meaning your personal assets are not at risk.

Limited liability corporations (LLCs) and limited liability partnerships (LLPs) are relatively easy to structure but do require you to file articles of incorporation with your state. This can be done through sites like LegalZoom.com, or you can hire an accountant or attorney to file for you. Sometimes they require yearly taxes if your income is high enough; other times they do not. Fees vary by state. An LLC provides you with pass-through income and also provides you very similar protection as a C or an S corporation.

Unless you are selling something that is risky or you feel you could be sued and have a lot of personal property at stake, you may want to stay with a sole proprietorship, for a while at least. An attorney or accountant is the best person to answer this question, though, because it very much depends on what your business is.

WHICH COMES FIRST—THE DOMAIN NAME OR THE BUSINESS NAME?

What should you create first—your business name or your domain name? Well, if you are an established business entity and are seeking an online presence, then the first step will be to do a search at a domain registrar for your business name and see if you can acquire it as a domain name. If your business name is quite common, you may find that the domain name is already taken. At that point you need to get creative and choose something that is close to your business name, or abbreviate your business name, use syllables, or append some logical or appropriate letters or numbers to the end.

Imagine this frustrating scenario: Your business is based in California and is named Staples Food Store, but staples.com is already taken. Your next step is to try staplesfood.com; that, too, is already taken. Next you try staplesfoodstore.com, and that is already taken. What about Staples-Foodstore.com? You guessed it, already taken. Now it is time to take your creativity up a notch. It's time to try staplesfs.com. If it is actually available think about this carefully and try to take your target audience into consideration. Does the name have a ring to it? Is it easy to remember? Is it easy to pronounce? If the answer to those questions is yes, then go for it. If the answer is no, then try again until you find a domain name that best represents your business name and company brand. You can also search online auction sites for domain names that are in high demand if you are willing to pay for them.

Do you find yourself needing help coming up with a domain name? Bring up your dilemma with friends and family, or even complete strangers. Let them know the name of the business and see what kinds of ideas for domain names they can come up with. You could even take it one step further and hold a little contest: whoever comes up with the best domain name gets taken out to dinner or a baseball game (yes, paid for by you). Another option is to consult with a company that markets businesses and helps them launch. Many can help you design a logo, a name, a domain name, and so on.

On the other hand, searching for a domain name if you have no business yet established gives you tremendous flexibility.

First, think up what you plan to do online and then, based on what your online business needs are, toggle with a few names that may be appropriate and then search for the respective domain names online. For example, if you are interested in selling hip clothing online and your business is based in Florida, you may want to search any domain registrar for hipclothingfl.com, where *fl* represents *Florida.* Or, you may want to first search for hipclothing.com and if that is not available, you can try hipclothingfl.com, and if that is not available, keep searching until you find something that has a ring to it, is intuitive, and is easy to remember. Getting the idea?

When you have selected a domain name that you feel would best appeal to your target audience, then you can name your online business using your domain name as a guide. This way your domain name and your business name are the same, like Dell Computers and dell.com or Kmart and kmart.com.

In each scenario, there is no need to get desperate and try to buy your domain from another domain name owner for high sums of money, unless you have the capital to do that. Simply rely on your creativity in order to find reasonable alternatives or, if you feel you are not creative enough, simply hire a web consultant to help you with that particular task—or ask friends with a great sense of humor! Let's look at some methods you can use to find a business name.

Business Name Brainstorming

Thinking of a business name is harder than starting the actual business for some people. You can tell I have struggled with it when the name of my own company is my name! Lots of others do the same thing, and that is certainly an option. But here are some other things to consider first: Try looking through some keywords or clichés for what you do. Are you a scrapbooker? *Scraps* is a keyword. Are you an accountant? *Bean counter* is a cliché. Try to think of as many of these as possible and write them all down. See if something is catchy. If you find it catchy, chances are your customers or clients will also.

If that isn't working, try writing down some ideas that represent what clients will get from using your service or buying your products. Will they get faster time to market? Will they get better advice? Ask yourself what types of demographics will buy your products. Busy professionals? Stay-at-home dads? Try to write down as many of these ideas as you can, and put them together with the clichés and word associations you have already listed. Also think of what clients have to say; most of my clients tell me I have "contagious enthusiasm," and so I incorporate that into my business plans and business model (although as of yet, not the name). Try using synonym tools online that allow you to find words similar to what you have come up with but that are a bit more creative.

While you're thinking of your name, chances are you'll end up creating your tagline, too, because the name you don't choose might just end up portraying whom you represent, whom you help, who your clients are, and what you do. The name you settle on might also be generic, like The Scrapbooker. Your tagline, motto, or slogan will help you separate yourself from your competition.

When all else fails, there is always your own name, and if you have a catchy one or one with a double meaning, like my maiden name of Wright, then you might find something there. At the end, be sure you google the name and check to see if it already exists in your state or nationally and is already essentially taken. I recommend having two or three names ready just in case. So how do you check and see if the domain is taken? I go to NameSecure.com, which is my host for several domains. Begin on the homepage to see what is available and to check which extensions are available, too.

Domain Name Brainstorming

The importance of a domain name is often underestimated, and people sometimes overthink it, trying to make their business name and domain name

Your Domain Extension

Once you have a domain name figured out, don't forget there are other domain extensions beyond the most common: *.com*. They range from *.net* to *.mobi* to *.biz* and even country-specific extensions like *.us* and *.au*. The more extensions you add onto your domain during initial purchase, the more protected you are from others who want the same domain name. Imagine if you owned ABC.com and sold letter blocks and you woke up one day to find out that someone else that sells letter blocks just launched ABC.net, ABC.us, ABC.biz, ABC.org. Even though your .com is still the preferred extension, the other guy now has an increased potential for gaining clients over you through sheer statistical calculation.

Each extension will cost you a few bucks more each month or year, but it is well worth it to protect your piece of the pie!

exactly the same. Sometimes the domain name *becomes* the business name. Working a bit backward isn't always bad. Who would have imagined ten years ago that a random name like Google would become a household name? Or that Amazon would be equated with books? Domain names are absolutely critical to the success of your business, but they don't have to be the business name, they just need to be catchy and easy to remember.

There is so much hype about search engine optimization (making sure search engines find you) that a basic consideration is eliminated from the equation: *intuition*. It's so easy to remember a domain name that has a ring to it and seems familiar. Just think about it; if your domain name were intuitive, known, and remembered, would there be any reason to search for it? People could simply enter your domain name into the web address bar of their browser and go directly to your site. This is ideal. For example, there really is no need to google "IBM" in search of IBM's website when you can simply enter "ibm.com" into the address bar of your browser, press Enter (or click on Go), and arrive at IBM's website directly. Under ideal circumstances, having a domain name that either replicates your business name or your main product or service will bring your target market closer to you, more quickly. The other option, of course, is something totally unrelated that is catchy and gets attention. Other than that, you want to try to keep your domain name easy to remember; this means that it is best to keep it short, easy to spell, and easy to pronounce.

Watch Out for Bad Domains

So what are some of the worst examples of domain name selection? The following examples are from the good folks over at MarketMe.com, and the list is from their public site in an article written by Tim Paulino, published March 20, 2008. The name of the article is "8 Worst Company Domain Names Ever Created" (nawh, you'd never make this mistake).

8. F.A. Gray, Inc. has been in the paint and wallpaper business since 1902. Clearly they weren't thinking about how to market themselves online back then: fagray.com
7. Looking to get a custom pen created? Look no further than Pen Island: penisland.net
6. Need a therapist? Try Therapist Finder: therapistfinder.com
5. Welcome to the First United Methodist Church in Cumming, Georgia. Their website? cummingfirst.com
4. Need some artistic direction really quick? Try these brainless art designers: speedofart.com
3. Find the latest mp3 hit albums at: mp3shits.com
2. Need an attorney? First thing I'd think of is: mofo.com
1. I've always wanted to know the name of the agent that represents Britney Spears. Now I can find it through a site called "Who Represents." Their domain of choice? whorepresents.com

Notice that although you can print all of your marketing materials using your domain with strategically placed capital letters, the actual address (or URL) bar in an internet browser won't show them.

OK, so you won't make such a serious mistake, but be sure that you read your potential domain names thoroughly in every context before you select one. Since you are probably the one who created the domain, you may want to enlist the help of friends and family again for this one—let some fresh eyes have a gander at your URL and see if anyone picks up on anything out of the ordinary.

REGISTERING THE DOMAIN NAME

So how do you really set up your business online? It starts with the domain name and, yes, formally registering your online business is also recommended, but it isn't a prerequisite. As stated earlier, the internet is not regulated. All you need is a domain name, a web host, and a website in order to conduct business online. Be prepared to fashion your registered business name after your internet business name. There are many reputable and accredited domain registrars that offer affordable domain names on the web; GoDaddy.com offers domain names at $9.20 a year; NameSecure.com at $8.95 a year; 000domains.com at $14.95 a year; and 1and1.com offers domains for as little as $2.99 a year, to name a few.

What's the difference? Besides price and support, there is no difference really. Each registrar must report to the same governing body, the Internet Corporation for Assigned Names and Numbers (icann.org), and must enforce the same common (and transparent) policies in order to protect your domain name subscriptions. You, as a domain name owner, are responsible for renewing your domain subscriptions accordingly. Perhaps you are now wondering what is meant by subscription. Well, you do not own the domain name. You own the use of the name to represent your business online. Once your subscription expires, given a 30-day grace period, any other entity is legally eligible to purchase the subscription from a respective registrar. Most domain registrars will remind you by e-mail to renew your subscription starting from 90 days in advance up to 30 days before. So you don't even have to mark your calendars if you don't want to (although I still do recommend it—just in case).

FINDING A WEB HOST

You have acquired the domain name, so what's next? You now need to acquire a web host that will be responsible for hosting your website. Your domain name has to be mapped to a hosting space reserved specifically for the website that represents your online business. In other words, when someone enters your domain name into her browser's address bar, your website (once published), should appear in the web browser. How do you know which host is best? Again, this would depend on the type of hosting you need or want. There are several types available: shared hosting, reseller hosting, semidedicated hosting, and dedicated hosting. Shared hosting is normally the most affordable for startup online businesses in particular and it runs anywhere from $4.95 a month to $9.95 a month in best-case scenarios, if purchased annually. Let's face it, about $60 a year for hosting is not bad.

The deciding factors when purchasing any hosting account are disk space, available bandwidth, website backups, and the availability of customer support; everything else is usually standard for all hosts, who are basically responsible for the maintenance and administration of the respective web server. Reseller hosting is more appropriate for web developers who want to offer hosting services to other website owners who want to acquire managed hosting; it usually requires that you understand the basics of web server administration. Semidedicated and dedicated hosting are appropriate for the more advanced web developer or application developer who understands how to manage and maintain the web server from the ground up and is usually more costly in both managed and unmanaged scenarios.

If you want to learn who's the best host for the respective hosting categories, you may be interested in visiting sites like Top-10-Web-Hosting.com, Best-Web-Hosting-2008.com, and HostCritique.net, to name a select few found from a basic Google search for "best web hosts." These sites will steer you in the right direction, their reviews are quite accurate. If you chose one of the top ten you may very well have made a good choice.

> Many domain registrars also offer single-site basic hosting and hosting packages and may offer a better deal for your dollar as you are already an existing customer, versus going through a secondary host.

You have now acquired the domain name and the hosting account; now it's time to select the right web designer or developer to build the website for your online venture. This website will be uploaded to your allocated web hosting space and, *voila*, you'll be the owner of a website that people can access from yourinternetbusinessname.com. It is almost as simple as that—but not quite.

FINDING A WEB DESIGNER OR DEVELOPER

What's the difference between a web designer and a web developer? A web designer is cheaper. Choose a web designer if you want to save on cost and still want an attractive presence online that adequately represents your business and appeals to your target audience. Again, this depends on the type of website that you need built for you. If your design needs are minimal, then a web designer is the one to hire. If design needs are more complex, a web developer may be more suited to customize or build web applications for the purpose of meeting your business objectives online. If you feel it is all too difficult to sort out on your own, hire a web consultant or information technology (IT) consultant. A Google search should bring you desirable results. Access the top ten results as a starter, call them all up and ask for free initial consultations. They want your business so they will help you. But don't be afraid to ask as many questions as you need in order to gain the understanding necessary to make the best web development choices.

ELECTRONIC COMMERCE EXPLAINED

Electronic commerce is the process of conducting business online but using electronic facilities like real-time processing in order to complete business transactions in real time. Be prepared to understand exactly what the electronic commerce model entails. Let's start with merchant processing. Visitors come to your website wanting to purchase a product or service, so what happens next? How do you encourage them to reach into their pocketbook, pull out a credit card, and use it to conduct the business transaction at your website? I go into this further in Chapters 8 and 11, but for now begin thinking of the basic customer service you want to offer, who your base demographic is, what they represent, what you represent, and how you want to be perceived in the public.

There are also some good shopping cart programs available. We'll talk about this in more detail later, but here is some information for you to begin

Getting People to Buy from You and Not Just Browse

How many times have you told a store clerk that asked, "May I help you?" "No, I'm just browsing." That is the last thing you want at your e-tail store! All of the issues and concerns in this chapter will play a role in whether or not visitors actually buy when they come to your site.

digesting and sites for you to begin exploring. You want a company and cart that are both highly integrated. Three that quickly come to mind are ClickCartPro.com, TurnkeyWebTools.com (sunShop), and Shop-Script.com. These are all cleanly written in W3C-compliant code and blend commerce with W3C compliance–who can ask for more?

Online retailer CCNow writes: "CCNow eliminates the need to struggle with merchant accounts and shopping cart software. CCNow provides a credit card processing, merchant account alternative, shopping cart, secure checkout, risk and fraud management, customer service." What does this imply? That the process of conducting payment processing is very complex and must be adequately managed (and your web developer or architect needs to thoroughly understand it, too); there are many responsibilities involved. You have to ensure that your shopping cart does not get hacked into and the data stored therein compromised; you therefore have to invest heavily in securing transactions and securing the web server. You also have to ensure that people aren't using someone else's credit card to make purchases at your

Helpful Companies

Companies like CCNow and PayPal will help alleviate the burdens of credit card responsibilities. They act as a mediator between you and the client and thus use their human resources accordingly.

site. You are responsible for handling chargebacks, returns, and everything else credit card related. It really is more intricate than it is made out to be.

CHOOSING A PAYMENT SYSTEM

In the online world, you have a lot of options with regard to how you get paid by your clients. Here are the options:

- By snail mail with check, money order, or cash
- By money wire–such as MoneyGram, Western Union, or direct wire into your business checking account
- By credit card
- By online check
- Through PayPal or Google Checkout

Maybe waiting for snail mail for checks, money orders, and so on wouldn't be as appropriate as it seems. You would have to wait for checks and money orders to clear before shipping the product or delivering the service. This then delays the delivery, which may be extremely frustrating for customers who are eager to get what they paid for immediately or as close to immediately as they can. In some instances it may be appropriate: if you have a business relationship with the customer and you have extended credit to her accordingly (like terms of net 30, meaning she has 30 days to pay). But, if this is not the case, you may want to exclude this as a payment option in your e-commerce environment.

Choose the Best Options for You

While you do have many options for getting paid, oftentimes handling money orders and checks and waiting on potentially lost snail mail, bounced checks, and so on is more hassle than it's worth. Chances are you won't lose clients by taking only credit cards, Google Checkout, and PayPal. I highly recommend weighing the pros and cons here.

Accepting Credit Cards Online

Payment by credit card is the most convenient form of payment for online processing, especially if you offer real-time processing online. The downside? Some customers wanting to scam you (or otherwise impatient customers that don't want to wait for you to take care of an issue) may dispute charges, holding up funds in your account.

Money wire is a very appropriate option, but the customer will have to pay a fee for sending funds this way and that does raise the cost of investing in your product or service. In some instances this is very convenient, particularly when the customers for whom you have extended credit need to pay you immediately. Though wire transfers via MoneyGram or Western Union are almost instant, direct wire into your account may take anywhere from one to three business days depending on where the money is being transferred from. Additionally, your bank will charge a processing fee for completing the transaction. Do you want these added costs when studies show most consumers don't use this service anyway?

If you want to offer credit card payment and don't use an online processing system, you will have to store credit card credentials either on your local PC (which is not safe) or your merchant's server (which is safer), and process manually (off-line) and resolve transactions at the end of the business day. Yes, this is time consuming. If you invest in real-time processing services, the whole process is automated for you: the credit card transaction is processed in real time, is authorized, and funds are deposited into your business checking account once resolved by your merchant bank. This enhances the user experience, automates the entire online payment process, and most importantly saves you time, which we know equals money.

Billing Systems or Shopping Carts

Next you must look at investing in both a billing system and a shopping cart system. Billing systems are more appropriate if you offer services and product lines with fewer than 20 products and do not require a sophisticated database. Shopping cart applications are more appropriate for merchants that have a database of products and need a more sophisticated system for managing their product lines and selling products online. Billing systems are to bill clients; shopping carts let customers add items to their cart online.

Either way, once you find the most appropriate option, you should get some leads for finding the right merchant bank. This may seem backward, but it's actually easier to start with the right payment processing application than to first get a merchant service and real-time processing services and then look for the shopping cart application that has already integrated the chosen real-time processor into its application core. It might be best if you consider the following steps in order to broaden your options:

1. Find the right application for payment processing, be it a billing system or a shopping cart system.
2. Look at the real-time processing applications already integrated into this payment processing system.
3. Find a merchant bank that offers real-time processing services in sync with those native to the application of choice.

Virtual Shopping Carts

Shopping cart applications are popular and reputable real-time service providers. It serves the best interest of the shopping cart application developer to design an application that would serve as a one-stop place for every online business need.

Thus, you will find that shopping cart applications come equipped not just with popular real-time processing software but also with real-time shipping applications like FedEx.com, UPS.com, DHL.com, and USPS.com, which are a few of the most reputable shipping companies available to online business owners today. It would make sense that beyond setting up the merchant services, you also apply at one or all of these sites for shipping options if you intend to sell products and not services. Again, call up each and consult with them toward how they may best meet your shipping needs. That being said, some of the most popular shopping cart applications are Shop-Script.com,

X-Cart.com, and TurnkeyWebTools.com, all affordable out-of-the-box solutions. Some of the popular open source applications are OsCommerce.com, ZenCart.com, and CubeCart.com.

With all these turnkey solutions ready to use out of the box, do you really need a web designer or developer? The answer is actually yes and no.

It doesn't end when you have selected the right shopping cart application. You still have to design for the user experience. You have to answer so many questions about exactly what would make your audience feel comfortable buying from your website, and you have to answer those questions honestly so that you can bridge any gaps between where your customers are in their purchasing decisions and where you want them to be. So what exactly are those gaps and how do you identify them? Before we can go any further, you really have to address and resolve this very important group of issues. You will save a great deal of time if you simply hire a web developer to help you, especially if it is your first time building an online presence; take notes and perhaps do it yourself the next time. Watch and learn from your web developer as the user experience is strategically carved into the web design process; yes, this is what you will ask the developer to accomplish for you, if you want your customers to feel comfortable and safe conducting business through your online storefront.

Real-Time Processing

If your decision is to process in real time, then you need to make another decision:

Do you want to become a merchant vendor using your own merchant bank (brandable) or do you want a merchant vendor to process for you using its merchant bank (non- or semi-brandable)? If you prefer not to assume the expense of becoming a merchant vendor, you can use a service like CCNow.com, PayPal.com, or 2Checkout.com, to name a few. They may require a minimal setup fee and service fees for the convenience. In most instances they offer you customer service support and protection for transactions, so it really saves time, is convenient and affordable as a first-time attempt at merchant processing. That is, it's a good option if your intent is to take the cheaper way out or simply get your feet wet before committing fully.

Just remember that the customer experience is what you have to focus on and you need to establish trust. Most established businesses online are merchant vendors and handle their own payment processing independently, and you want to come across as established. This lends to good credibility and fosters trust.

Now if you want to focus on establishing that trust between you and your customers it comes with a higher price. You will have to be responsible for becoming a merchant vendor and handling customer relations issues particularly charge backs. This is a somewhat tedious process and requires that you take the following steps:

1. Get an Employer Identification Number (EIN) or use a personal Social Security number, which may require registering your business with the state or local authorities.
2. Get a business checking account.
3. Get a basic website in place—enough for the merchant bank to see that you have a presence online.
4. Apply and be approved for a merchant account.
5. Obtain a real-time processing account.

One question you may be asking is "How do I get a merchant account after I have set up my website, and will this increase the cost of building my website?" Look at it this way: Whether you have a storefront or not, you still need to present your company information to your customers in order to legitimize yourself as a business entity and address any concerns they may have toward that end. You simply put this information up first: your first draft of your website would simply be a homepage, an About Us page, a page for your products/services, a Contact Us, and a Policies page. This should satisfy the

ONLINE PREREQUISITES

As you can see, some pre-requisites complicate the process of setting up online. Get your ducks in a row by having a legitimate business and a business checking account set up.

bank's requirements for applying for a merchant account. Stage this information in preparation for meeting their requirements. Then, the process for payment processing solutions continues and it becomes time to find the right application for electronic commerce. This ultimately helps you to determine which merchant bank you will solicit for merchant services.

Real-Time Processing Vendors

A few real-time processing vendors that are popular with most applicable storefront applications are Authorize.net (will work with most merchant banks or will find you one that does), LinkPoint (offered by Card Services International: cardservices.com), and WorldPay.com. A good starting point would be to consult with them about your merchant services needs. In most instances you will find that each may be able to handle both your merchant and real-time processing needs. At the same time, their real-time software is already integrated into the most popular shopping cart applications. And by default most merchant banks will deposit collected funds into any banking institution with which you have your business checking account; at least this is how it works in the United States. Whether or not funds are collected from international buyers, your merchant bank will deposit them into your U.S. business banking account. All this will be established in the beginning when you first apply for their merchant services.

CHOOSING THE RIGHT MERCHANT VENDOR

There are many vendors out there today that offer merchant services for online business owners. Your goal is to be able to accept online electronic payments, and you need merchant services to do that.

You have the option to choose the cheaper and quicker approach or the one that is more expensive and more time consuming. Some of the cheaper options would include CCNow.com, PayPal.com (owned by eBay), and Chrono Pay.com. These merchant vendors will take a percentage of your sales and per-transaction fees, in exchange for the real time and merchant processing services that they conduct on your behalf. There is also Google Checkout, which is absolutely free.

The average per-transaction fee is about $.30 each, and commission fees range from 5 to 8 percent of your total sales. The benefit is that you have no startup costs and can still cover merchant services. The problem is that it is almost impossible to assume your own branding and completely hide the merchant vendors. As a result you may come across as one of the less developed online business owners that simply cannot afford anything but the free services. This does not say much for the success of your business, does it? It may serve you best in the long run if you simply invest in becoming a merchant vendor and offering your own branded merchant services in real time.

You probably are wondering exactly how you get started and what this all means—and how complicated it really is. It isn't extraordinarily complicated, but if you have a good web designer or developer, you might want to rely on him to help you navigate.

Really what this means is that you have to start with your bank and open a business checking account. This is the prerequisite to eligibility for a merchant processing account. Then you want to ask your bank if it offers both merchant and real-time processing services to its business banking customers, with the hope that it can offer you some competitive service rates. But don't stop there. Shop around. The average one-time setup fee for a merchant account ranges between $99 and $199; the average per-transaction fee is $.25 to $.35, and the average service fee ranges between 2.17 percent and 2.75 percent.

This is the initial price that you have to pay for offering your customers real-time processing services online. It is therefore vital that you shop around for what's most suitable for your budget and needs. The trick to shopping around is to first ask for real-time processing options. Why? Because the real-time processing service that you acquire will come with special software that acts as middle ware between the shopping cart application that you use at your online storefront and the merchant bank that will ultimately be processing your online transactions. The real-time processing software online replaces that credit-card machine that you would traditionally use in brick-and-mortar stores, but instead of dialing into the bank (or connecting by Ethernet) in order to process transactions asynchronously, transactions are processed over internet protocol (IP) via your storefront's interface. So this software must be integrated into your shopping cart software.

By default most storefront developers do this for you and sell you a product that is already capable of incorporating your real-time processing credentials. If you really want to save money, save it on web programming fees, which range anywhere from $50 to $150 an hour, and acquire a shopping cart application that has already integrated your real-time processing software. If you have to choose between saving on merchant services and saving on web programming, choose the latter—web programming for electronic commerce is very expensive.

Selecting Merchant Services

First you need to determine whether you want to sell products or services and how many of whatever it is you're selling—how frequent your transactions may be. Next you decide if your target audience is local to the United States or, instead, the international marketplace. Then you find a shopping cart application that best suits the products or services according to your selling and business needs. After evaluating the many powerful applications available on the web programming market today, you want to look at the real-time processing software that is already integrated into the shopping cart application that you have chosen.

This is the real-time processing service that you need to seek and it must be compatible with any merchant service that you acquire thereafter. Before you decide upon that particular real-time processing vendor, consult with them as to whether or not they offer merchant services to international buyers, if this is vital to your online selling needs. Once you have made the decision, approach your regular bank to see if its merchant services work in sync with the real-time processing service that you need because it might be the most straightforward and easy solution. If your bank does not accommodate your real-time processing merchant, then you may not be able to acquire merchant services from your bank. At that point, continue to shop around.

Check out these two organizations:

1. payonesolutions.com/merchant-info/broker.php
2. merchantaccount101.net/merchant_account.html

If you are working with a web developer or architect, now is the time to begin looking at these two organizations.

WHAT ABOUT AFFILIATES?

An affiliate program allows you to be paid when consumers click a link on your homepage or buy a product. You can offer money to other companies when they bring you leads. The thing about an affiliate program is that it is a finicky thing to offer. It's easier to join an affiliate network and make residual income from your website traffic as opposed to actually starting one. In order to make an affiliate program work, you've got to invest in graphic design because you then have to create a series of banners that promote your products or services or both, and that can serve as a distraction at first.

First, set up the business online, make it work, and then, in later stages, start an affiliate program. Besides, most of the very good shopping cart applications have integrated affiliate programs or they integrate the more popular affiliate web applications like POSRAffiliatePro.com (qualityunit.com/post affiliatepro/) and IDEVAffiliate.com (idevdirect.com/idevaffiliate.php). So when the time comes, you can simply set up and customize the program accordingly.

FEES

One thing's for sure: there are expenses beyond development fees. So far you have an annual domain name subscription fee; a monthly or annual web hosting subscription fee; merchant processing fees; and shopping cart application and installation fees. Next you must assume an annual secured certificate subscription fee. Conducting e-commerce is not cheap, though it is generally affordable. The same principle applies to making money online: in order to make money, you have to spend money; the internet is not exempt and neither are you. Secured certificates range from 128-bit to 256-bit encryption, and subscription prices range from $29.99 to $599; it all depends on the level of security that you need based on the products and services you are offering and the extent to which you feel security is vital to your customers' buying experience, in terms of verification and encryption. For instance, if you are selling cars, you will want the priciest, most secure applications. If you are selling antenna balls, perhaps not so much! Some of the reputable digital certificate issuers include Twarte.com, VeriSign.com, Geotrust.com, and Comodo.com, and one of the cheaper and more affordable providers is GoDaddy.com.

MORE TIPS FOR GETTING STARTED ONLINE

You will need to get your idea written down, whether it's for your web developer, someone funding your business, or just your own planning purposes. As any traditional business would, you need to research what and who your competition is and what your competitive advantage or niche is going to be. You also need to name your company (remember if you sell widgets, it doesn't have to be Widgets R Us—think of eBay and Google, which have become household names). Find an available website domain name that is that matches your company name and then find a hosting site. I recommend HostGator for great service and exceptional plug-in Web 2.0 capabilities.

Then you need to work on your shopping experience; getting your ducks in a row is critical here.

First, you need a bank checking account in your business name. Next, you need a merchant account; Authorize.net has some great options. Make sure your web developer knows how to work with these tools. Decide if you also want to support Google Checkout and PayPal and integrate these tools as well. You also need to be sure your web developer optimizes your site for search engines, and be sure you are listed. Use pay-per-click search engines like Google AdWords to build your targeted traffic fast.

There are many threats in an online environment—particularly if you are working from home—to your new business. Here is how to avoid some of the worst offenders. Knowledge is power!

Make Sure the Work Gets Done

One downside to working at home is the ability to procrastinate—indefinitely, in some cases. If you're torn between home, work, family, and lots of other obligations, you might be inclined to let work slide until you have more time. Making sure you don't procrastinate is vital to your success in your online business.

Remember to Take a Break

Many people suffer from not working enough on their business when they work from home. Others, though, suffer from working *too* much, thinking that there is always more to be done! And since your office is upstairs, why not go for it instead of watching some TV and hanging out with the kids? This is putting your own stress, potential for burnout, and business at risk.

Avoid Working When Others Are Playing

It sounds crazy and perhaps one reason you *want* a homebased online business is so you can work odd hours, but if you are working when others are playing, you may soon begin to resent your new baby—your business. While others are going to Vegas on the weekends, having barbecues with friends, and hanging with their kids, you are stuck up in your loft trying to get new clients and not enjoying life. This is a major downfall to online work, and something you need to think through before diving heavily into your work. Think through the days and times you want to work and stick to them. You still might find yourself totally out of sync with the rest of society, discovering that your best creative times begin at 2 A.M. You are now waking at noon and breakfast and the gym are out of the question—there are only five "business" hours left in the day, and before you know it, you're off schedule with the rest of society. This works for some people, but not for others. Think first how this scenario will play out for you, and if it doesn't fit your lifestyle or personality, be sure to set your time boundaries clearly, up front, with your clients and your family.

Create a Separate Work Space

In the next chapter, I discuss the potential need to create Mom's or Dad's office or space that is free from traditional home-based distractions. Some people like to put their computer in their bedroom—bad idea! You may soon find yourself an insomniac, unable to put work to rest, listening to the hum of the hard drive all night instead of

> Of the survey respondents, 98 percent had an office in the home and 2 percent had an office outside the home for their online business. Some indicated they fit into both categories.

focusing on sleep! You need your energy to get your business building—plus you need a separate area in order to keep your focus.

You may not have the space or money for a full separate office. A guest house or casita house is ideal, but most of us don't have that luxury. Do your best to try to make what you do have into a functional separate space, using fake walls or room dividers to create areas. You can buy cubicle walls, perhaps not the most aesthetic, but an option. Be sure you have sufficient filing space, a place to back up your data, and an office environment that is suitable to your personality. Have space for common office equipment like fax machines and printers, though if you don't have the room for those, I do have suggestions in Chapter 5 on what you can use online instead, taking up as little room as possible.

Effectively Manage Your Time

You need to put the time you do have to great use. Sometimes this can take years of practice, but be sure that you devote your strongest, most engaging hours to those items that need the most creativity or focused work time. Find the time that you are most fresh and capable of making decisions and try to put away the e-mail and cell phone for hard, intense work. E-mails can always wait until later in the day. I've found that it takes me 10 to 15 minutes each time I am interrupted to begin to focus again, so if you remove those distractions you won't have to contend with getting back on track.

Visualize a Path to Success

While it's vitally important to focus on what will keep you from becoming successful, we also have to spend considerable time on what *will* help make you successful! Here are some great strategies from pros across the nation.

First, make sure that your personal boundaries are set. You need to find the job that fits within those boundaries, not make your boundaries fit around your job. If you focus on what you enjoy and where your passions are before how you're going to make money, then the money will follow. You have to be practical and outline what your goals are and then find jobs that align with those goals.

Also remember to visualize the steps you will take. A study by Alan Richardson, an Australian psychologist, found that there was a 23 percent improvement in performance in his subjects when they visualized their basketball shot, golf shot, or tennis shot beforehand. Richardson wrote in *Research Quarterly* that the most effective "visualization occurs when the visualizer feels and sees what he is doing." Apply this to your own business. Imagine the steps you need to take when you have some time to unwind, and then take those steps. Write them down and compare your actual process with the required steps for success. Also remember not to push yourself so hard that your passions become your nightmares. Take your dreams one step at a time and deal with each obstacle as it comes.

Maintain Relationships

The more you work independently, the more you will value relationships—personal and business. Almost no new business owner is successful without the help of others to some degree; this is also true with regard to life in general. Be sure to spend time with others who are important to you personally, and cultivate business relationships. Just because your work is online doesn't mean that anyone who isn't an online buddy is eliminated from your life. I have personally suffered from this myself, and I know how hard it can be to make time when there is always so much work to be done. You aren't the only one who will suffer; so will those close to you. You may find that as you dedicate more time to your latest endeavor, those who care about you will start to feel like they have lost some importance and will long for more time with you, which of course brings up the issue of distractions again.

Don't Fear Failure—or Success

Most people know they fear failure—they imagine themselves failing and therefore never start. But another way to sabotage your success is to secretly fear success—what will you do and what will you fight for if you *are* successful? Be sure you define it clearly for yourself; it might be more about freedom than money. Whatever your definition of success, fight for it, but don't be afraid of it. I can promise you new lessons will arise and you will never be bored.

YourOnlineProfessor.com

Getting started can be the most difficult part. Looking for inspiration? Procrastination is like a giant hole that will eat at your time and energy. Visit Your OnlineProfessor.com to get motivated and learn what others did to get off their behinds and onto their keyboards!

You will also need a darn good domain name. Don't know where to buy one? Want to brainstorm your ideas with other caring entrepreneurs? Visit YourOnlineProfessor.com for some help.

As you get into finding a developer and a web hosting partner, merchant vendor, payment system, and so on, you'll want to get some guidance. Feel free to jump onto your virtual professors' website for more information and for some help in choosing the right vendors for the right job.

PART

II

SETTING THE RIGHT TONE FROM THE START

CHAPTER

4

SETTING BOUNDARIES AND FLEXIBILITY

Keeping Home, Work, and Clients Separate

There is an online job for *everyone*. But, each person must determine what his boundaries are and know where his flexibilities are. I will discuss the pros and cons of working at home, how to set up boundaries, and how to make sure you don't feel like you live at work. Having firsthand experience here, I will share my own personal coping mechanisms and the mechanisms of hundreds of individuals I surveyed myself (I have a doctorate and

teach quantitative methods, so my research is sound, reliable, and valid), and will help you figure out how to set up your personal and work-related boundaries. In this chapter we will talk about how to tell clients what restrictions you have; how to screen clients based on personal boundaries; how to communicate familial needs; and how to know when you need to make changes—the warning signs that issues are arising before they become big problems.

THERE IS AN ONLINE BUSINESS FOR YOU

No matter where your dreams and passions are, there is an online business for you—and your online business can make you big money.

SETTING YOUR BOUNDARIES AND KNOWING WHAT WILL WORK

When you are eager to get new business and start with your new endeavor, it is relatively easy to begin just piling on clients and taking on work, asking everyone you know for referrals, offering affiliate fees, and building your business *fast.* This is great, but you need to determine what your own boundaries are, and methodically so, before just engaging in lots of new business.

Here are some examples of personal boundaries you need to consider. They assume you are a stay-at-home parent looking to add to your income, and you'd like your business to grow slowly over time. Because of these obligations, the examples listed here are the more restrictive ones. I'll later move to a looser set and you can see how they differ.

- From 6 to 8 A.M. I need free time to take my kids to school.
- From 5 to 9 P.M. I need time to make my family dinner and put the kids to bed.
- I am available to work from 9 to 11 P.M. but I need to be in bed by midnight.
- I need an hour per day to exercise.
- I don't enjoy working with obnoxious people or with unreasonable deadlines.

- I want a job that keeps me in the house at least 50 percent of my working time.
- I don't want to spend more than 30 hours per week working.
- I don't want to spend more than $5,000 on technology.
- I don't want to have more than three conference calls per week.
- I want to be able to take a vacation yearly, for at least two weeks, without clients being able to reach me.
- I want the freedom to travel while my business maintains itself.

Assume now you are a single person without family responsibilities, and your goal is to grow your business as fast as possible with few boundaries or restrictions. You may still have some, such as these.

- I want to be able to go out Friday and Saturday nights and have a social life.
- I need time to travel but don't mind working on the road.
- I don't mind waking up early to begin working but I'm shutting down at 5 P.M.
- I need more interaction and don't want to be tied to my home 24/7; I want at least 50 percent of my working time to be outside the home.
- I don't mind conference calls or technology, but I'd like to keep super-busy working at least 60 hours per week until my business really takes off.
- I want to grow my business with staff at some point; I want to run something that will take off and be my primary source of income.

While these boundaries are drastically different, they are still boundaries, and either set or anything in between needs to be understood completely before approaching your business. Your boundaries may even dictate which business you go into, because some online businesses will require more time than others and some will require more in-home time and less face-to-face time.

To help you determine your own potential upsides and downsides to online work, let's examine for a bit what the survey respondents said were the most challenging aspects to owning an online business. Keep in mind that most worked primarily from their home—a whopping 98 percent! That bias is reflected somewhat in this data.

So what did they say? Some had difficulty staying in touch with the outside world while working at their desk all day. Some worked too much because time flew by (not necessarily a bad problem to have). Some felt isolated at times from other colleagues. Some fought procrastination and had trouble keeping themselves motivated and disciplined. Others cited their own obsessiveness and working late hours. Some noted that separating personal from work life is tough, and others noted disruptions from family. Some noted time management issues, knowing when to stop, and losing track of time. Some cited difficulty gauging how many projects they could take on at once, while others noted that managing and remembering their schedule was cumbersome. Many business owners said responding to so many e-mails was overwhelming, but that being able to do it 24/7 was very helpful (although checking e-mail every two minutes wasn't on their list of most fun things to do). Many missed the camaraderie of peers but found it worth the flexibility of living and traveling anywhere. Most noted that taking a day off was tough. About 5 percent noted that finding new contracts or work was difficult at times and that internet issues severely affected their work. Importantly, over 30 percent noted no difficulties at all working purely online.

What about the rewards for these same participants? Plenty to brag about. Flexibility in hours and income, the ability to travel anywhere, anytime, the clients they choose to work with (keyword–*choose)*. They also mentioned having time to formulate effective helpful responses to people, freedom from direct supervision, the ability to care for children and take vacations and attend school functions without the guilt of co-workers' pressure, the opportunity to meet people from all over the world virtually, fewer expenses (clothes and gas, to name two), the ability to set their own hours, and notably, the ability to work independently as fast as they wanted without others in a group setting interfering with personal success. Many noted they felt they had more control over their destiny being their own boss, and two noted physical disabilities that are embarrassing and being thankful for not having to work in person with others.

HOW YOUR JOB MIGHT AFFECT YOUR PERSONAL BOUNDARIES

Take my full-time job of online teaching, for example. It allows me flexible time in the morning (I can schedule conference calls around my insomnia), but 95 percent or more of my work is conducted in the home, which means beyond e-mail and my assistant, my human-to-human interaction is limited. This can be frustrating at times, which has led me to speak at seminars, go to residencies, and otherwise find ways to engage in human relationships beyond my computer. I can travel anywhere I want whenever I want, but I must work from my computer in my hotel room and must be available by e-mail about 14 hours per day every day, regardless of whether it is a weekend or weekday, the middle of June or Christmas Day. While tiring at times, this fits within my own personal boundary checklist.

There are statistical models that are very easy to use that will help you determine what type of business will flow nicely with your own boundaries. I'll show you an example first comparing my needs against online teaching and book writing (Figure 4.1), and then provide a blank worksheet (Figure 4.2) that you should fill in as you think of jobs that interest you.

One benefit to this table is that the value of the boundary on a 1 to 10 scale changes the score, as does how well that job fits with your boundaries. This means that the numbers at the end are weighted not only for how important a particular boundary is to you, but also for how well the job fits that boundary. This makes this type of tool incredibly useful in decision making.

In this particular case, book writing actually scores higher for me than online teaching, which means if it came down to picking one, I would probably be happiest as an author rather than as an online teacher. Of course my real spreadsheet has far more boundaries with far more variables, and my actual numbers show the two so close that I decided to do both, teaching people how to make their own livings online!

Try using Figure 4.2 as you work through your own job idea.

Boundary (A)	Importance (B) (1-10, 1 unimportant, 10 very important)	Teaching (C) (1-10, 1 doesn't fit, 10 fits very well)	Book Writing (D) (1-10, 1 doesn't fit, 10 fits very well)	B X C (score for teaching)	B X D (score for book writing)
Need to be able to wake up late because of insomnia.	10	9	10	10 x 9 90	10 x 10 100
Need the ability to build my business fast.	8	6	7	8 x 6 48	8 x 7 56
Need the ability to earn significant income to pay the bills.	10	9	5	10 x 9 90	10 x 5 50
Need the ability to raise a family.	2	5	10	2 x 5 10	2 x 10 20
Need the ability to have time to exercise during the middle of the day.	9	7	10	9 x 7 63	9 x 10 90
Score				301	316

FIGURE 4.1 **SAMPLE JOB EVALUATION WORKSHEET**

Boundary (A)	Importance (B) (1–10, 1 unimportant, 10 very important)	Teaching (C) (1–10, 1 doesn't fit, 10 fits very well)	Book Writing (D) (1–10, 1 doesn't fit, 10 fits very well)	B X C (score for ______)	B X D (score for ______)
Score					

FIGURE 4.2 **JOB EVALUATION WORKSHEET**

WRITING IT ALL OUT

There are many reasons to write this all out—and it isn't only for planning purposes. If you are more logically oriented and less inclined to take risks, sometimes weighing the pros and cons on paper can help you remember why you made a particular decision and ease your anxieties.

Your final scores will be weighted just like mine were in my example. Ultimately your numbers will help you weigh the pros and cons of each job in which you are interested.

Now, you can decide to go against the numbers—your business and your life that will be affected—but know that numbers are hard to argue against. The previous model actually quantifies happiness, or at least the potential for happiness given specific scenarios and criteria.

SCREENING CLIENTS

After you have your jobs tallied and you know which online job interests you most, it is time to begin working on screening clients with regard to your boundaries. Of course first you will need to get your business up and running, and have a good advertising and affiliate campaign launched. But you will also want to know how to screen clients as they begin coming in based on your own personal boundaries.

Here is an example of my own client evaluation worksheet (Figure 4.3), just for online teaching. Each school is anonymous here but will give you an idea of how each compares with my needs.

In this case you can see that School X is a better fit for me than School Y. It doesn't necessarily mean I will not take on School Y as a client, but if I am choosing one or the other, I'll go with School X. You will want to take your boundary sheets and plug clients in to make sure they are a good fit. Remember that they should meet most of your boundaries that are very important, generally those you gave a 7 or above. If not, you may be miserable and sacrificing the very reason you decided to run your own business to begin with.

Boundary (A)	Importance (B) (1-10, 1 unimportant, 10 very important)	School X (C) (1-10, 1 doesn't fit, 10 fits very well)	School Y (D) (1-10, 1 doesn't fit, 10 fits very well)	B X C (score for school X)	B X D (score for school Y)
Need to be able to wake up late because of insomnia.	10	2	7	10 x 2 20	10 x 7 70
Need the ability to build my business fast.	8	4	4	8 x 4 32	8 x 4 32
Need the ability to earn significant income to pay the bills.	10	9	5	10 x 9 90	10 x 5 50
Need the ability to raise a family.	2	3	10	2 x 3 6	2 x 10 20
Need the ability to have time to exercise during the middle of the day.	9	7	3	9 x 7 63	9 x 3 27
Score				211	199

FIGURE 4.3 **SAMPLE CLIENT EVALUATION WORKSHEET**

Use the following worksheet (Figure 4.4) for your own clients as you begin to build your business (you will ask clients questions and lay out your terms and conditions to help make your boundaries clear—no mistakes or misunderstandings).

Boundary (A)	Importance (B) (1–10, 1 unimportant, 10 very important)	Client X (C) (1–10, 1 doesn't fit, 10 fits very well)	Client Y (D) (1–10, 1 doesn't fit, 10 fits very well)	B X C (score for ______)	B X D (score for ______)
Score					

FIGURE 4.4 **CLIENT EVALUATION WORKSHEET**

SETTING FAMILIAL BOUNDARIES

One thing that comes as a surprise to many work-at-home entrepreneurs, particularly those in online businesses, is how demanding a business that is supposed to be running itself can be, particularly within the first few years. This is, of course, entirely dependent on your choice of business and the resources you have while you are establishing your new venture. If you have unlimited financial resources and can afford to hire a complement of employees and your business takes off, you could spend very little time and effort and simply reap the rewards. This is less common than those of us who are often limited in resources, and start the business ourselves.

One area that can cause tremendous stress is familial boundaries and setting aside real office space and work time for yourself at home, particularly if you have a spouse and/or children. Both men and women complain of this affliction and intrusion into their working lives, so it doesn't appear to affect one gender more than the other.

There are some common misunderstandings, particularly with spouses or living partners, that seem to occur when one decides to have an online business:

- My significant other will be home all day and have more time for me.
- My significant other will be home all day and have more time for household chores.
- We can fire the nanny and save money on health care because my spouse quit his "real" job.
- We can have more free time and travel without interruption now that a pesky boss won't be calling my husband.

None of these is true; in fact, in many cases the opposite is true. Once you decide to become responsible for your own success and endeavors, in many cases you spend more time and feel more endeared to success and making things happen for yourself than you do if you're working to make "the man" rich. Many spouses think that since you're home, you must have time to do other things. This simply isn't the case. A homebased business, online or not, is still a business—and it's your job. You must clearly lay down boundaries before you embark on your endeavors or you and your significant other will suffer. Better yet, make your significant other part of the boundary setting,

Separating Work and Home

How hard did survey respondents say it was to separate their work from home life when they worked from home? Forty-three percent said it was extremely difficult, 18 percent said it was very difficult, and 38 percent said it was not at all difficult. How did the participants handle the separation? Some said that home and work were the same—both going everywhere! Others noted that they built their home around their business need. Some converted a bedroom into an office or moved as a result of needs. Some noted that distractions were tough because of the reminder of errands and housework. Others required a physical separation in an office outside of the home to be successful but some used their laptop to do their work in the kitchen with kids running around! Some even said it was fine all year except during the holidays when they felt pulled in multiple directions. This truly shows it all depends on who you are and what you do!

and even include his or her boundaries, too. For example: "My office needs to be separate from the main house" or "My spouse must give me ten hours per day of uninterrupted work time"—whatever your personal requirements are. Without doing this first, you may become so stressed that you'll be begging for a corporate America boss again in a year. Evaluate jobs and clients based on boundaries within your family, too.

CHOOSING A PASSIVE OR ACTIVE ROLE

One thing you need to ask yourself in the work-life boundary area is how passive or active you want to be in the process of setting up your business. Remember that running a business that grows well isn't for wimps or people with no passion. In Chapter 5, I go into detail on how much work it will take to get going and what you can contract out (essentially all of it, if you want) and what you can do in-house (also essentially all, if you wish). But you must consider your other work and life demands when you make this decision.

At this point, you will want to decide how active or passive a role you will want to take because it will affect decisions you need to make about starting your business.

If you want to take a passive role, you can just hire a web developer and let him make all the decisions for you. If you prefer an active role, then go out there and stage things for the web developer and let him make only those decisions that he is more qualified to make.

Web development has evolved to the point that you do not really need to know the technical details in order to complete the technical tasks. Let's look at some options for content management systems (CMSs), which have changed the way we develop. Some are commercial and others are open source and therefore free. Some of the good free ones are Drupal, Joomla, and Xoops. These are the most widely used and supported CMSs and because they are basically modular, they can include shopping carts and billing systems that are equally supported by the open source programming community. There are some powerful commercial CMSs as well.

A very powerful CMS that comes in start, standard, small-business, professional, and enterprise editions is Bitrix (bitrixsoft.com). It is modular, which means that beyond its application core, site owners can add modules based on how they want to extend the capabilities of the CMS. Some of the modules that can be integrated are a help desk, private mail, web forms, polls and surveys, e-learning, blogs, a photo gallery, an e-store, commercial catalog, advertising, web analytics, newsletters, and discussion forums. Sound exciting? It is!

Once this application is installed on the web server, it's easy to simply add modules as needed from a user-friendly web interface that makes e-mail seem difficult. Some web developers would argue with this, but I've seen individuals create their own sleek sites firsthand. If you can use Microsoft Word or you can use e-mail, then you can manipulate a CMS. It's as easy as picking and choosing what you want to add and implementing accordingly.

All this technical stuff happens within an administrative, intuitive back end, and once implemented, the changes are reflected at the website on the front end in real time. So you really do not need to have technical knowledge and you can build a very powerful website. The only thing you might need is a web designer to design your interface. Bitrix has a database of hundreds of interfaces that they can install and customize for a nominal fee, and which allow you to make your site plug and play.

In other words, whether you are developing an e-commerce or a non-e-commerce website, you may very well be able to assume an active role toward establishing your internet presence even with limited time. The next chapter goes into more detail about all the technology you may need to run your business.

YourOnlineProfessor.com

It isn't always easy to set boundaries. Many people do it—they work from home with a family to boot! Want to learn how to do it? Visit YourOnlineProfessor.com and chat with others doing the same.

You want clients? Who doesn't? But you want the RIGHT clients. Bad clients are worse than none at all. Share experiences and learn how to screen your clients at YourOnline Professor.com.

CHAPTER

5

TECHNOLOGY

What You Need to Get the Job Done

In this chapter, I'm going to help you decide what kinds of technology you'll need for your business. One tremendous advantage of working online is that you can have a truly green company. With energy-efficient electronics and little need to print and copy documents, this is your chance to let your green monster shine through.

There are so many technological options out there that most people don't know where to begin. In many instances, simple technology that you may already have is sufficient, but in other cases an intense, data-driven online business may require more. I'll first focus on front-end equipment, meaning what you'll need in your office to answer e-mails, get creative, focus on advertising, and so on.

What did survey respondents think was absolutely essential technology for their business? Here are the results (the percentage of people indicating what is essential):

1. A laptop, over 87 percent
2. A cell phone, over 68 percent
3. A calendaring system, 47 percent
4. A scanner, 45 percent
5. A desktop PC, over 38 percent
6. A fax machine, 37 percent
7. Automated backups, 35 percent
8. Dual monitors, 35 percent
9. A PDA, a bit more than 33 percent
10. Voiceover IP, 31 percent
11. Manual backups, 24 percent

Other responses included a high-quality digital camera, compatible software, an external hard drive, a voice recorder or online system like K7.net, and a webcam.

INTERNET ACCESS

When it comes to internet access, speed isn't everything; reliability is also important. If you live in a heavy storm area, you might not want to consider satellite because it may drop more often than DSL, ISDN, or better yet, cable. Definitely eliminate a dial-up phone connection as an option—remember you are an online expert! Try not to skimp, and test out the upload/download speeds once you get your new connection. If you aren't happy, move on. I recommend you always have a backup line, even a phone line you can use with a modem, in case something goes wrong and you still need to handle orders. Or

So Many ISP Options!

There are many options out there in terms of internet access: dial-up or accelerated dial-up (significantly slow), DSL, cable, satellite (high speed). T1 lines, in the past reserved for highly-profitable businesses, are quite affordable these days and something you should look into through your major telecommunications companies.

get a backup full-scale provider; if you are using cable, for example, you might want a backup DSL line.

If you are going to do business online, you need to invest in high-speed internet access. In selecting a high-speed internet service, remember that speed isn't everything; reliability is also important. It is a good idea to go with the more reputable providers who can offer you a dial-up account as backup in case there is failure on your data line. But remember, do not depend on a dial-up connection as your primary internet access.

PHONE SERVICE

You cannot completely depend on the internet to handle all of your business needs. People still want to call and speak to someone about customer service, billing, or support issues. Having a reliable phone service is important. Based on the type of online business you'll be running, you can choose between using a cell phone as the main contact phone number, investing in a dedicated business line, employing the use of an autoattendant to answer your calls whether or not you are available, or hiring a company to answer your phones for you. But people need to speak to live persons in many instances, so be prepared to accommodate them.

COMPUTERS

Now you have high-speed internet access, but you need something to access it with—and to convince all of those clients to come to your business, answer e-mail, and conduct other business-related activities. Of all the equipment in your home office, the most critical is the computer, and it needs to be efficient.

You really need to determine first the reason why you will be using the computer and then the minimal resources you will need. Any other suggestion would not be correct. For instance, if all someone is doing on the PC is browsing the web, accounting, word processing, and creating presentations using PowerPoint®, there really is no need for investing in a huge hard drive, 2 gigabytes of memory, and dual processors. If you plan to use your computer to store large files like pictures, images, audio files, and video files, or you plan to do audio, video, graphics, and multimedia production, then you are going to need upgrades.

This means your computer must be powerful enough to handle the many tasks that you may want to accomplish simultaneously, like check e-mail, open multiple browser windows, word processing, run malware scans in real time, and listen to music if this would make you more productive throughout the day. This requires a powerful processor (at least a 2 GHz processor; 25 GHz or more is better) and enough memory (at least a gigabyte).

Be sure your machine has at least 2 GB of random access memory (RAM); although some people do work well with 512 MB of memory, I have found it frustrating to run applications without 2 GB. Add as much cache as you can. Keep your hard drive at a minimum of 200 GB, but I really recommend a terabyte in today's marketplace. It might seem like a lot, but it will quickly be used with graphics and web design.

Also remember that disk space is cheap and you can always add more later, but it isn't so easy to rebuild your operating system, so don't skimp on the primary drive. Be sure your drive is at least 7000 rpm; a slower drive will be noticeable in how fast you access applications.

> When buying a computer, try not to get caught up in hype. Computer sellers tend to sell computers that far exceed the power that you need.

Whether you have a Mac or a PC really does not matter unless you intend to do heavy graphics and audio and video productions, in which case a Mac might prove better. Other than that, any affordable PC will do the trick. (Remember that while Macs may look nice and you may even be partial to them, more than 90 percent of your clients will be using a PC.) And, instead of having a computer consultant build a computer for you, buy from the manufacturer. It may save you a lot of money in support costs in the long run and preserve your business continuity.

If your business requires you to be mobile, you may want to invest in a laptop with docking station and monitor; otherwise, a regular desktop computer will do the trick. If you are going to spend a great deal of time online it may serve you well to invest in a bigger monitor and an antiglare screen. I recommend a 22-inch LCD monitor; they run for less than $300. Do invest in disaster recovery plans to ensure that even if you suffer a hard drive or software crash, you will be up and running again within an hour.

In some instances it may even be a good thing to get two video cards and two monitors, especially in instances where it is vital that the website is heavily monitored or if you are offering customer service options at the site. This can make it easier to multitask. For example, on one monitor you can have a browser open with your online support desk and on the other you can have the website up, but you are still running both off one computer, and it is very easy to set up. It makes life easier for one person to manage two separate tasks. So this is a good scenario for a one-man show. Another option is to have one monitor and two computers, which works well if you are hosting your own website.

When shopping for a new computer, do your research at reputable manufacturers, and be sure to purchase an extended manufacturer's warranty (especially if you have a laptop). Just remember that these warranties cover hardware only and not software issues. The trick is that 90 percent of computer problems are software related, so be sure to maintain your computer software, as this may reduce the likelihood of software-related problems and therefore reduce your software support costs.

Your computer must be able to take full advantage of high-speed internet access and must be capable of multitasking well enough that you aren't frustrated, nor are you waiting for your machine to catch up while you have ten web browsers open and your e-mail up constantly. The speed of your computer will truly affect how fast you work.

If you choose to work with a laptop, know you will be sacrificing speed while perhaps gaining flexibility. If you go the laptop route, try to choose a name brand with good support and fast response times because being down means you're out of business until you get your machine back up and running. PCs can be taken to the local Best Buy, but often laptops are more difficult. See Appendix A for three PC companies I recommend buying from.

DISASTER RECOVERY PLANNING—A MUST FOR *ANY* BUSINESS

Backups are the second most critical item, next to internet access, that you will need for your computer. You absolutely must have backups, and many new online companies like Mozy and iBackup make it easy to retrieve data even if you are traveling. Remember there are two types of backups: full, which backs up your hard drive every time you add anything whatsoever, including applications, to the drive; and incremental, which updates the backup every time a piece of data is changed. Plan when you want to do a full backup and when you want incremental backup ahead of time.

First invest in an uninterrupted power supply with surge protector in case there is a power surge, install an internet security suite to protect your software from malware, and connect a second hard drive to which you will back up your data.

I have remained brand loyal to American Power Conversions and use the Smart UPS 1000 on my server and my desktop and laptop PCs. I even have one connected to my internet router, which has kept me running when the power was out for hours. The investment cost is between $300 and $700, depending on which model you get, but there are many options available and it will save your equipment, keep power flow regulated (which prolongs the life of your equipment), and keep you running in an outage.

UPS—Not the Shipping Company!

Don't run your PCs and laptops without an uninterruptible power supply (UPS). Not only will a UPS protect your equipment from power surges and lightning, but your system will continue running even in a power outage.

A good disaster recovery plan would start with creating an image of your hard drive and storing it to either another hard drive partition, a hidden hard drive partition, or another hard drive; this way, if your hard drive crashes you will be able to restore your computer software within 15 minutes, depending on the size of your hard disk image. In preparation for this, a good practice would be to store all of your data externally, either to another hard drive partition or an external drive. Beware of pen drives as a primary backup source because they can easily get lost, and if they fail, retrieving your data will be virtually impossible or significantly expensive. The traditional external hard drive is the best primary data backup drive to use; the pen drive can be used as secondary backup. It is always a good idea to store your data in two places anyway.

You should keep at least one backup hard drive at your home office. You should have the hard drive bootable and use it as a spare. A laptop drive with a 200-GB drive in it connected by USB cable is an excellent way to back up data and store it off-site.

Invest in a powerful internet security suite that will protect your computer software from malware; software maintenance software to keep your computer software tuned; and disk cleanup software to remove any unwanted software and data that may be threatening to your system.

One backup option is an application like Norton Ghost, which makes an exact replica of your drive and also stores files. While you can retrieve file by file, you can also quickly re-clone your PC if your hard drive data becomes corrupt or your drive dies completely. There are some flaws with Ghost. For instance, it can be tough to recover after a crash or Ghost may restore to an incorrect drive letter without making you aware of it. Ideally, you will have two computers and the data will be pretty close to the same on both, if not identical. There are lots of free applications out there that will let you copy data from one computer to another for $30. Remember if you do store data locally and your home office gets robbed, you run the risk of losing all of your data, so a once-monthly off-site backup stored in a safe-deposit box is a great idea.

ORGANIZATION SYSTEMS AND PDAS

It doesn't matter whether you use Outlook, a Treo, or some no-name product you got free online, but use something to remind yourself when tasks are due and when you need to submit proposals or information to various clients. You can even use it to manage meetings and tasks that you need to do each day, making sure you don't fall into the procrastination trap. Remember that your technology should help keep you on track, so if it's making your life more difficult and not less difficult, it might be time to find a new solution.

This brings up yet another requirement. Whatever you choose, it *must* synchronize to a PDA. This can be a Treo, a BlackBerry (both of which will let you get e-mail, too), a Windows-based device like an iPaq from Hewlett-Packard (HP)—whatever you choose. However, it's recommended that if you're on the road a lot and consulting, too, you seriously consider a device that lets you get e-mail remotely so that your clients aren't left hanging waiting for your reply. This is particularly true if you still have a day job and you're checking your e-mail from work.

CELL PHONES

About 20 percent of the population has completely replaced their land-line, old-school phones with cell phones—after all, you get free long distance and some companies offer unlimited plans that allow you to do as much calling as you like. If you are going to travel a lot, choose a phone company with access throughout the nation that won't require you to pay roaming charges, and if you're going to travel internationally, consider that, too. While lots of people like the integration of a cell and a PDA, I personally prefer to keep them separate so I can be taking notes and managing information (even answering e-mails) while on conference calls.

An advantage to having more than one cell phone is potentially being able to keep business and personal lives separate. A friend of mine used to carry two cell phones on him; one was for work and one was for everything and everyone else. When he was not on call, he would leave the work phone at home when he went out.

VOICEOVER INTERNET PROTOCOL (VoIP)

VoIP is the ability to route telephone calls over the internet and although it may be nice to have, it can also save you a lot of money. All the major telecom providers offer voiceover IP services and the quality is now really good. The quality of the call depends on bandwidth and the extent to which the voice packets have to be compressed in order to accommodate the transportation of these voice packets. If you have limited bandwidth on your high-speed line, then the quality of your voice call will suffer, but that is hardly the case these days. Vonage and Magic Jack are both great; and check out AT&T's voiceover IP plans for local service. Skype is an inferior product, but its price makes it popular.

UNIFIED MESSAGING

Whereas some might think unified messaging is a luxury, I consider it a requirement. Unified messaging is a system that sends voice mail into your e-mail. This gives you several advantages: 1) if you are traveling out of the country, you can forward your cell phone to the unified messaging system and still check your voice mail and not miss messages; 2) you can retain your privacy and not give out your cell number except for emergencies if you wish to do that; 3) it's nice to have everything in one system, particularly letting you forward or reply to voice messages in standard .wav (Microsoft and IBM audio file format) or other formats to other individuals. The service I use is called K7.net. I haven't missed a call in two years and can access my messages from my Treo. It also works as a fax if you wish. In addition, if you want to remain more anonymous (depending on your online business, you may wish to retain anonymity), this is a good way to do it.

Most VoIP providers forward voice messages to e-mail. Local phone companies and cell phone companies do not. In that instance, K7.net would be the way to go if you want anonymity. But a mini PBX system is the way to go if you want a more traditional system. There are even some hosted versions where you get a virtual phone number (so you don't even have to invest in the hardware) and they route calls, or offer voice mail if there's no answer and then send the messages to your e-mail, or you can call in and get your messages from any phone. If you are not using the hosted version, investing in the hardware is equally affordable using talkswitch, which can act as a call router, voice mail system, and autoattendant. You can route calls from one main location to wherever you are and give out just one phone number.

CONFERENCE PHONES

If you intend to take calls from home, consider an inexpensive solution from a company like Polycom for a small conferencing system or a voice conference system from your favorite VoIP provider. This will allow you clear, office-quality conference calls for far less money than a traditional system. I purchased one on eBay for a fraction of the retail cost and it works very well.

WIRELESS HEADSETS

If you are on the phone a lot, a wireless headset can be a godsend. True wireless headphones that switch between cell phone and business lines are excellent, and they free up your hands to continue typing on long conference calls or if you're a superb multitasker. I always recommend buying such equipment from computer superstores or office stores so that you can get some warranty protection in a convenient and efficient environment if possible. Jabra and Plantronics have some excellent products and you can pick them up at computer superstores such as Best Buy, CompUSA, or even at Staples, OfficeMax, or Office Depot. But some of the real fantastic ones you have to buy from the manufacturer. Check out this product: headsets.com/headset/Plantronics-Calisto-Pro.

ERGONOMIC WORKSTATIONS

You will be on your computer a lot—probably far more than you imagine and than you are in corporate America. If your online business is supplementing your income, you're adding even more computer time on top of your day job. Natural keyboards can save your wrists and hands, and you can bring in ergonomic specialists for anywhere from $300 to $500 to take measurements, make sure you have the right chair, workstation height, and so on. You may not want to have such expenses, but if you are like me and suffer pain from years of using the computer, the $300 can be the best money ever spent. Really, it is a personal decision. The other option, of course, is to simply invest in an ergonomic chair that is adjustable, and an ergonomic keyboard and mouse tray that is also adjustable (that is attached to your desk), and then adjust things to be sure you are pain free. Here is a great site with products to check out: imakproducts.com. For resources visit safecomputing tips.com. There are also sites with advice about setting up your work station. Look at positioning here: scsite.com/sclabs/menu.htm; check out the swivel options on this CPU holder: ergoindemand.com/cpu_holders.htm; consider the anti-glare filters (which increase privacy and minimize glare) here: ergoin demand.com/glare_filters.htm; LCD filters for laptops are available here: ergoindemand.com/Filter_for_LCDs.htm; and CFT filters are available here: ergoindemand.com/Hanging-Mount.htm.

INSTANT MESSAGING

One option for communicating with your clients is entirely free: instant messaging (IM). You can use any of several systems, including America Online (AOL) and Microsoft (MSN). Using an IM system will help you keep people from phoning. Some find instant messaging more annoying than phone calls, though, so this is a personal decision. Using a system like Trillian will let you have one IM application but several IM addresses. This is important if you want to keep it simple but offer multiple solutions for your customers. Sometimes customers will want to use IM to get hold of you, but they are using AOLs Instant Messenger and you are using MSN Messenger. While they are not incompatible, receiving messages from both means you have to have two login IDs and two systems running all of the time. A system like Trillian (and there are several out there for free) will let you use one software solution to log in to all of your accounts. Just remember to have a security suite installed—particularly a firewall application to protect your system; using these applications will compromise your system but most firewall applications allow you to configure the use of IM programs like these and ward off unsolicited attacks.

ELECTRONIC VERSUS TRADITIONAL FAX SYSTEMS

Electronic faxes will allow you to send and receive faxes by e-mail and via a web interface, which is particularly useful if you travel frequently or if you move—your number doesn't change even if you go out of area. I use MyFax online, which offers a toll-free number, too, which allows my clients to fax me at no cost.

Many online businesses will still need and want traditional fax services, especially in verification instances. So you can invest in a fax machine or a fax service. Fax services like jFax.com and eFax.com are very valuable because they save a lot of time; faxes are delivered to your e-mail in box and it's equally easy to send documents. You also get your own local virtual fax number or toll-free fax number if you want, without having to invest in a dedicated fax line or fax machine, and you get a copy of the fax in a digital format for archiving. Ultimately, though, I recommend choosing only one; as long as you have a scanner you can scan documents and fax out.

Traditional fax machines act as copiers and also let you send out quickly. I have both a traditional fax machine for sending and receiving large files or contracts and a MyFax account for smaller faxes or if others are sending to me. Many of you may choose this because of the convenience. It is nice to get the file already in electronic format, particularly if you want a paperless office as I do.

PDF CONVERTERS

Adobe's Portable Document Format (PDF) has become the standard for sharing documents and information. Even official documents are being sent online this way. PDFs are more difficult to tamper with than Word or Excel documents, for instance, and most people are able to view them on their equipment, although PDF editors are becoming more common in the marketplace today. PDF readers are free online or you can purchase something a bit more versatile with more features, like ScanSoft's PDF Convert. A PDF converter lets you take, for instance, a Word file and save it as a PDF file and vice versa. This lets you manipulate PDF files to sign contracts and easily send them back; it also lets you save, for instance, a Word test file into a PDF that students can't copy and paste from. This software has a multitude of uses and is relatively inexpensive. There are also lots of free software products like primoPDF, which prints your document into a PDF file. ScanSoft does a great job at character recognition and at creating editable PDFs. Your choice will just depend on what your business needs.

SCANNERS

Your scanner will serve many purposes including scanning documents that you need to save in electronic form, scanning graphics, and copying documents.

While I don't recommend spending a lot of money here, items like an automatic document feeder (ADF) can save you a lot of time if you have multiple pages to scan for one file.

PRINTERS

Even though you're working online, you'll find yourself printing files and contracts and reading off line, so you'll want a fast printer that uses inexpensive ink. Find one that will use cheap paper, too, because some printers will jam with lightweight paper.

BACKUP INTERNET PROVIDERS

It might not be a bad idea to have a backup internet provider, such as T-Mobile (which also works great when traveling) or a cell phone company's PCMCIA or USB laptop card that you can use at local coffee shops if your internet access goes down. Without internet access you are dead in the water. Look for high-speed options that work across the nation. You will be amazed at how much work you can get done while taxiing at JFK International Airport. Sprint and Verizon also have good plans, so check them all out. This has saved me many times at airports and even allowed me to do work in the hour-long taxi ride from JFK to Manhattan.

WIRELESS ACCESS POINTS

Consider using wireless in your business in addition to your hardwired connection. I would not recommend replacing your desktop's connection with wireless only, but having it as an option for your PDA and your laptop is great. Note that there *is* always speed degradation between wired and wireless. Your home desktop and even your laptop, if that's your primary computer, should have a hardwired connection. But wireless lets you roam about the house and teach while cooking dinner, for example. D-Link makes excellent wireless routers, but so do Belkin and LinkSys. Today's standard is the n+1, which has the best access and ability to penetrate walls with a superfast connection. Note that some wireless network cards are not forward compatible and some routers are not backward compatible, so to take advantage of speed upgrades and so on you will want to choose one that works with your current router.

VIRUS PROTECTION

Virus protection sounds simple enough, right? But many small businesses don't use virus protection and are forced to stop running for days out of each year. This is a must-have on any machine. Virus writers write destructive forces faster than we can keep up. Get a good virus protection program, pay for it, and have it autoupdate its definition files daily while you're not using your computer. Let it autoscan every morning sometime before you start work. Unless you are on a serious energy conservation trip, just leave your computer on and let it scan while you're sleeping. I know this makes a lot of people nervous; they have nightmares of burning down their house or sky-high electricity bills. You can just turn off your monitor but let the PC run. It has jobs to do at nighttime, particularly while the room is cool; it's better for the drives to churn away in ideal temperatures so that you don't overheat your machine.

ANTI-SPYWARE SOFTWARE

Spyware will take down the best system. Spyware is software that runs in the background of your machine, doing a variety of not-so-nice things. This includes monitoring your activities and even reporting to a marketing server what you did, where you went online, and what you bought. Often it's distributed within downloadable crippleware or freeware products. Several solutions are out there to help you manage this nightmare. AdAware and SpyBot Search and Destroy are the two that I use regularly and have used to fix others PCs. Either way, update them regularly and run them on a schedule and anytime you notice your computer slowing down; this is another good nighttime activity for your computer.

ANTI-SPAM PROGRAM

Spam can bog down your e-mail system, as you already know. The best solution is to turn on anti-spam protection from your internet service provider so that you don't receive junk mail at all. The trouble is, sometimes there are messages that get dumped into the spam box that shouldn't be there, so check it often and be sure to unblock domains of companies you work with or business partners. You might still miss the anonymous e-mail; just be sure to check your spam folder.

A quick tip not many people realize: Spammers will usually find you because you bought something online, put in your e-mail address, or downloaded some application that tracked you. The mass spammers also just randomize letters and send to major known providers, so having a tricky e-mail address keeps you somewhat protected from spam. There is a positive correlation between browsing the web or buying online and spam. Be careful to which sites you provide your e-mail address and look at their policies.

Be careful downloading software, especially the free kind. Read the license agreements, boring as they are. If they are tracking you or installing spyware, don't use them. It's rare to get something for nothing these days.

I recommend avoiding crippleware at all costs because it will work for a while for free and then ask for payment before continuing. Anything that says it works "partially" or "is somewhat locked" should be avoided. It's a scam.

If you do not really understand the differences between viruses, worms, Trojans, spam, and so on, take a look at grisoft.com/ww.product-avg-internet-security, which explains the following types of protection:

- Anti-virus: protection against viruses, worms, and Trojans
- Anti-spyware: protection against spyware, adware, and identity theft
- Anti-rootkit: protection against hidden threats (rootkits)

SHAREWARE

Shareware (software that you pay for on an honor system, like Simon's) often opens an annoying message like "Register me!" every two times you start it up, but it will continue working without registration. When you pay the usually small fee to register it, the messages go away.

- Anti-spam: filters out unwanted and fraudulent e-mails (anti-phishing)
- Web shield and LinkScanner: protection against malicious websites
- Firewall: protection against hackers
- System tools: for easy system management

The candidates for virus and hacker protection are Symantec/Norton, McAfee, and F-Secure. All very powerful, but often, the least popular and the least well-known is the less attacked and the more effective. In my view, Norton is the weakest of them all, and I've found the company to be the slowest to respond while the product is the worst resource hog.

E-MAIL ACCOUNTS WITH IN-BOX HIGH LIMITS

You may want an e-mail account with an in-box high limit, which really means virtually no limit. Some of the files you will work with will be many megabytes; I have sent 80 MB to 100 MB files to my web development team. Hotmail and GMail have nearly unlimited accounts at many gigabytes, and you should get one of these accounts in addition to whatever comes with your internet service provider. You may have to pay a small fee for unlimited or very high use access, but it is well worth it. Also, if you get a domain such as mydomainishere.com, you will want an e-mail account for that domain. However, you can always use a forwarding system within your domain system to forward the mail to your Hotmail address, keeping only one address that you need to maintain. Forwards are easy to set up.

OFFICE SUITES

By office suite, I mean Microsoft Office. It is expensive, but it is also a standard. Buying 2007 will ensure backward compatibility, but if you have an older 2003 version you can download a free compatibility pack to open 2007 files.

Consider using a PDA that supports at least a reader of each of these products so that if you're checking e-mail remotely and need to answer something with an attachment, you aren't pressured into rushing back home. Any Windows CE device should come standard with pocket versions of Word, PowerPoint, and Excel.

There are cheaper options, of course, but you may run into compatibility issues when working with others. Free Office is available at openoffice.org and Word Perfect Office (not free but cheaper) is available at corel.com/servlet/Satellite/us/en/Product/1151523326841. IBM Lotus Suite Symphony is actually free and is a decent product; it was out before Microsoft Office.

ONE WEB ARCHITECT'S OFFICE SETUP

What does a web architect use at his place of work to design and build hundreds of websites? Here is a setup, including ergonomics:

- Two 22-inch LCD monitors attached to one computer
- Back cushion
- Nonskid wrist cushion for keyboard
- Nonskid mousing combo
- Adjustable footrest
- Adjustable keyboard and mouse tray
- Adjustable chair
- Adjustable monitor arms

Other than that, you need a reasonably fast computer with 5 GB of memory—that is it. Even the most sophisticated developers don't have to spend thousands upon thousands for office equipment.

A GREEN OFFICE

An online business is perhaps the ultimate in green. You probably won't have mounds of paperwork, hours of incandescent lighting and office time, or the need to cool a 10,000-square-foot building housing your hundreds or thousands of employees, as many of them will be virtual. You will be cutting out fuel costs and will provide the ultimate in efficiency for commuting for your team members or contractors. Going green online is, in fact, quite easy.

First, have a plan in place for conducting meetings online. NetMeeting (free from Microsoft) or tools like GoToMeeting will allow you to hold virtual meetings, not requiring airline travel or commuting, which will save on gas and help the air quality.

Your online business will probably also be hosted on an external server somewhere—chances are in a location where power is cheap. And while these server rooms are cooled, they also host thousands or tens of thousands of businesses in one room! This is the ultimate in power saving.

This is also the time to look at things like the wattage on your computer's power supply (keeping in mind that USB devices could power down your computer if you overload it), but also getting the minimum that you need (which should not exceed 300 watts in most cases). You can run monitors and video cards in power save mode, and turn off your computers when they are not in use. This all saves a tremendous amount of energy. Being the boss also means you set the rules for how efficient you want to be. You can implement a "no print" policy if you want to—saving trees and power all at the same time. Buy recycled ink for that printer if you wish, and use only cell phones. If you want to buy all recycled products, that is your call, although you probably won't have much need to print for an online business anyway. Most of your marketing will be virtual—talk about saving money for print advertising. Except for business cards and about 500 pieces of stationery a year, I haven't needed much.

YourOnlineProfessor.com

Technology technology, and more technology—staples of the online business owner. From internet access to conference phones to VoIP, visit the forums at Your OnlineProfessor.com and take advantage of Dr. Danis years of technology experience to get the best possible goods.

Want to see what others are saying is the best color copier under $400? Do you want to know what other entrepreneurs are using for Bluetooth? Visit the YourOnline Professor.com forums for more insight and information.

There are a ton of tools out there, so how do you separate what you need from what you could live without? Visit the forums, ask others, and read Dr. Dani's articles on the topic all at YourOnlineProfessor.com.

PART

III

A ROAD MAP TO SUCCESS

CHAPTER

6

SETTING YOUR PRICE

Determining What to Charge

Sometimes the hardest part for people in their own business is figuring out what to charge for their work—essentially, setting a price! It sounds easy—just look at what others are doing. But there is a fear that if you charge too much, no one will buy, and if you charge too little, you might be perceived as having an inferior product or service or may not make enough money to make it worth your time.

Chances are you want to differentiate yourself, so you cannot simply charge what another site is charging for the same service or product. You need to do your own research and poll people—find out what they'd be willing to pay for what you're offering.

You have to determine what price is right for the unique product or service that you offer. Document what the buyer or client will get for that money, and advertise why it is worth the price you set. This topic can get a bit tricky, so this may be a good time to jump onto the Entrepreneur Press blog for this book and share tips and tricks for setting your online price!

> Charging less than your competitors can be (and usually is) a good thing, particularly if your target market is price-conscious. What you lack in profit margin per unit (per product or hour of service) you can make up for in quantity of orders or work.

This chapter is designed to help you entrepreneurs figure out where your starting price should be and help you set realistic (but appropriate) expectations. It will also help you determine when you need to change your price and whether you are priced too high or too low. It focuses on services offered, boundaries set, availability, the type of service offered, the type of client appealed to, and the relative price for similar services in the area.

LURK IN PUBLIC PLACES—GET THE SCOOP!

One way to feel out your potential customers is to post to blogs and forums; you can either "lurk" and ask questions, or you can introduce yourself as a new business owner and entrepreneur and ask others what they would expect to pay for your product or service. Both are good ways to get started.

What are other ways to determine how you should price your product or service? A site called SmallBusinessNotes.com has some good tips and techniques for pricing your product. It notes that it is crucial to determine who your target market is and then what they are willing to pay—which is one reason I recommend going to fanatic sites (for example, sites for wine connoisseurs are great for testing out a good price on various types of wine or for advice)—and then add a profit margin that you can live with. The authors of the site know that there are many approaches to pricing, some scientific and some, well, not so much. They note one model for creating a starting point for price: They assume cost is the total of the fixed and variable expenses (costs to you) to sell the product or service, and price is the selling price customers pay. One method is to use the perceived value approach, which is somewhere between your cost and what the market generally charges, making you a bit more competitive yet still able to make a profit.

CONSIDER AN ACCOUNTANT'S POINT OF VIEW

There are a few key definitions that need to be noted here; one is the value basis and the other is a cost basis. *Value basis* is used to set a selling price based on what the customer will pay for the service or product. The value basis for pricing is a bit risky because if someone comes in cheaper or can find alternative suppliers, the market rate for the product can go down fast. This method requires you to continually look at the benefits and downsides to others' businesses and determine how your pricing strategy is and know when others are offering lower prices.

Cost-based pricing is based on a financial accounting calculation that creates the gross profit margin that is required given a certain expected sales volume and fixed overhead costs. Sales prices set using cost basis would be the amount paid plus a percentage, or the profit margin. When competition is hard at play and a strong differentiator in the market is price, this is often what is used to determine the price. This method is very sensitive to price fluctuations, but does take into consideration service levels, which is important.

HIGHEST PROFITABLE PRICE—FINDING THE BALANCE

You will want to create the highest profitable price that does not negatively affect sales, so market research is important. The highest level you can set a value basis price is dependent on the customer base, the demographic of your customer, and the product, service, quality, availability, and benefits you provide.

Your goals are to generate the highest profit margins you can, while remaining competitive and not getting a reputation online as a rip-off.

HOW YOU CAN LOWER COSTS FOR GOODS—AND LOWER PRICES, TOO

Obviously, the cheaper you can buy your product for, the lower you can sell it for and still make a profit. Large businesses have a distinct advantage here because they buy in large quantities or source cheaper products from overseas and, therefore, can sell at a cheaper rate. They also build economies of scale and efficiencies into their work, which helps drive down price. It isn't wise to compete with products that people can buy at Wal-Mart if you cannot beat Wal-Mart's price because of their ability to buy in bulk.

People are still willing to pay a bit more if their products will be delivered promptly, they will get good service, the site offers live chat, and so on. Consider Zappos: Free returns for a year! Free return shipping! Automatic price adjustment by typing in the URL of the lower-priced competition. Now that is service. They have built quite a loyal fan base.

You can also set different prices for different customers. For instance, customers who pay for a monthly membership may be entitled to 10 percent off their purchases or great coupons that you send via e-mail to remind them about your site and encourage repurchasing! Think of what brick-and-mortar

Beating the Low-Price Leaders

Unfortunately once one company goes low price online, if you don't follow you may lose customers who care mostly or only about price. You will have lower overhead if you have an online store, particularly if you have an online store that ships directly from the manufacturer or distributor, but you still need to make a profit! Often the margin on just pure sales is so low that people have a hard time making money, so you will want to consider how you will differentiate on service and then do that.

stores, like drugstores and grocery stores, do. They have club cards to encourage purchasing, and they are able to keep track of what you buy most and when you buy; your web developer or designer can give you that type of data, too. Using analytics, you can get information about your buyers and their buying patterns that will help you market to them. Also, you may want to offer bulk discounts for customers who buy in large quantities. The more you buy from your suppliers, the more leverage you will get to have prices adjusted downward for you for future purchases.

Also, keep an eye on supply and demand. When demand is going up or if supply is going down, you can often raise your prices without much repercussion. Just be sure you do so incrementally so as not to hurt your business.

KEEP TRACK OF COSTS

It is very easy to think you are making a profit; you see the bank account balance rising and have high hopes! Then you pay the bills, and are left with next to nothing for all that work. It is essential that you keep track of all costs throughout the entire process of building and growing your business so that you know what is being spent. Sometimes we think costs are fixed, but they are really variable. For instance, say you pay an employee by the hour to handle orders. This seems like a fixed cost—but as the volume of orders goes up, so will the number of hours the employees work—therefore it is really a variable cost. By keeping track of this in a spreadsheet or by using Quicken or another product to manage your

WHEN TO HIRE AN ACCOUNTANT

There generally is no need for an accountant in the early and mid stages of your business growth, but it is something you may want to consider after your inventory and sales become incredibly large. (Yes, it will happen!) I got to a point about two years into my business where my taxes were very complicated, and while I could have figured them out, I wanted a reputable person protecting me and making sure things were done right.

expenses, you can keep tabs on everything and limit surprises. If you know what contracts are outstanding and which companies or clients owe you what, it is easier to plan and maintain your business.

BUSINESS-TO-BUSINESS SALES

If your product or service is business-to-business, you are in a different boat. The cost you ask for your service affects the price the buyer of your goods or services must charge their consumers: often B2B sales are priced differently. Many companies already have a predetermined budget for what they can spend on a product or service, and they simply go with the provider that offers the least cost. So, if you're providing B2B, you will want to be careful of the pricing strategy you use. Remember that businesses that buy from you may not need the level of service or hand-holding that a consumer would, so you may not be able to charge more for added services. Often companies *will* pay for ways you make their cost of doing business cheaper, like automated invoicing or sending data to their database systems automatically.

PRICE LIKE AN ENTREPRENEUR

Entrepreneur.com has a fabulous article written by Ian Benoliel: "How to Price your Product and Determine what Calculations are Right for your Business" (available at entrepreneur.com/money/moneymanagement/financial managementcolumnistpamnewman/article53786.html). Bendiel focuses on whether you are a market leader or follower, which is very valid regardless of the business you are in. He writes:

> Pricing products is something every businessperson thinks about. You don't want to price yourself out of the market, but at the same time you want to provide sufficient margin to cover overhead and generate a profit. Therefore, in pricing your products you must consider these two factors: what the market will bear and your profit margins. These factors apply to pricing both products and services. To find out what the market will bear, ask yourself this question: Is my product or service unique? If it is—meaning there's little in the way of

direct and indirect competition—then you're a market leader and you have more leeway in setting the prices.

Just because your product is unique, doesn't mean you can charge very high prices. When you have a unique product and you set your prices high, your customers can still pick an alternative product or not buy at all. In addition, your high margins may give incentives to competitors to copy your product and then undercut your price. Take Apple Computer: The product was unique, the company charged very high prices and it was the market leader. Of course there were other factors that led to Apple losing market share, but one factor was that new entrants like Dell and Compaq offered alternative products at better prices.

You can be a market leader if you sell a product that is not necessarily unique, but where you are the only available outlet for that product. If you've ever been on a cruise ship and visited the on-board convenience store, you know what I mean.

If you are a market follower—meaning your product is not necessarily unique and you're not the only outlet—then setting prices is easy. Your prices simply can't be higher than that of your closest competitor. The question you should then ask is this: Should I be selling this product? The answer lies in your profit margin for this product.

There are three different profit margin calculations one should consider: direct costs margin, break-even pricing, and profit pricing.

The direct costs margin is the margin generated after paying for costs that are directly associated with the product or service being sold. Examples include costs of sales, commissions, and so on. The formulas for direct costs margin and direct costs margin percent are:

- direct costs margin = sales price - total direct costs
- direct costs margin percent = direct costs margin ÷ sales price x 100 percent

You can also use the direct costs margin percent to calculate the break-even volume as follows:

- break-even volume = (fixed costs ÷ direct costs margin percent) ÷ selling price

You must at least cover direct costs to continue carrying the product. You may accept a price that is greater than direct costs in the short-term (such as a slow month). Over the long term, however, you must also cover your fixed costs and generate a profit—otherwise, you're just trading dollars.

Fixed costs are costs that do not fluctuate with sales volume like rent, depreciation, administrative employees and so on. Break-even pricing is related to the break-even point, but instead of having the volume as the variable, selling price is the variable as follows:

- break-even price = direct costs ÷ unit + fixed costs ÷ volume

Setting the price at the break-even price will give you a profit of 0. If you're at least getting the break-even price, you're not losing money on the sale. However, all that work and investment still won't pay off. This brings us to profit pricing, which is calculated as follows:

- profit price = direct costs ÷ unit + (fixed costs + desired profit) ÷ volume

So now you have a price that will make you a profit. Ask yourself this: Can I sell my products and services at this price and still be competitive? If the answer is no, then you have two alternatives: lower your direct costs, fixed costs, or desired profit, or consider not selling this product and focus your attention instead on products that have a better profit margin or less competition.

YourOnlineProfessor.com

Pricing! KEY to success? Perhaps. It is very important. What is your product or service worth? Want to find out how others priced their work? Go to YourOnline Professor.com for more information and to get help from others.

Lower your costs and outsource. It isn't as bad as it sounds, and you will (if you do it right) create more jobs than you lose. Visit YourOnlineProfessor.com to learn how others have done it and what partners they use.

CHAPTER

7

UNIQUE WAYS TO SELL

Different Strategies for the Online World

One thing it seems most online entrepreneurs discover rather quickly is that they have to find very unique ways to sell and market in the online world! From meta tags to new pricing strategies, online entrepreneurs must be top in the game of beating out online competition.

HTML TAGS

Let's take a look for a moment at something very important: HTML tools and tags. Search engines and other optimization tools (search engine optimizations are referred to in the online world as SEOs) need to be able to find your site. How do they do this? Through meta tags. This is something that your web developer or architect must build into your site to make it searchable. You may also want to consider buying advertising space from a company like Google, which I discuss later in the book.

For now, though, be sure that your web developer has meta tags—that is, descriptions about your site content—and that everything from pictures on the site to stuff you sell is indexed with a tag that will allow everything to be searchable and found online. This is very important. Also remember that the more hits your site gets, the faster it will move up the search engine ranks. Many of us have paid for a while for higher-ranking results, which is something you can do by clicking on the Advertising link on Google or Yahoo!'s homepage. These are the two top search engines, so buying into another probably won't be worth your money.

PRICING STRATEGIES

You may need to take a totally different approach to your pricing strategy, depending on what you are selling. Here are some creative ideas that are worth considering, particularly those unique to online businesses.

Hold Auctions—With or Without eBay

Even if you aren't in the auction business, you might have an item available for auction each month or each week, something on the homepage that has no reserve and a low starting amount, something that gets people excited to go to your site. Another thing to consider is creating an eBay account and selling one

Good Products for Skimming

Think iPhone or Wii—price the item high while it's hot, then drop it while it fades and availability becomes greater. This will require some time and effort on your part in making sure your price is right, at the right time. You may even have to make multiple adjustments during the day.

item at a time. In your item listing, direct people to much higher-priced items on your site.

Price Using the Perfect Market

One creative pricing strategy is to find the "perfect price." The first ever perfect market was eBay, because at any given second, literally, an individual will buy a product for exactly what it is worth to the public at large, including international buyers. Truly, when you buy something on eBay, you are buying it for its exact value at that time. You may experiment with pricing models by first trying to sell your product on eBay and seeing what it goes for. Does it sell for more on certain days? Does it sell for more if you write certain words in the auction information section? This might help you define your meta tags when you get to that point. I have personally used this strategy before to price products, and it worked well for me.

Undercut the Price Leadership

Another option is to go out there on the web and find the most expensive company for a similar product and then price your product, including shipping and applicable taxes, $1 or $2 less. This is, of course, assuming you offer comparable service. If you do, you will beat your competitor.

Undercut the Value Pricer

Another strategy is to do the exact opposite and undercut the value pricer. This would be similar, in brick-and-mortar terms, to building a 99-cent store next to Wal-Mart, then carrying a lot of similar products or the same products for pennies less. Whom will you capture this way? Individuals who are buying strictly on the basis of price, and you will be surprised how many do. If you do this, you'll need basic customer service or you will risk getting a bad reputation. Be sure you are making a reasonable profit also. It is tough to compete with a Wal-Mart-like store if you aren't buying in Wal-Mart-like bulk.

Offer Bulk Discounts

Do people buy in bulk from online stores? Yes! Try purchasing something at vistaprint.com (great site, by the way, for your new businesses needs–I use them all the time) and checking out. You'll be asked at checkout, if you want to "add 250 more business cards for only $7.99 more," for example. Of course you just paid $50 for the first 250, so it is a steal. But it costs them very little to print more, so their profit margin on the second 250 is higher than on the first 250. You can also offer discounts if your customers buy more than one product.

Sell Loss Leaders

This is a common tactic in the used car business, and has a bad reputation because of it. But, low-price loss leaders do work, which is the reason they continue to be in play in today's most savvy marketing plans. Advertising a few low-cost items, particularly in newsletters, helps drive business. Think TigerDirect.com or even big sites like Target.com that have cheap items right there on their homepage. While you are there, it directs you to other products that may be of interest—and of course have higher margins.

Set Prices at the $.99

How many gas stations do you see with gas for $2.99? And think of sale items for $29.99 and televisions for $499.99? While it is a penny to you, there is a psychological impact of not rounding to the next number. Paying $30 for something is paying in the thirties, which has a psychological effect on consumers. This is hard to do in some brick-and-mortar stores because it leads to bunches of odd prices, but online it is easy as the transaction is all web-based anyway.

Skim Profits on New Products

Another method of pricing is to skim. Let's say you sell cell phones. When a new product comes out, you charge high profit margins but guarantee availability (particularly if an item is hot—people will come to you just because you can get it) and then drop the price very quickly as you see the item penetrate the market.

Price Line

When you price line, you set a quality level for each product type and then set the price entirely based on quality. This is commonly done in businesses where there are only three of four qualities of parts, and you want to keep consumers shopping because figuring out price is simple and straightforward. You might offer four types of cell phone chargers with different levels of reliability and features.

Up-Charge for Services

Think of Southwest Airlines' new way of doing business: you can buy a cheap seat (what the airline is known for), but you can also pay a premium to get priority boarding. Virgin America did a similar thing with very low prices for the coach seats and high flat-rate prices for the first-class seats. While service is far better in first class, the basics—leather seats, navigation, and internet access—are the same. Offer a base service level to everyone, then charge for the extras and let people decide what is right for them. Perhaps most importantly, make it easy for people to upgrade. This way you capture the low end and the high end of the market. Just be sure your brand doesn't get stigmatized with a Wal-Mart-like low-cost-leader but poor-service retention by making certain your base service level is decent.

Follow the Single Pricing Strategy

A single pricing strategy is a bit difficult to do successfully but it is when you charge a customer the exact same price for everything on your site. For example, "Everything on my site is $19.99." Obviously some items have a 2 percent profit margin while others have a 300 percent profit margin, and you want to steer customers to those higher profit margin items. There are no surprises when customers go to check out, and they come to your site always knowing what to expect.

Take Advantage of Returning Customers

Although a great amount of your time will probably be spent on spreading the word about your new business and gaining additional customers or clients, this doesn't mean that you should lack in the area of serving your current customers and clients. Let them know that you appreciate their patronage and dedication to you and your business. Offer returning customers discounts on your products or services.

A great way to retain customers and gain new ones is to offer referral discounts. You can offer a discount to the referring customer or to the referred customer or to both. The power of saving does a great deal to motivate sales and return patronage.

UNDERSTANDING THE IMPACT OF PRICE

While we like to think that our product and service differentiate us from our competitor, the fact is that price has an impact on competitive advantage, whether we like it or not. This is especially true when we are trying to build our brand and reputation, which requires a lot more work in the beginning. This is another reason you need to thoroughly brand yourself with the online community, participate in online discussions, and be known as an expert—your free advice will pay off in the form of very loyal customers.

YourOnlineProfessor.com

Pricing strategies are important, particularly for various times of the year. There will be times your product is more desirable than others. What are some ways to find out? Visit YourOnlineProfessor.com for information on how to price, HTML tags, and the impact of your pricing models.

CHAPTER

8

ADVERTISING

Your Online Business in a Global Market

Advertising is the key to starting and growing your business. You can have the best business idea in the world, but if no one knows about it and no one is drawn to your site, it is irrelevant. You will want to advertise to lots of individuals—locals that want to buy local, other web businesses, affiliates, businesses (business-to-business or B2B), consumers (business-to-consumer or B2C), international, national, you name it. In times when the dollar is

strong (meaning interest rates are generally higher), your focus might be more on domestic sales than international; as the dollar weakens, you may shift to a more global focus. One great thing about the internet is that you can advertise to everyone and anyone, and you can accept online payments and ship anywhere, so your market is literally limitless. Using global shipping companies that are automated (like PayPal's multiship function or the postal service's USPS.gov automated shipping service) makes shipping a snap. If you are handling inventory, having Priority Mail boxes handy makes flat-rate shipping super easy and takes the guesswork out of shipping costs. But, we'll get into details later; right now we'll focus on how to get that business as "out there" as possible. This chapter is devoted to teaching you, the web entrepreneur, how to advertise, where to advertise, what the key ingredients in the advertising recipe are, and how to begin getting clients. So, let's dive right in.

MAY I HAVE YOUR ATTENTION, PLEASE?

An understanding of how the human attention span operates is something all advertising and marketing professionals strive for. Once this understanding is achieved, you can use the knowledge to your advantage, exploiting the ins and outs of what works, what doesn't, and why. A great article on this subject was written by Gloria DeGaetano (2008) and published on the Parent Coaching Institute's website. Although the article is based on the child's attention span, the primal concepts are the same. You can read "Attention Span: A Fundamental Human Requirement" at thepci.com/articles/degae tano_Attention Span.htm.

Television Assumptions

Many television network producers have told me that the viewer has about a 12-second attention span. If topics aren't changed in 12 seconds or something pretty isn't on the screen within that time, they lose the viewer either mentally or via channel hopping.

TRADITIONAL ADVERTISING METHODS

Traditional advertising is still viable and valid today even if you have a web-only business. A web-only business doesn't mean you should be advertising only on the web. You need to push your website and e-mail address on your business card and your domain site on your business card and in any flier, classified ad, newspaper ad, or even traditional radio and television commercials if you decide to go that route. Do you own a business that is becoming "webified"? Have you been mailing fliers and leaving calendars on doors? Do the same (unless it isn't working), but be sure your domain name is everywhere!

CLIENT AND BUSINESS PARTNER GIFTS

It sounds simple enough: offer gifts each year around the holiday times in a nonoffensive manner (you don't know the religion of your clients, most likely). "Season's Greetings" is certainly appropriate, and you should consider doing this for your clients and even business partners each year. I budget $2,000 each year for client gifts and gifts to producers in the media; it has never been a wasted effort or expense. First, I truly appreciate their loyalty and I want to show it, genuinely. Secondly, I am reminding them I appreciate them. Why can this be a bad thing? Third, I am getting my name out there. One year I sent a basket of Mrs. Fields cookies to a major television cable news anchor, and he wrote me back a personal signed thank-you note; I haven't missed a month on his show since. I didn't send the cookies to get more hits, but it is good business practice and it was genuine gratitude on my part. I also happen to know he likes sweets.

PRE- AND POST-WEB 2.0

There is a pre-Web 2.0 era and a post-Web 2.0 era. We already know that Web 2.0 is dynamic, customer driven, and consumer and community focused. But the way we advertise in both spaces is different. In the pre-Web 2.0 era, people still promoted their websites through newsgroups instead of blogs, or through Bulletin Board Systems (BBS); all of these small promotions paid off. You should still be doing this. Why not host a newsgroup? It might take 20 minutes of moderation per week to remove spammers, but you build loyalty by offering a free place for people to gather. Better yet, have this integrated into your site.

Now of course there is Web 2.0, and you have social broadcasting, social networking, social blogging—notice a key word here? *Social.* Follow your target audience around and know what Web 2.0 sites they are drawn to. The Web 2.0 internet generation lives in a collaborative world where people associate engagement with being able to contribute to a blog or share a video or a file or comment; they don't like being fed information with no method of remarking. They want to synchronize their cell phones and bookmark their PDAs, and their world revolves around this low-attention span, younger target audience that, whether they are today or tomorrow, will eventually be your consumers. They like innovation, and innovation attracts them to you, your product, and your site. This is the group spending an hour a night answering MySpace bulletins to learn more about their top friends, and they don't have a phone at home because they are entirely mobile by cell. You need to determine if your web ventures appeal to them, which I discuss further in the next section.

AUDIENCE PROFILE

The key to any of the campaigns I talk about in this chapter is really knowing your target audience profile. If you are selling music and genres, who is your target audience? Where do they live online? Yes, *live* online! If most of your sales are from pop, R&B, rap, and rock, maybe your target audience falls within the 13 to 25 age group or maybe it's 26 to 35. Either way, you need to know. Then you need to research where these people hang out online, and advertise there. Find out what concerts they go to and where they buy the tickets, and advertise there. What else does the younger generation buy? Ring tones, games, music, DVDs, Facebook and MySpace profile editors—you name it. Understand your target audience like there is no tomorrow, because if you don't, that just might be the end of your business.

CONNECTIONS WITH ESTABLISHED BUSINESSES

One quick way to get established quickly is to connect your business with others that are already, well, established. I did this with my book *Finding*

Advertising with Complementary Businesses

If you sell airline tickets, partner with hotels and taxi services, tour guides, and so on. Find complementary products and then advertise with those businesses.

Foreclosures by getting to know the fine folks at RealtyTrac really well and then finding ways we could sell each other's product. They gave my data credibility, and I helped sell memberships. I would talk about their data on television, promoting them, while they had a reverse link back to me. Is there a local restaurant you frequent where the staff knows you and your order by memory? That would be a good place to start. Maybe the owners will let you leave brochures around.

ONLINE ADVERTISING METHODS

Before we get into too many details, be sure that you have an advertising budget set aside for buying ads online. Buying banner ads and offering affiliate links is going to cost you money. Much of what you can do is free, as you will see, but you will need a budget, too. We also need to go over some basic advertising methods: cost-per-click advertising (CPC), cost per impressions advertising (CPM), and cost-per-action (CPA) advertising.

CPC Advertising

Cost-per-click advertising is the most common method of advertising out there, and when you think of buying ads, this is probably what you associate with it. With this type of advertising, you place an ad on another site, and you pay a fee each time someone clicks on the ad to get to your site. Web users are becoming more and more frustrated with banner ads and buttons though, so this isn't always the best form of advertising. Some have even called for boycotts against sites that have too many ads because they are annoying to users, and you don't want to pay for an ad no one wants to click on. How many times have you visited a site that won't let you even continue looking at it until you close an ad, thereby forcing you to look at it longer? Many blacklist these sites (so don't use this method on your own site either). The ads appear on sites in the same manner as other advertising methods, such as CPM (cost per 1,000 impressions, for example, or for the amount of times an ad appears on a page), but the difference is in how you pay. In CPC ad campaigns, you pay only for the number of times people actually click on the ad, as mentioned earlier. It might cost more per click than it would per impression, but at least you're paying only for what draws traffic to your site. You also set a price ceiling–a maximum amount you will pay each month–so that you can balance and protect your fees each month or year. This will help you with budgeting as well. Your ads just automatically run until the number of click-throughs you paid for is reached, which also means your ad will stay up for awhile and get greater visibility for your company, even though you may not get a click-through for it.

Where to Set Up CPC Advertising

So where can you find CPC services? Google AdWords is the most commonly known CPC seller. With AdWords, you pick the keywords that you want to use and pay for as many clicks as you can afford and want to pay for–with no surprise bills.

CPM Advertising

Although CPC advertising continues to be very popular, cost-per-impressions (say 1,000) is another effective way to reach your customers. Instead of paying per click, you pay for a set number of impressions, or appearances, on a website.

Of course one downside here is that we know click-through rates in general are going down as people become annoyed with ads, so you may be paying for brand recognition more than immediate customers. This is often a nice idea on a popular site coupled with other methods that require you to pay only once you get a customer from the click. For example, say you have some CPC-based advertising for which you are spending $.50 per click. If you get 10 clicks, you'll spend $5. In a CPM-based ad campaign, you may pay $10 for 10,000 impressions, meaning once your ad is shown 10,000 times, you'll pay $10. Which is the better value? The key here is click-through ratios. You need to monitor those numbers to see which approach is a worthwhile method for you.

Interestingly enough, we are seeing that often text-based ads actually receive more attention and click-throughs than banner ads. That probably seems odd, since banners are graphical and we assume people would prefer to click on a graphic. But data shows that the average view time for a text-based ad is about 7.0 seconds (people have to read it) while the average for a graphical ad is about 1.6 seconds. If you decide to pay for an ad, you may see if the site offers text-based advertising. Also, if your keywords are very popular and expensive, CPM-based methods might be better for you. Remember that clicking through to your site isn't the be-all-and-end-all of ad campaigns. It might garnish attention and help build brand awareness and recognition, but if people don't buy, what is the point? Remember also that an unclicked ad that is viewed can be valuable, because people will tend to remember your site if they see it advertised often, particularly if the name is catchy.

Another alternative is to ask that your ad be seen on particular pages that are geared toward your audience. Click-through ratios improve if the audience is targeted rather than general. You should be able to find good advertising options if you ask the advertiser; they want your ad bucks and are willing to make modifications to get them. I recommend buying into low minimums first so that you can see if the ad campaign is going to work before you pay a lot for it. Do your homework and don't pay for a large amount of impressions up front, and be sure you are very clear on your budget. Make sure the contract clearly states your maximum amount paid out monthly.

CPA Advertising

In cost-per-action advertising, you pay for performance–i.e., you won't pay unless you actually make a sale off the company's referring ad. Sometimes the advertisers will charge you for registration or subscriptions (even if subscribing is free) because it means more targeted leads for you, so read the contract carefully. When you select this type of advertising, your ad is put into rotation and then it begins to display as soon as it's added. You decide what actions you will pay for—sale, registrations, newsletters, and so on—and then budget for that. If you pay for 100 sales, your ad will continue displaying until that goal is reached.

You should use this method if you want to test your ad before starting a large advertising campaign online. This will let you see how many people actually purchase your products after viewing your ad; if you want to go with bigger CPC- or CPM-based ads later, at least you'll have the ad type, graphics, wording, and so on fine-tuned. Be sure to pay careful attention to the common mistakes discussed in Chapter 12 so you don't make the mistakes of not tuning your advertising. Also, you should note that most affiliate systems are basically CPA advertising systems. If you are an affiliate, say, of RealtyTrac through their affiliate system, you get paid each time someone subscribes to RealtyTrac. The same holds true for you as a business owner; you pay only your affiliates for people who actually buy. If you want to test an affiliate program, this is a good way to do it. Also, if you aren't experiencing great sales from your existing methods, you may try offering affiliate dollars; you may also try this method if you have a limited advertising budget because you set the threshold and you pay only for real clients. (See the "Affiliate Networks" section below.)

Affiliate Networks

There are two ways to attract targeted visitors to your site through affiliate networks. The first is to participate in an affiliate network. This means that as an affiliate, you place a link on your site and the merchant of the site to which you are referring people pays you compensation for all visitors arriving through the link or for those who purchase an item, depending on the agreement. There are thousands of affiliate programs out there, and some great directories for these are the iBoost Journal Directory and the AssociatePrograms.com system, as well as Commission Junction. Affiliate networks help boost your revenue and also associate your site through keyword searches with other sites that have similar interests or target bases of customers.

Another option is to create your own affiliate program. If you offer others money to list your company then you are paying them for each new membership or each click-through that they send to your site. Be sure you are careful here, though; some will require payment for every click even if it doesn't result in a sale. For a refresher, review the sections on CPCs, CPMs, and CPAs. If you offer affiliate money, be sure you pay promptly and as promised. It is recommended you go through an affiliate system (one of my favorites is Commission Junction) so that this is managed and traffic is reported correctly. Appendix A has some great sources for affiliate networking.

Banner Ads, Pop-Up Ads, and More

Let's face it—advertising your business can be one of the most difficult things to do because there are so many options and choices available to you. There isn't a lot of data with regard to which ad type works best, because it is incredibly industry specific and very focused on the type of business, the mood of the user, the originating site, the type of product or service, how long the ad stays on the page, the hosting site, and numerous other things.

Animated ads and pop-up ads have the highest visibility, but they also have the lowest click-through rates, probably because people are saturated with online ads and tend to discount them and not pay attention to them as much as they used to. We also know that textual or in-line ad campaigns work best. People are experiencing what the business refers to as "banner blindness"—growing so

Avoid Hijacking Ads

One thing is for sure: If the ad is going to "hijack" the customer's computer, don't buy it! In other words, if you're being offered an ad that will require the user to close or click off it to make it go away, you will annoy your potential customer base to no end. Instead of focusing on the ad, people will focus on how to *close* the ad.

accustomed to ads that they ignore them. AdBrite and Google's AdSense will allow you to use simple text ads, which is very valuable. In the early stages of these types of ads, you can see hit rates of 70 to 90 percent, depending on the study that you read. That is an incredible percentage. Use graphics for branding, but text ads if you want actual business.

Advertising on Google

Google is synonymous with *search*; *Google* is a household name—and for good reason. Everything from Google Earth to searching is done through a vast company with incredible reach. Google offers two advertising programs: AdWords and AdSense. AdWords is for advertisers, and AdSense is for web publishers. If you go to the Google homepage, select Advertising Programs underneath the Google Search section, then select AdWords or AdSense.

AdWords targets people actively looking for information related to a particular product or service that your business sells; this means that those who visit your site from AdWords are targeted—prescreened, if you will—genuine leads. It uses CPC pricing, which means you pay when your ad is clicked on. There is an activation fee, then a per-click fee. You tell Google how much you are willing to pay per click and per day. Ads for your business appear alongside or above results on the Google search results pages, too, which is great for building your brand.

AdSense, on the other hand, is for web publishers to earn revenue from their websites. AdSense will deliver an ad that is targeted to content pages, and when Google WebSearch is added to the site, AdSense also delivers targeted ads to the search results page. This allows your company to make residual income when visitors click on ads that are associated with your business, which also means the ads you're selling and making money from are targeted leads as well. Ads that appear are those relevant to your own company and your own business, and you can manage your AdSense account and track earnings online very easily.

Free Internet Advertising

If you have been looking around, chances are you are finding all kinds of free advertising online. But you will get what you pay for. The ads may give off the wrong impression for your company, so be careful. Sometimes these advertisers will attach words you don't want associated with your business. This is considered a guerrilla marketing tactic, and while it may have some benefits, it could really diminish your brand. Such advertising techniques used to be called "link farms" and there are still quite a few of them out there; unfortunately while you may gain a few clicks, you may sacrifice your quality and image.

Link Exchanges with Colleagues and Friends

I got started with my online businesses by exchanging links with colleagues and friends–offering free advertising for them on my site if they put ads up on their sites. It is a good way to get started in an internet marketing campaign and you certainly can't beat the price! I would recommend doing this immediately, no matter what type of ad campaign you ultimately choose for your business model. Just be sure you are connected with businesses that you want to be affiliated with.

Monitoring the Effectiveness of your Online Ad Campaign

So you just spent your entire first month's profits on a new ad campaign. Someone asks, "How is the advertising going?" Your answer should not be "Um, I don't know, actually. Let me find out." Or worse yet, just a plain old "I don't know." You must have the ability to track ad performance. There are many sites now using tracking programs that produce reports on every imaginable aspect of your online campaign. The basics include the number of impressions your ad has received and clicks it has earned. If you are doubting or just want to double-check (always a good idea) the validity of the data that the company you are advertising with is sending you, using these third-party companies can help validate information (and it's also keeping companies more honest knowing there are systems out there they can tell if they're being truthful). You want to check conversion ratio reports from your ad companies by using redirects or a link program. If you use a newsletter program that embeds links and reports to you how many click-throughs you had, this is probably the method it is using, too. When a customer clicks on an ad for your business, while she is taken directly to the

FREE FEEDBACK

One option is to put a referral box in your website shopping cart, which asks the customer how he found your site, but then you are relying on the user for information. You could include a drop-down list with all the places you advertise and hope customers answer the question. You might want to do this even if you collect data using other methods.

site, you are able to see how she got to you. Often your own website has a log that shows where your business came from, and you definitely want this data.

If your ratios are low and your click-throughs are low, it might be time to rethink your entire campaign. This might be disheartening, but it is important information to have regardless. You can also usually tell through your web hosting provider how many hits came from Google, and even which browser your clients used. This will help you be sure you're tooling your site for all of your potential clients.

There are also sophisticated systems called web analytics, like Clicktracks at clicktracks.com or OneStat at onestat.com. The data here is overwhelming, particularly at first. Go through their tutorials and don't be afraid to ask for support if you need help interpreting the data. After all, you need to be sure you are getting what you are paying for.

NEWSLETTER ADVERTISING

Traffic is very well targeted if an e-zine or newsletter includes a link to your site, especially if it personally endorses you. Often these newsletter companies are bombarded with requests, though, so it's best to make personal contact. Suggest cross-promotion, too. If you scratch their back, they will be more inclined to scratch yours!

WORD-OF-MOUTH ADVERTISING

Talk. Talk a lot. Enlist the help of your friends and family to help get the word out, too. Just think about how many people you know and can mention your new business to. Now consider if each person you tell had the same number of friends and family to tell, and so on. See how quickly you could have thousands of people talking about (or at least hearing about) your products, services, or both?

MAXIMIZING SALES

What are some things you can do to make your site most enticing and encourage people to buy? Have you ever checked out of a site like VistaPrint, only to be offered last-minute deals for literally pennies or only the price of shipping? Remember, online sales are exceeding $220 billion. Why not get your piece of this pie?

One way to maximize sales is to create more buyers of unplanned purchases. People are more comfortable than ever buying online, even big-ticket items. People buy big-screen televisions and cars online using feedback ratings! Recent studies show that about 10 percent of online sales are purchases that the buyer never planned on making—spontaneous purchases like CDs, DVDs, books, or clothing and accessories. Think of what would work with your site, and then make it supereasy for buyers to indulge. Create online promotions; create a hook and a reason to make that unplanned purchase. A quick and easy one is a holiday promotion. Mother's Day right around the corner? Upon checking out, right before they see a subtotal, remind your buyers which holidays are approaching. According to a Harris poll, shoppers who had bought something spontaneously indicated the top factors that affected their decision were sale items (66 percent) and special promotions (59 percent). Amazon and other brilliantly run sites create a great tie-in, such as the infamous "85 percent of people who bought this book also bought . . . ."

Another thing you can do is reward your repeat sellers. Create a frequent buyer program or keep track of purchases using a unique identifier, like an e-mail address. Offer a $10 gift card for every $200 spent, or whatever works.

Also, offer traditional *and* nontraditional payment methods. Accepting PayPal and BidPay in addition to credit cards will maximize purchases; 53 percent of online shoppers say that they use electronic payment systems to complete transactions.

Be sure that your advertising lives up to your delivery, too. Do you advertise prompt and efficient service? Be sure you deliver. Ship on time, offer automated tracking information, and fulfill the orders quickly.

Additional Ways to Draw in Buyers

What are some other things buyers consider? The cost of shipping and if tax is part of the price. Some companies offer free shipping but offset their costs with higher prices, in addition to using coupon codes (instead of free shipping in general); this sometimes creates an illusion of savings. You don't want to be deceitful, but you do want to give people a reason to shop with you. Is it a holiday season? Charge a dollar more and offer free gift wrapping services or free rush delivery, or free personalization. If you are shipping directly from the manufacturer, be sure that you have a method of handling returns set up that is fast and efficient, and monitor whether packages are delivered and arrive on time.

Consider also added perks like two-way free shipping; Zappos has become wildly successful with this. It makes the returns hassle free and ensures that your return product is trackable, which is in the best interest of both you and the buyer! Anytime you give your buyer additional confidence in your shop and your reputation, you will be promoting your own success. Making returns cumbersome via return merchandise authorization (RMA) and so forth, while helping you track incoming returns, adds inconveniences for buyers. However you handle back end processes, make sure you advertise the best aspects of your business.

ARTICLES

Many people say that traditional article marketing, being noted as a subject matter expert (SME), doesn't work today. I would tend to disagree, since I have built a good portion of my business using this model. It may help to hire a publicist at first, but once you are quoted in 20 or so magazines or newspapers, reporters will begin to call on you. I also recommend subscribing to a service called ProfNet that shows you what reporters are working on and what topics they need experts for. Being noted as an expert and building your credibility—how can that possibly be bad? Also remember most articles are posted on the internet, so your name begins to be searchable and noted with your business name. Asking a reporter to list you as "owner, XYZ Company" is reasonable; in fact, they should ask you how you want to be referenced. This builds brand awareness on the internet and also makes you searchable in more than just one category.

TRADITIONAL PROMOTION

Just because you have an online business doesn't mean you should ignore traditional promotion methods! Trade shows, the Yellow Pages, direct mailers if applicable, television infomercials or commercials, radio and print in magazines and newspapers can and do readily advertise online companies nearly as often today as they do traditional brick-and-mortar stores. Also consider partnering with a traditional brick-and-mortar store; you may have to pay an affiliate rate but the business is worth it.

BUYING MAILING LISTS

There are many companies out there from which you can buy mailing lists. By now you've done research on which individuals represent your primary demographic, so you already know the answer to that question. You can buy mailing lists and then plug the membership information into newsletters or mass e-mail, commonly referred to as spam. You run the risk of paying for a lot of invalid addresses, and annoying your customers, so be careful if you choose this route.

CONTESTS

Offering a decent cash prize or products to generate some buzz to your site and additional traffic or member sign-ups is a great idea. Also, if you run your own newsletter or you buy ad space in someone else's newsletter, this is a great thing to promote there. You can also hold contests for your affiliates—those that refer the most traffic win a prize.

AD ROTATION AND FACES

If you are using any form of banner advertising, ask the company that is hosting the ad if they allow ad rotation—you give them four or five ads and they change them up frequently. That way, frequent visitors don't look at the same ad all the time, which leads to ad blindness. Be sure to incorporate new tag lines with each one, and the more you can make your ad look like content, the greater the chance it will be clicked on! Also, statistics show that ads that use faces (if you have to use a graphic ad and not a text ad) have a higher click-through rate.

ORDER DEADLINES AND ADVERTISED PRICE INCREASES

Are you trying to encourage people to buy by a certain date to boost sales for the month? Follow the common practice at x10.com and give a certain date people must order by (or say they must order within ten minutes of the last order) to receive an extra discount. Also, if you plan to increase your price on a certain date, make it known. This will create a better sense of urgency to buy now. I frequently use this method when advertising seminars; it does cost me more to book more seats late, and I pass that cost onto customers. I make them aware that as of a specific date, costs go up. I see higher order rates the last two to three days before the price increase deadline. Again, savings is a great motivator!

TRIAL MEMBERSHIPS AND UPGRADES

If you are selling services, you might offer an introductory or trial membership for free. Take a look at the RealtyTrac model (go to my website at drdaniellebabb.com and click on RealtyTrac); you will see an offer to buy X months and get X months free, or buy one month and get the first week free.

This gives you a chance to try out the service with no obligations, which makes people feel more comfortable before they pay. Offering money-back guarantees helps, too. You can also offer a free upgrade, particularly if the item is a service or membership, for buying before X date. This creates a sense of urgency and of stronger value. If you are selling a product, say a cell phone, adding an extended-life battery or car charger can help boost sales.

STATING THE BENEFITS—AND THE TESTIMONIALS

People want to know that your product or service works. Did you get an especially great e-mail last week from a client? Ask if you can post it online, and offer the writer something free in return. If you are new and have no testimonials, you might want to give products away and ask for testimonials in return. Whatever your product or service, state, restate, and restate again the benefits of not only buying your product or service but buying it from you!

PRESS RELEASES

We've been using press releases for years, right? You may not think they can benefit your company, but positioned right, they can! Press releases are typically very factually written, information driven, and provide quick talking points. Yes, it is true that most likely your press releases won't get read, but they do two things that are very important: They help with search engine optimization (you aren't going to send out your press release without including your website address somewhere) and they will help position your brand by showing that you are constantly growing, particularly if you create a press release every time you create a new product or service line. You can also hire a publicist to get you out into the world of media as a subject matter expert in your particular area, but that can be quite costly.

YourOnlineProfessor.com

Advertising in the online world doesn't mean you ignore brick-and-mortar advertising. Check out YourOnlineProfessor.com, and learn from your virtual professor what has worked for her as well as other entrepreneurs and what hasn't.

Word-of-mouth advertising is still critical for any business today—even those online. Think about Zappos and its famous one year return policy, which spread like wild fire. How? Word of mouth! Network with other entrepreneurs and learn what choices they made and what impact it had on their business. Visit YourOnlineProfessor.com for more information.

Remember that bad news can spread many times faster than good news. Want to stop the bad news at its source? Network with others at YourOnlineProfessor.com to learn how the experts have done it.

CHAPTER 9

SOCIAL NETWORKING

Creating a Buzz in the Web 2.0 World

A big form of advertising and promotion today comes from social networking—a relatively new phenomenon that has accompanied the Web 2.0 world! I find this personally to be one of the most fun aspects of my online business—and to think it's actually work!

So what is social networking? It is the art of using community spaces to network with other people and to provide interactive

content that will ultimately lead to loyal followers—followers who will hopefully turn into customers.

There are a lot of tools in the social networking sphere of the online community. MySpace, LinkedIn, and Facebook are three that come to mind for most people. There are, of course, others and many are generationally dependent. Other forms of social networking are blogs and online forums or communities—any place that has content that isn't just dictated to users but allows them to participate, too. They are all vital media for you in your business.

USING SOCIAL NETWORKING TOOLS

Chances are you've heard of Facebook, MySpace, and other tools that Gen Yers tend to use to communicate with each other. But did you know that Burger King has a MySpace account? And just about every major company out there? Creating a public MySpace account that associates you with your user base also creates instant viral marketing for you, which is a method of posting one item and having it reposted by others or seen multiple times.

There are many things you want to make sure you do, and some mistakes to avoid. First, make sure that you are consistent with who you are and what your company represents. Don't be someone different on MySpace than you are in your business. The social networking site does reflect who you are. You always want to maintain your appeal and not create trust issues. Use social networking to build your brand. Also make sure you separate business and pleasure. I made this mistake early on in my MySpace work. I had my business partners linking to my personal page with vacation pictures—not smart. I soon had to create a public MySpace profile. Create one for your own family and friends, and one for the world to see. The same holds true for your online photo albums: don't make your Shutterfly album public! Also, be sure that you own up to mistakes. There is nothing that bloggers and social networkers hate more than for someone to make a mistake and then try to cover it up. Just be honest and upfront about the error.

We'll take each option separately, go through the pros and cons and the merits, and whether you should consider using it in your business advertising model.

Facebook (FaceBook.com)

A great article at MarketMe.com asks, "Is Facebook a time suck or a viable marketing strategy?" (Cummings, 2008). It's a very good question and one we must answer here. Tools like Facebook allow you to market to all kinds of people you might not otherwise have access to, particularly the Y generation, which uses this site as a common method of communication. You can also find like-minded business owners or even those with similar products and help one another. One thing you'll want to do is set up some automatic note where you create new posts, create video, update, and talk about your product but don't get sucked into answering every e-mail. Encourage users to interact on your blog or your forums (which hopefully you are charging for, or at the very least, promoting products in) because you don't want this to be yet another avenue to eat up time.

MySpace (MySpace.com)

MySpace is by far the most popular social networking site, and it has strong financial backing as well. MySpace allows you to create a public and a private profile, and you should be sure to keep the two separate. You can talk about your business, your passions, and what your business stands for, and be sure to create ties to something people can believe in and feel good about, whether 2 percent of your revenues go to going green or you donate a lot of money to a charity for children, be truthful and genuine and share great information. People linking to you will generate a viral marketing.

LinkedIn (LinkedIn.com)

LinkedIn is a far more professional site; instead of focusing on tweenies and Gen Yers as its starting point, LinkedIn from day one has focused on professionals. By entering in schools you have attended, companies you have worked for, and businesses you've started (as well, of course, as friends), you create a connection-based system that allows you to be introduced to others and to contact them and grow your professional affiliations. It is definitely worth a look. Setting up an account and getting started is easy and free.

YouTube (YouTube.com)

It is great to create videos about your product and create brand awareness by posting infomercials (particularly those that are educational, but keep them short) on YouTube. Hold a roundtable session with experts and post it on blogs and on the internet, but be sure you keep the relationship component and that you don't lose that in the communication era. Keep your message consistent and on par with the type of business you want to run and the type of business owner you are.

Blogs

So you think blogging is only for teens and political pundits? Think again. Blogging is your way of sharing information with the world–and guess what? Often content for other blogs is reposted by blog originators, so your material becomes viral very quickly. I ran into this myself when I posted a controversial post on my Finding Foreclosures blog (at findingforeclosures.entprepreneur.com) about real estate agents hindering the market recovery. It was reposted on thousands of blogs, mostly by angry real estate agents (they aren't my target audience anyway). As a result, hundreds of for sale by owner and investor sites also picked it up as an article that validated their message, and my website hits doubled over the following week. If you run a blog and use an RSS feed (meaning the material can be automatically fed into other blogs) it can be incredibly rich and powerful. It is quick and easy to type up messages, and you can and should integrate it into your site so that people don't need to leave your site to see the blog. Perhaps they can even click on products or services you talk about in posts to buy right away. Take a look also at blog.hubspot.com, an interesting site about blogging and marketing. Another reason to blog is for the potential for your site to become the aggregator of information or specialized data on a specific topic, particularly if your product or service is unique.

The Elements of a Blog

A blog has multiple elements in play, each one making the blog special, unique, and perhaps most importantly identifiable to the blogging community and to the individuals that post on the blog.

What Is a Blog URL Exactly?

The uniform resource locator, or URL (or permalink), is the full article that you want to display to your readers.

One element is the title, which is the headline of the post. Next, the body of the blog post, which contains the content you want viewers to read consistently; this is often referred to as the element that is pushed (Babb and Lazo, page 30, 2007). The interactivity is what sets blogs apart from traditional newspapers.

The post includes the date and time, and may include comments, categories, and/or trackbacks that refer to the original entry (Wikipedia, 2006). Sometimes what is posted is a repost and not the original. Blogs are often seen as a way for non-mainstream media to get around the filter that exists in the mainstream today. Recently mainstreamers have also joined the blogosphere (the community of blogs and bloggers) and have created blogs themselves. A published blog software comparison chart available at ojr.org/ojr/images/blog_software_comparison.cfm shows you lots of various options for bloggers to host and maintain their web logs.

Blogs are a great way to market your expertise and services and to share your knowledge with others. This builds a sense of loyalty. I see this happen all the time on my car site forums. The shops that do work take pictures of how to do repairs and modifications yourself, share them online for free, participate in the car rallies, and give away product, and they build an incredible base of followers who buy even if their prices are higher than their competition!

If nothing else, you should host a blog on your site with weekly updates and let other people respond. Generate some buzz on your area of expertise and your topic regardless of what it is; most likely there is a blog out there that fits your expertise. This is also a good feedback loop to try to understand what your visitors are thinking and what they are interested in, and it's a good way to attract other professionals to your site who may have business for you or

A Blog Equals Money? It Sure Can!

There are some who have made a business out of blogging. Take Perez Hilton for example. He started blogging about celebrity gossip on his own time, and now he gets paid for it. Where does the money come from? There are advertisers that pay him to have space on his blog, and money is generated for referral fees and purchases made through links on the site. You can check out more about Perez Hilton by visiting his blog yourself, at PerezHilton.com. Talk about an easy domain name—see how everything is tied in?

with whom you may be able to partner (Babb and Lazo, 2007). In fact, the term *blog marketing* is receiving much hype nowadays and advertisers are paying attention to it.

One of your goals, of course, is to increase traffic and sales from your website and your blog is one of many ways that you can accomplish that—another good reason for hosting it on your primary site (where you sell stuff). You want to be sure that you establish yourself as an expert, first and foremost, regardless of how casual or formal you want your blog to be. You need to use your blog to define yourself from your competition, and you need to be an authority figure in the area that you are writing on. People will respect you and will come to value your opinion, which you make clear through your blog writing. Blogs are a relatively new phenomenon used by businesses, though they've been in play now for a few years in the social networking world.

Tips for Setting Up, Designing, and Hosting Your Blogs or Podcasts

Just as with the web in its infancy, there really are no rules for how to set up and host your own work. However, there are tried-and-proven methods that have become accepted and have formed a sort of protocol—best practices, so to speak. If you decide to venture outside these norms for the sake of innovation and sexiness, you risk being perceived as an amateur. It's a fine line that you have to be careful not to cross.

"Keep in mind that blogs and podcasts are tools, not solutions. This means that if you have something meaningful to say, they can help you say it in an exciting and innovative way. However, if your words are not of much value to start with, they probably will not add value to them" (Babb and Lazo, 2007).

As you are working on your blog and podcast, keep asking yourself the following question: "Is my content useful and unique?" If it's useful but not unique, then why should an individual read your blog over another? If it's unique but not useful, you may get only an initial surge in traffic followed by a drop-off, or a lot of one-time visitors. However, if it's both useful and unique, people will come and keep coming back.

As with all the other marketing activities you may be doing, keep the customer as the focus. Can you distinguish the subtle difference in the following two statements?

1. Provide the customer with what she wants.
2. Provide the customer with what you want her to know.

The first statement starts with the customer and understanding what the customer needs (and knowing who your customer is), while the second statement starts with you and what you want the consumer to walk away with and what you want her to know when she leaves your site. "Showcase yourself as a dynamic resource that can be used to fill the gaps of knowledge that customers may have. Each customer is different, so make sure that your content is appropriate and interesting to a wide spectrum of audiences" (Babb and Lazo, 2007).

Setting up a blog or a podcast is like setting up any business. You need to start with a mission statement. Basically, you need to answer the following question: "What do I want to accomplish?" The more lofty your goals, the more critical the mission statement becomes. Two other vital considerations are your budget and your technical abilities going in.

When you begin to record your blog, you need to have a plan. How many times do you want to post in a week, a month, a year? When will you consider the blog a success? The same questions hold true for podcasts or roundtables that you push online. What is success to you? Defining it up front will help

Baby Steps to Blogging

The first step in designing and setting up your own blog is to determine if you want it to be stand-alone or part of a platform. Do you want this on a website that is dedicated to your blog or would you rather just make it part of an existing website that provides blogging services (e.g., Blogger.com or WordPress.com)?

Better yet, would you rather integrate it into your website where customers buy products, thus keeping them on your site longer and allowing you to push ads on your own site and keeping them there. Do you really want to miss out on all those potential revenue-generating opportunities?

make it certain you meet your goals, and therefore your advertising goal for this portion of your business, which hopefully will lead to business goals.

Customizing and Writing to Your Blog

Writing to your blog can be tough, I struggle with articles on occasion. But try to write every week at a minimum. I don't think anyone but the best ever really masters it, but that shouldn't keep you from blogging. You have to decide what kind of tone you want your blog to take. Informal? Formal? If you want it to be formal and more on the serious side of things, you cannot write sloppily. If you want it to be informal and allow people to feel more free to share opinions rather than just facts, you should do the same. The tone you set will carry through your work. One thing that helps us get started writing is to brainstorm. This may be especially useful for your first post. Take out a blank sheet of paper and write words all over the page: What comes to mind? What dots did you connect? These may be things to help you begin. If you want to spruce up your writing, go to the old thesaurus. Just be sure you are mostly free from grammatical mistakes. Everyone makes one here and there, but you don't want to discredit yourself, and making many mistakes throughout may do so in the eyes of some.

Are you ready to enter the blogosphere? Then here's what to do:

> The first step is to set one up. You need to come up with a blog platform. This refers to the look and feel of your blog. You need to first decide whether you want to start with a personal or a business blog. In either case, there are many sites out there that can help. On the personal side, Wordpress. and Blogger are common platforms (and they're free!). On the business side, you can also use Wordpress (not the free version, though), but try Typepad and Movable Type. For business owners like you, Active Rain, RSS Pieces, Tomato Blogs, and Blogging Systems are relevant. (Babb and Lazo, 2007)

When it comes to hosting a blog on the web, you can do one of two things: 1) simply pay for a hosted blogging solution; or 2) install a blogging platform on your own hosted server (GoDaddy and DreamHost, for example). If you choose the first option, you'll find the setup process to be easy because much of the work will be done by your service provider. Even if you choose the second option, you won't have much difficulty as it is normally done with a one-click install.

A lot of anxiety appears to come from setting up the hosting solution. Remember that many great companies do this for a living; you need not fret over the technological side. Focus on content and advertising, and your blog will be a success. You can even have your web designer put the blog directly onto your site and make it super easy for you (although a bit more costly in development).

Customization of your blog is very important because you need and want your site to look and feel unique and you want it to be user-friendly and have a high usability factor. To do this, you need to edit the template that you're using, if you are using one, or have your web designer custom create something for you. There are many free templates out there that can be acquired from the websites mentioned earlier. Modifying the templates is a bit tricky. Usually, you're going to want to modify the sidebar portion. This is the part that displays the information that you want all your users to see regardless of which individual blog post

> WordPress is a name that comes up a lot when you talk about blogging and bloggers, and there is good reason for that. Check it out online and see what use it may be to you.

they happen to be reading. A sidebar should provide your readers with a good high-level introduction to yourself and the content. It can include links, contact information, and a subscription link. Check out the following blog, which focuses on creating blogs: emilyrobbins.com/how-to-blog.

A useful tool to have in your sidebar is a search box. This is a quick way for viewers to search the contents of a particular blog they may be interested in by subject, phrase, date, and so forth. Every good blog should have one!

Be sure there is enough information in your blog that readers get a sense of who you are and what you and your business are all about. Remember this is about creating a relationship with the reader, albeit a virtual one. To some who are people persons, this may seem intimidating. It can actually become quite fun, and it is a bit of an art form. Being able to express yourself with the written word is a unique way to show a bit of your character and personality. "Some people prefer it to face-to-face communication because they can explore other facets of their personality that may be naturally introverted without leaving their comfort zone. Don't lock yourself in too tightly with a method of blogging and see what comes naturally to you." (Babb and Lazo, 2007)

Blogs and Copyrights

You are not allowed to post copyrighted material in your blog without first obtaining permission from the copyright holder. Sure First Amendment

Make Sure Your Blog Doesn't End Up Where You Don't Want It!

I have had my blog information replicated over and over by people who were free to beat me up and take my words out of context simply because I failed to include a simple disclaimer: "You may not repost this information without the author's permission." This is a lesson learned, but one you can avoid.

rights can come into play with regard to the fair use doctrine, but this does not give anyone free rein in posting.

Section 107 of the Copyright Act mentions four factors that should be considered when determining fair use:

- The purpose and character of the use—commercial or nonprofit educational?
- The nature of the copyrighted work
- The amount of the portion used in relation to the entire piece
- The effect of the use on the market value of the work

Talk to an attorney if there are any potential problems.

This is a sticky subject. Since you are ultimately trying to benefit financially from your blog, you need to be especially careful. When in doubt, obtain permission. Most of the time none of these issues will come into play. However, there have been cases where problems have risen to the surface. Be sure you talk with your attorney if you hear any grumblings that you think may be an issue, and follow the law. Understand your audience and what they are looking for prior to starting to blog. It's important that you remain on topic and always include a key word phrase that should be repeated throughout the post. (Babb and Lazo, 2007)

> Believe it or not, Wikipedia is a great resource to find out what is protected under the copyright laws. Wikipedia staff take copyright infringement extremely seriously and do quite a bit to prevent it from happening on their site. They have a very thorough, yet elementary explanation of what is and is not protected. Visit en.wikipedia.org/wiki/Wikipedia:FAQ/Copyright for more information. Don't rely on it as your only source, but it is a good place to start.

Inbound Blog Links

Inbound links to your blog are probably the most effective method to achieving high ranking in search engines because the activity is noted by the crawlers and the search engines. In fact, both inbound and outbound links can be beneficial. Use links all over your blog. It's OK to link to other blogs because it often results in return links back to your blog.

Using creativity and having good content are key fundamentals with any blog. With these two foundations your blog site will be poised for growth. Don't discount creativity and freshness.

SEARCH ENGINE EXPLORATION

In order to help search engines discover your blog, you can do some of the following–the more, the better:

- Make the content easy to subscribe to by using feed buttons, and make sure that the content is relevant.
- Use only one URL or web address rather than multiple addresses. Try not to have one for your blog and one for your company. Integrate as much as you can.
- When writing your URL on any page, don't use underscores. If you have to separate out keywords, use hyphens, which look like this "-" and not this "_." Underscores are often mistaken as hyphens or people don't know where to find them on the keyboard.
- Try to avoid using generic title tags that the blog provider gives you. Change them to reflect your specific blog for better searching and user-friendliness.
- Use categories for the posts in your blog and be sure to include keywords when choosing categories.
- Use content that is "sticky" in each category–a sentence or two that contains key words to describe what that category is for. This also reminds people what they should be talking about in a specific category.

BLOG BUZZ

Now you need to spread the word about what you have written. Most readers of your blog will have gotten to it through an RSS feed. Here's how you can make it easier for them to read it:

Subscribe to your blog in Technorati (technorati.com) and other blog subscription services that you can find in your favorite search engine.

Make sure that each category in your blog is subscribable and then subscribe to all the categories. You want to know what others are saying. You won't necessarily automatically be kept abreast of the writing in your own blog, so subscribe to your own blog.

Allow others to subscribe to each category, thus eliminating junk e-mail, giving them a sense of control and using Web 2.0 dynamic preferences.

Make sure to post full text and not just summaries. People want to have the opportunity to read all the text.

Include a site description, just as you would for any website.

> The setup of the blog really is one of the easiest parts if you use the right tools. Focus your real time and effort on a great looking site, on lots of useful links and tips, and in our opinion most importantly on the content and the message that you convey. Not just the actual words, but the inarticulate message you are sending to people visiting the blog. What do the colors say? Soothing or powerful? Does it matter? Sure it does! (Babb and Lazo, 2007).

People who want a professional to provide them with incredible advice on a very important subject matter may not want a website full of flowers and butterflies. On the other hand, a stay-at-home parent may find this appealing (or not—that is for you to decide). Know your client; that is the key message here and one that is weaved throughout this book! You may even want to ask a few test subjects what about your blog appeals to them. Ask what message they get from the site without words (that is, a page that's blank other than the layout and design). Be sure it reflects your personality; the more real it is, the more attractive it (and you) will be.

Enticing Conversation

Comments are really the reason people like blogs—they can say whatever they want without being edited (within reason). It is our Constitution at its finest! You may want to edit content though, as I do, for vulgarity or hate speech.

> So how do you entice a conversation in your blog? First of all, make sure that you do that. Do not turn off or disable the comments functionality. Comments are really what separate a blog from a regular website. Allow reader comments to become an integral part of your

website. This is free content that comes at no effort to you! In addition, it provides you with a method for measuring the appeal of your topics. A topic that receives many comments, even negative ones, is one that's of great interest. Comments are the equivalent of "letters to the editor." (Babb and Lazo, 2007)

Listening to Your Bloggers

When you are reading blogs talking about you or your business, don't feel that you have to be perceived as having all the answers. On the contrary, your site visitors are going to be more apt to post if they feel that they can educate the community. It's OK for you to ask questions like "What do you think?" Be open and honest with your bloggers. Respond quickly to keep interest alive, and try to respond to every question if it's feasible. "If someone corrects a factual error that you make (hey, it happens) correct it quickly and publicly thank the person who corrected you—this is no time for defensiveness!" (Babb and Lazo, 2007)

> Always listen to your audience. Again, this is free advice that would otherwise cost you a lot of money. Don't second-guess the feedback that you get unless you think there is a serious flaw in the way it was collected.

There will be times when it's better not to respond. There is no point in beating up or putting down readers. Never take negative comments that are directed at you personally, even if the person meant for them to be taken that way! Take the higher road. I've run into this many times when my blog comments were taken out of context. Your gut reaction is often to defend yourself, but ignore them and you'll actually feel better about it over time.

Remember, you are the moderator of your blogging platform. This means that you have the ability to keep the blog tidy. Always delete SPAM and, whenever possible, block spammers from commenting further. You can always force users to register and log in to your blog in order to comment. This will reduce SPAM, but may deter legitimate participation, so it's probably better to not do it. (Babb and Lazo, 2007)

Blog Trolls

Trolls can be worse than spammers. All they do is criticize, and they are impossible to please. I have a number of them on various sites that repeat information I post. They will use every opportunity to harm you and try to discredit you. Again you can jump in and try to defend yourself, or you can just ignore them. I highly recommend the latter, having been experienced with both.

The trolls have the right to do this, but it's best to ignore them and encourage others to do the same. Most people are smart enough to spot a troll, and often your fellow bloggers will take the person on verbally without you having to do anything. This will make them go away eventually.

The following can be considered "silent comments." These are methods other than actual comments by which you will know that other readers have been there before you.

- Trackback (en.wikipedia.org/wiki/Trackback)
- Digg (digg.com)
- Five-star rating
- Subscriber count
- Meebo (38.meebo.com/index-en.html)
- Chat widget
- MyBlogLog (mybloglog.com/) avatar

Remember to always comment on other blogs. Actually, as a new blogger, that should be the first thing you do; comment on other blogs before working on your own. When you leave a comment, you can link back to your own blog. (Babb and Lazo, 2007)

Paid Reviews on Blogs

In addition to writing blogs and writing on others' blogs, you can pay for a review on a blog, particularly those that are popular within your industry. Be sure that you pick a quality blog with good content and excellent integrity, or else your brand will be tied to that issue or special interest for a long time. Usually bloggers disclose that the review was paid for, but if you can find a quality blogger that, for a few extra bucks, won't disclose it, that is generally better for your product or service. Don't forget about posting a link to your blog on Twitter, too.

YourOnlineProfessor.com

There are many tools out there to socially network you and your business! Visit YourOnlineProfessor.com for links and advice and learn from Dr. Dani's technical expertise and entrepreneurs from around the globe.

CHAPTER

10

WHERE TO WORK

Working from Home or an Office

What a decision to have to make! You've made the choice to work for yourself, now you need to decide where to do it. There are pros and cons to both working outside the home and working in the home. The decision will be based largely on personal circumstance, budget, and preference. Throughout this chapter I outline the pros and cons of working at home, but it's up to you to make the decision. It will drive the technology that you will need

and the budget you will have to work with. Owning an online business doesn't mean you don't need an office unless you truly have a business that is entirely based on residual income and you don't have to run anything. But that is probably not the case.

BENEFITS TO WORKING FROM HOME

So what are some pros to working at home? You definitely save money on gas, dry cleaning, and car maintenance. I only have dry-cleaning costs for television clothes; otherwise it's laundry for my gym clothes worn 95 percent of my working day. I drive about 5,000 miles per year, down from 20,000, which has reduced my insurance and car costs—and allowed my car to maintain its value. I am stuck in traffic about 30 minutes per week going to personal appointments instead of being stuck two hours per day and having very little time to attend personal appointments.

Too Many Benefits to List

While I do my best here to list the largest of benefits (and downsides) to online work, some of them cannot be quantified—peace of mind that you won't lose your job (are you going to fire yourself?), stability, never again having to worry if you can leave for an hour to take your sick child to the doctor. For most people, online work would be a dream come true. Also note that many benefits are particular to you, your lifestyle, and your business. The positive and negative aspects of online work, custom to your situation, will make themselves known in time.

A Lighter Footprint (No Pun Intended)

Since your commute will be a matter of feet rather than miles (or hundreds of miles), you will ultimately save on both time and gas.

Working from home equates to a very, very short commute and the ability to get to work quickly should the need arise. If you have small children and need to be close to them or you are caring for another individual, this can be a great option for you. This whole issue of no commute could be one of the best advantages, considering the recent rise in fuel and other transportation costs. Undoubtedly as underdeveloped nations become developed, we will see even more demand for oil, which will increase costs for everyone.

Ability to Work When You Are Creative

Are you a night owl? I am, which is why working from home is a great option for me. I can work until 2 A.M. and then sleep until 10 A.M., should I choose to. I typically do my best thinking late at night. In fact, it was quite late as I wrote this section. Not having to report to an in-office boss at a particular time or make an early morning appearance at a meeting allows me the option of working as late as I need or want to, and I can still sleep in so long as I don't have any meetings, travel, or media spots lined up for the next day.

Once your business is up and running, you get the opportunity to work during *your* most creative times, not the times set down by your manager. If you want to exercise in the morning, take your kids to school, start work at noon, and work until midnight, so be it. If you want to sleep until 5 P.M., get up and have dinner with a friend, and work from 10 at night until 7 in the morning designing websites, go for it.

When and where you work are completely up to you, of course, as long as your business allows for it. If you are a web designer and you have a notebook PC, you can work all night from a 24-hour coffee shop if you prefer. If you are making and selling custom screen-printed T-shirts, however, you will probably be tied to wherever you set up your screen-printing press and design station, but the hours in which you are producing your one-of-a-kind fashion statements are still completely up to you.

PJs and Slippers (or Gym Clothes)

Another great benefit to working from home, which I take full advantage of, is no dress code. If you can conduct your business either primarily or entirely out of your home, you can wear whatever you want. I often spend a great majority of my day in my gym clothes, they are simply more comfortable to work in. If I need to do an on-camera interview, most of the time the only thing that changes is the hair, makeup, and the top part of my outfit. Sometimes when I appear on television, I wear a jacket and nice shirt with gym shorts or jeans.

The downside to this is I don't often get to see myself fully dressed in any of my many business suits, which make me feel empowered and capable. Having to get dressed up in my fancy threads does provide me with a sense of accomplishment and success that I don't get when I forego them for gym clothes. Of course going out to special events, speaking engagements, residencies, and in-studio interviews takes care of that problem right away. Too many of these in a row and I quickly remember how much I love working in my comfortable sweats and T-shirt.

Tax Benefits

There are tax implications for both working at home and working outside the home. Homebased business write-offs are determined like this, in general: Determine the percentage of your home that is used for business (square footage of business portion, and only that used exclusively for business, divided by the total square footage of the home). If you use the space for business and personal activities, figure out what percent of the time you use it for purely business and not online family e-mail or family sharing, for instance. Here is an example:

2,000 square foot home
200 square feet used for office space
10 percent of the home is used for business purposes

Of that, you spend 60 percent of your time doing work things in that space and 40 percent doing personal things. Sixty percent of 10 percent is 6 percent, so you can write off 6 percent of your home expenses.

What are home expenses? Mortgage interest. Association fees. Insurance. Utilities that are commonly shared with the house. And so on. If you use separate phones they are fully deductible.

Again, talk with a tax accountant about this because home offices are one of the biggest reasons returns get audited.

If you have an office-based business then all costs associated with rent, utilities, and so on will go on various lines on your Schedule C of your Form 1040 tax return. Again, consult with a qualified accountant for all of the possible deductions and implications.

A Solution to Daycare Issues

Are you tired of your daycare provider flaking or getting sick, or tired of changing your schedule at the drop of a hat around child-care providers? Since your home is your work, and your work is your home, an online business is a quick and easy way to solve that problem.

More Time with Family

In a 1998 study published by Janet Attard at careerknowhow.com/office survey/intro.htm, 72 percent of respondents cited that they have more time with family in their stay-at-home job than they did in their corporate America job and saw this as a benefit.

Higher Income Potential

In the same study by Attard, a full 48 percent of people surveyed said they earned more money working at home than in jobs in corporate America. Keep in mind that not all of these people are full timers. This is an incredible boost for potential income. Like any entrepreneurial activity, your potential for income is as high as you set your sights and your business model and demand will take you.

Healthier Lifestyle

You may find yourself more invigorated and healthier if you work at home. I have suffered for many years from severe primary insomnia, often going an entire week on 2 hours of sleep or less. Getting up in the morning for mandatory 8 A.M. meetings was grueling, not to mention taxing on my health. In my case if I have a bad insomnia night and work from 2 P.M. until 2 A.M. to get rest in the morning, that is my decision. That pressure of knowing "I must fall asleep *now*" is no longer there. I have many friends who have left their day jobs for health reasons—to allow themselves more flexibility with when and how they work.

Many find they eat less fast food and move around more often, or take walks around the block. You may also feel less stress because you have more control over your day, though some people feel more stress because they feel pressured by self-imposed deadlines (which are important for success in the online world, so you need to evaluate your own personality fit).

I am generally much healthier now that I work from home. I don't have to cram all of my personal errands and lunch into a one-hour block of time, and I am not restricted to the local fast-food stop. I can actually cook a healthy meal or take the time to go to a real restaurant, which in turn has provided me with an overall healthier lifestyle. Keeping with this same benefit, I am awarded more flexible time to visit the gym at a time I feel most strong rather than at a specific time my employer deems is OK. Whenever I have a block of time, I can take the five-minute drive to my local gym and work out.

Flexible Workload

In corporate America, when a boss piles on more work, you really have two options: speak your mind and risk getting fired, or say, "Thank you, ma'am, may I have another?" What about the alternative—selecting which projects you will undertake by balancing your desires and need for income, and then making your *own* decision?

Many people also report being able to add and delete jobs from their workload as they see fit, which is a great benefit (although your customers or clients may not be too keen on the notion). You can turn down contracts with people you don't enjoy working with if you can financially afford to do so. The flexibility is really a great advantage.

You also, of course, have more flexibility with regard to operational costs—not paying for expensive office rent, office furniture, business phone lines, and business internet access. This lack of overhead will free up money for advertising and marketing, which is what many online businesses are affected by most, either negatively or positively.

Just how flexible is an online business? Let's go back to our survey respondents. A whopping 94.7 percent of respondents indicated that online work was more flexible than working in a brick-and-mortar environment! Only 3 percent said it wasn't, and 1.8 percent said it was about the same.

DOWNSIDES TO WORKING FROM HOME

Although the benefits, in my opinion, astronomically outweigh the downfalls of working from home, I will address them, in the interest of full disclosure.

Distractions

You may also find yourself distracted by the very reason you decided to work from home–your family. For people lacking self-discipline or feeling torn between home and work responsibilities or those with young children, finding time undistracted by everything from laundry piling up to a sick child can be tough. When you are working from home, it can be difficult, at times, to get into work mode if you don't set a routine and stick to it. Once you find one that works, do your best to keep yourself and your routine stable.

Technology

You also need technology, though depending on what you do, you may not need much. You absolutely do need dedicated office space. I have been on hundreds of conference calls where I consistently heard other participants' dogs barking, kids crying, and husbands yelling. It is distracting for colleagues and the worker and can create stress that you didn't have before, it can even cause discord in your relationship. To get around this, set aside very specific work areas, and make it clear to everyone in the house that this is *your office*–your work! Install phone lines if you need to, buy more computers–whatever you need to be sure that your kid isn't hanging out in the same room where you're trying to write a business proposal. You may also have to teach children and spouses not to answer your business line and to stay away from your cell phone. If you need to meet clients in person consider renting office space, which is usually available at everything from a FedEx Office to large office complexes that rent conference rooms for that professional look. You may wear your pajamas all day, but you can't meet clients in them.

RISKS AND REWARDS

If you are concerned about the risks mentioned in this chapter or the potential downsides, I highly recommend writing down every one of your concerns along with at least five things you can do to mitigate it that are within your own control. This might help ease your mind and become a fallback plan should something negative occur.

Office-based businesses, particularly rented small suites, may also give you luxuries like a shared administrative assistant, cubicles if needed, conference rooms, mailing services, access to technology (fax machines, copiers, etc.), and so on. It is often more expensive, however, and is another added cost to your startup, which you may not be able to afford immediately. Sometimes entrepreneurs start at home and, when they get too big, then move into an office. This is a great alternative, particularly if to accommodate your office you will need to move to a much more expensive home. However, you won't have your work at your fingertips should you need it, and rolling into work in your pajamas won't be quite as easy.

Lack of Regular Paychecks

Another big worry, particularly in the early stages of a new business, is the inability to have a regular paycheck and the stress of living project to project or client to client. This was very stressful for me, in the beginning. Eventually you will have more consistent work, but this fact may require you to load up slowly and transition when your income is stable. You will need to be incredibly disciplined to manage your finances. Also remember that you should stick with what you're good at, because taking on lots of extra work (particularly if the pay isn't so hot) will stress you out to no end. It helps to create spreadsheets or databases showing when you expect income, and then noting on the same spreadsheets which bills you will pay with which checks. Investing in bookkeeping or accounting software will also be appropriate. Applications like Quicken or Quickbooks or Peachtree can prove to be very useful to you. You usually have the option of using a template of a business profile that resembles yours or using interactive wizards to help with setup and customization. For hosted solutions online, FreshBooks.com is powerful; not only is it fully brandable, offering online bookkeeping, invoicing, and help desk tools for both you and your clients, but it is free. There are methods you can use to help yourself manage your money until it starts flowing regularly. In Attard's 1998 study, 29.9 percent said that not knowing where the next job would come from caused some angst.

Healthcare Costs

Cited as a major drawback in multiple studies, the cost of healthcare and the lack of automatic health insurance consistently ranks as a concern. In Attard's study cited earlier, 33 percent of respondents said that lack of health benefits was worrisome.

Reduced Human Interaction

Of course like many other online workers, particularly homebased ones, you may find yourself craving human interaction. Most of my interaction now comes from travel and speaking engagements and trips to my local studio for live shots rather than colleagues that I develop relationships with. It takes a genuine effort on your part to create those relationships and to make time to interact with people. It is easy to hole yourself up in your house and just work all day. Sometimes the only interaction you get is with your chat buddies, which can be tough and frustrating at times. There are ways to help you out of the feeling of isolationism, which I go into later.

It might sound so nice at first. Not having to deal with co-workers and being able to wear your pajamas most of the day. Taking web calls with PJ bottoms and a dress top–ah, the freedom. But, there can be some loss felt without human interaction and without a team environment, so that is something you need to prepare for. Twenty-six percent in Attard's study noted that they felt isolated working at home. You may miss some of the feeling of feeding off another's energy without a team environment, but look at it this way: the more your business grows, the greater the chance you can build your own team. When I first began my business, for two years it was just me; now I work with numerous people and they are individuals I choose to work with, not individuals I am forced to work with!

The walls of my loft and my computer screen were all I saw for hours and days and months on end, and my only interaction with others was with the random front desk staff at my local gym and my husband when he got home from work. Now that I have consistent contractors, I actually have someone to talk to during the day, bounce ideas off, laugh with, strategize with, and even have lunch with when time permits. Life is a little less lonely this way.

Of course it is important to note that in Attard's study a full 20 percent cited no drawbacks whatsoever to working out of the home.

Blurred Boundaries

A common complaint or critique I hear from individuals who leave corporate America behind for online life is that they don't have a clearly defined boundary between home and work. This phenomenon could commonly be compared to cabin fever. When they walk into their office, are they officially back at work? Setting work time boundaries is critical to feeling successful and feeling as though you have control over your work. You don't ever go home, leaving work behind, unless you create that transition for yourself, which is not easy to do.

The upside to an office-based business is the feeling of being able to get away from work—when you leave the office door and go home, you're home, not at work.

It is also easier to expand in an office-based environment because usually you will have room to expand the suite or add desks, at the very least. Even in my new casita-turned-business-office, I have room for two desks. Should I will have to go, and it will definitely be a cramped space. I may be able to add onto the structure itself but that is expensive.

You also get the feeling of ownership in a different way than a homebased business provides. There is something about walking up to a building with your company name on it that gives you a sense of pride and empowerment that, in my view, a homebased business doesn't give you. Also, if you need to meet clients and customers, you automatically get additional credibility.

Running your latest venture from home means that your client meetings may need to occur at Starbucks. I certainly don't have room for a conference table and I don't know many who do in their home businesses. I once recently went to a meeting at someone's home, where she converted at least three of her bedrooms into offices for her employees and the conference room was the kitchen table. It didn't feel the same discussing business on placemats with the kitchen sitting next to us. You'd be surprised how much the setting of an environment actually influences the actions taken—a meeting over a dining room or coffee table will often prove less productive than those in a boardroom, unless you employ great discipline and focus.

YourOnlineProfessor.com

The decision whether to work at home or work in an office is vital—not only for your sanity but for your profit margins and net income. Network with others and see how they made the decision—or when they changed their minds—at YourOnlineProfessor.com.

CHAPTER

11

GROWING YOUR BUSINESS

Identifying Additional Opportunities and Making Lots of Money

Each business has an opportunity to grow—some faster than others, and some of that may be your own desire to grow more slowly and enjoy life or to tackle numerous businesses simultaneously. An online bookkeeper may want to begin invoicing clients and handling bill pay, expanding later. An online eBayer may wish to take his eBay auctions to an eBay store where he buys in bulk from wholesalers (also provided by eBay) and kick it up a

notch with regard to pricing, inventory, and opportunity, or just sell for others as a trading assistant. The personal assistant may wish to add to his services. The online teacher may want to expand into higher-paying jobs as time goes on—or just add more schools.

In this chapter, I will help you, the web entrepreneur, identify additional opportunities and, perhaps more importantly, be ready to pounce on them when they're ripe for the picking. No doubt after establishing your business, growing it is the next hardest thing; some entrepreneurs say it's harder.

One thing you have to do right away is determine if your business is going to be based on Web 1.0 or Web 2.0. The differences are tremendous and really outline how you need to proceed. So let's start by looking at the differences.

CHOOSE BETWEEN WEB VERSIONS 1.0 AND 2.0

So why is the internet so powerful today—much more so than it was only a few years ago? For starters, Web 2.0 has taken hold, and it's bringing a new type of webosphere to the business world. To begin understanding what kind of business opportunities are at your fingertips, we need to first get a glimpse into the differences between Web 1.0 and Web 2.0? This simple chart (Figure 11.1) from O'Reilly's website has great information on what Web 2.0 is—and perhaps more importantly—is not.

Web 2.0 is still a rather ill-defined term, but it relies on user-generated content to create dynamic sites. You know the terrific sites that you visit that allow you to customize the page, become a part of a network of users, post your thoughts, save your favorites, link to other friends, and post just about anything you like? Welcome to Web 2.0! User-generated data or content became most popular in 2005 in the web publishing and media production circles (Lazo and Babb, 2007). Simply put, Web 2.0 refers to online content that is produced by users of a website rather than the traditional method—someone that works in a company or a marketing group displaying specific information with a specific purpose. Instead of a company pushing information out to clients and just providing them with information about a product or what marketing department wants out there, there is reciprocity in Web 2.0—people share. If you ask ten people about Web 2.0, you will be given ten

Web Version 1	Web Version 2
DoubleClick	Google AdSense
Ofodo	Flickr
Akamai	BitTorrent
Mp3.com	Napster
Brittanica Online	Wikipedia
Personal Websites	Blogging
Evite	Upcoming.org and EVDB
Domain Name Speculation	Search Engine Optimization
Page Views	Cost Per Click
Screen Scraping	Web Services
Publishing	Participation
Content Management Systems	Wikis
Directories (taxonomy)	Tagging ("folksonomy")
Stickiness	Syndication

(Lazo and Babb, 2007)

FIGURE 11.1 **COMPARISON OF WEB 1.0 AND 2.0**

relatively similar yet inconsistent messages. My job is to clarify the most important element–and that is what it *means* to you and how you can apply it. There has, within recent months, been murmur on some blogs regarding a Web 3.0 (how exciting).

Web 2.0 has given the average internet user not only new perspectives but unique control over her content. For instance, Top Ten Media, Wikipedia,

YouTube, and MySpace are all user-generated sites that are quite popular. "Some suggest Amazon and eBay's review system was an early form of Web 2. You can see quickly how these differ from sites that aim to push specific news or media worthy information to their site visitors. It allows ordinary people to publish their own content on websites they may not have had access to in the past. In fact, user-generated content is creating fame and fortune for people who may not otherwise have had access to media outlets." (Lazo and Babb, 2007) Companies are putting their profiles up. Even products! Did you know you can become a friend to the Whopper (as in Burger King's hamburger). The younger generations who use this technology frequently are identifying themselves and quantifying their personalities by whom they befriend. As a result, tech-savvy businesspeople are using the medium to get the word out about themselves and their products to a whole new generation of people.

TRY COMMUNITY SHARING INSTEAD OF UNIDIRECTIONAL MARKETING

Traditionally we got the word out about our companies through the television. There is a vast array of information that the television can provide, some of it more useful than others. We, as viewers, are completely passive when we watch, we don't participate beyond "E-mail us at . . ." and "We might use your words on the air!" Whoopee! We don't contribute anything to the various broadcasts; the television displays the emitted signal, which terminates in our eyes and ears. Whatever *they* want you to hear is what you hear, what they want you to see (product placement and advertisements) is done at your expense and for their revenue stream. But, what if you could push back? What if you and every other viewer could contribute to the broadcasts? Some television shows have become famous with interactivity—the ability to vote by cell phone, for instance. Why are these so successful? People are engaged; they feel as though their vote matters; it becomes viral.

> Growing the business is about expanding. It is about spreading yourself into different platforms, products, and services, and/or truly differentiating your business with products and services.

This is what Web 2.0 is to the internet. Instead of watching some anchorperson deliver news that someone somewhere has deemed relevant, you could provide your own input and be on equal footing with everyone else. The same holds true for your business and how you choose to use the tools is entirely up to you. This is the spirit of Web 2.0, best described as the "participatory web" (Decram, 2008).

It used to be that through an MBA program a businessperson learned all he needed to know to run a business and be a successful entrepreneur; he learned about sales and marketing, management, accounting and finance, human resources management, merchandising, advertising, inventory control, and so on. Once he knew these basic things, it was easy for him to simply branch out into any area of business because what was being sold wasn't important, but the supply and demand was, and niche finding was important. Repeat business was important; good control was important. But then, technology wasn't playing such an integral role in the process. Entrepreneurs began automating their offices to save money—from desktop publishing to word processing to accounting and bookkeeping.

Then we hit a new phase—the internet phase—and we entered a new realm and a new world that old-school entrepreneurs did not quickly adapt to because it was unlike anything they had seen before. This new world meant they weren't equipped from business school, and they often needed to outsource parts of their business, so many just didn't do anything at all. The web developer was not the entrepreneur and the entrepreneur was not the web developer. Today, though, the entrepreneur could be the web developer if he so chose; it is easier to build businesses online than ever before.

The objective to growing online is not just to grow one business. What percentage of people actually become millionaires and billionaires off one business, even in the traditional business world? OK, there are the exceptions—Donald Trump perhaps, but even he has expanded and made more money in doing so. *The Apprentice* is a good example of that. He knew that the reality show market was ripe for the picking and he picked it, and *voilà*—a hit. He found a niche and most importantly he understands business; the same principles apply to nearly any industry. Look at Oprah—she's more than just a journalist with her own talk show. She branched off into many areas: a magazine, a production company, and so forth. So the moral of the paragraph is this: Web business owners have to behave like entrepreneurs if they really want to grow their business. They need to know where to look for opportunities and they need to know how to pursue and exploit those opportunities at just the right time. Some may work and some may not. You have to learn to take risks while investing with minimal funds, but still getting powerful product to work with.

BUILD A FOUNDATION FOR GROWTH

If you want to grow your business, you need to see the future. According to Steven S. Little, "If you want to know what's coming, you need 'outstanding market intelligence.' This is your organization's ability to first recognize and then adapt to fundamental change happening in your company, your industry, and your community. You need to take the time to regularly consider the macro forces of change in the world as a whole" (2005). The question now is What can you do to stay on top of the changes happening in your industry and in your world? Little continues, in his article "Using 'Weak Signals' to Identify Opportunities": "Let's start with focus. Most business owners are great at internal focus. Knowing what is happening inside our own companies is one of the strengths that allow us to effectively compete with bigger businesses (because often, they aren't very good at this). However, we also tend to get mired within our insular view, and we ignore the importance of external focus. This is where big business, with their research budgets and market analysts, can often get the best of us."

Are You Getting Weak Signals from Your Clients?

Be sure you are keeping tabs on your clients from a high-level perspective. If you keep hearing something repetitive, chances are it will stick. Monitor the media, YouTube, and Google, and see what the most commonly searched for words in Google are, which it regularly publishes. eBay also publishes statistics on which products are doing best and which keyword searches are coming up most. Don't be afraid to ask for that information from your customer and statistics from your web hosting provider.

TAKE WHAT YOU HAVE AND MAKE IT BIGGER

One surefire way to begin expanding is to take what you have and make it bigger. This may require you to bring on staff if you have a service-based company, or it may require additional relationships with wholesalers and inventory suppliers if you sell products. For instance, if you sell coffee of a certain type, you may wish to expand your offering. If you run an eBay store selling women's designer clothes, why not add handbags? One way to figure out what your customers want is to survey them; ask them at the end of a purchase what they would like you to offer. This may give you a nice starting point to work from. Your online bookkeeping shop, for instance, may pay the bills, but what if your clients want CPA work, too? Knowing this will help you figure out what areas to expand into.

TAKE WHAT YOU HAVE AND FIND NEW TARGET AUDIENCES

So your online bookkeeping service is geared toward the one-man shop—the business of one person that needs some extra hands writing checks and paying bills. What about the small businesses of ten employees? Chances are they could use some outsourced work, too. When you do expand into new territory, be sure to issue a press release and be sure that you begin a new ad campaign with this targeted group of individuals, regardless of which advertising method you use.

What Can You Do for Your Country?

One area that can be expanded into that is often overlooked is the government or public sector. Local, state, and federal government agencies utilize private sector contractors for a multitude of tasks.

The United States Small Business Administration (SBA) provides information on the various programs that can help you position your business for contracting opportunities throughout the federal government. The SBA produced the document "Opening Small Business Opportunities: Federal Government Contracting" (2008), which can be found and viewed in its entirety at sba.gov/services/contractingopportunities/index.html. As you can imagine, the mere thought of becoming a government contractor sounds daunting, even a bit scary. The SBA lists the following myths and truths surrounding this often unrealized opportunity:

> *Myth*: Doing business with the government is too complicated, involves too much red tape, and takes forever to get paid.
>
> *Reality*: The government uses many commercial and business-friendly practices, such as buying off-the-shelf items and paying by credit card. Payments are generally received within 30 days after submitting an invoice.
>
> *Myth*: There's no one I can turn to in trying to obtain government contracts.
>
> *Reality*: SBA and its network of resource partners have programs and "hands-on" assistance for small businesses contemplating selling to the federal marketplace.
>
> *Myth*: I must compete head-to-head with large businesses and multinational corporations to win contracts.
>
> *Reality*: The government has many categories of contract opportunities set aside exclusively for small businesses to level the playing field.
>
> *Myth*: All I need to do is register in the Central Contractor Registration system and the contracts will come rolling in.
>
> *Reality*: Although the CCR is a primary way federal agencies learn about prospective vendors, it's up to you to aggressively market your firm to those agencies that buy your products and services. Remember, agencies don't buy, people do.
>
> *Myth*: The low offer always wins the contract.
>
> *Reality*: While price is always a consideration, the government increasingly awards contracts for goods and services based on "best value," in which both technical and cost factors are weighed in the final assessment.

The SBA has programs and services aimed at leveling the playing field so that small businesses obtain a fair share of government contracts.

The U.S. government is the world's largest buyer of goods and services, from spacecraft and advanced scientific research to paper clips and landscaping services. Military and civilian purchases total more than $425 billion a year. And federal agencies are required to establish contracting goals, with at least 23 percent of all government spending targeted to small business (SBA, 2008).

First, though, ask yourself, "Is government contracting right for me?" Government contracts can provide significant revenue, but they're not necessarily the right decision for every business. Here are some basic questions to ask yourself as you think of the opportunities: Are you willing to do ongoing and detailed research to find opportunities and present offers including bids on very strict deadlines with no opportunity to delay? Are you willing to act as a subcontractor, which may require you to lower your price? Are you certain your business can support the time and detailed requirements that government contracts often require? Do you have the time or the interest to learn the rules of federal funding for projects?

If you answered "yes" to these questions, then I would highly recommend that you contact your local chapter of the SBA to get more information, or you can download the organization's informational brochure at sba.gov/idc/groups/public/documents/sba_homepage/serv_pub_contracting.pdf.

OFFER CUSTOMIZATION

Another fun way (and high-margin method) to add product differentiation and grow your business is to offer customization. This is easy if you sell robes or towels: you can offer monogramming (which reduces returns, too, since customized products are generally nonrefundable). But you can do this with just about any business. Are you a graphics designer using templates to create new logos? What about creative out-of-the-box work for clients willing to pay for it? This may require additional staff, so the financial pros and cons need to be weighed, but no doubt this is a way to grow your business.

OFFER BULK DISCOUNTING TO RESELLERS

You may have turned off an entire segment of buyer—the reseller, particularly the brick-and-mortar store that often gets its inventory from online stores. By offering products to resellers on a net 30 basis and establishing credit terms, you grow beyond a business-to-consumer (B2C) model and move to a business-to-business (B2B) model.

TAKE REFERRALS SERIOUSLY—AND PAY FOR THEM

Chances are, the back of your dentist's card says something like "The nicest compliment you can give me is a referral to your family and friends." When I see that, I say, "That's it? What about a free cleaning? Or a free copay?"

> Provide incentives for those who refer business to you. It's perfectly OK to ask others to pay you for referrals, too.

Do you teach students how to build a website and know a great web designer? Does the designer make $5,000 per new client? Asking for 10 percent of any referral's first purchase is acceptable, and you should automatically offer this to people and businesses who refer customers your way who buy products. This is a fast way to build credibility and to encourage people to send new business your way. Who doesn't want extra residual income? When I hold workshops, I give an attendee 50 percent off for bringing in five people and a free seminar for bringing in ten people. Also don't forget to drop names when calling on new clients or asking for referrals from existing ones.

KNOW WHAT YOUR CUSTOMERS THINK

One of the best ways to grow your business is to know why people are coming to your business in the first place—and if they have to return something, whether they plan to continue to shop with you. If you return something to Zappos.com, you must fill out a questionnaire (very short, and they should keep it that way) on the free return label asking what the company could have done to prevent the return, and if you'll continue shopping with them. Not only does this portray a "we care about your business" attitude, but you can learn from this information, too. Don't collect it and sit on it, collect it and act on it. Know what your customers like—and don't like—about your store or services.

Try to stay away from annoying surveys. One thing I love to do is e-mail my customers directly and say, "Thanks for buying at my store. Can I ask you, what could I do to improve your visit? By the way, this is a personal e-mail from me, Dani Babb, and not an automated one. I will personally read it and reply. I care about your business." Don't just select the biggest customers either; all customers matter. Some smaller customers may be trying out your goods before making larger purchases.

TALK TO THE BLOGGERS

The more recognizable your company becomes, the more people will talk negatively and positively (more negative than positive) about it in public forums. It is easy to want to get defensive or to ignore them, but don't. Log in and reply to these customers, ask them serious questions about what could be done to improve the experience and let them know you are an enthusiast on whatever product or service you sell and you care about them. This goes a long way in the blogosphere.

SELL COMPLEMENTARY GOODS

Examine what complementary goods you may not be selling that you should. Do you sell special lavender pillows for insomniacs? (If you do, send your link my way) What about other products insomniacs might want, like alarm clocks that use light to wake you, or sound machines. Think of any complementary good you can sell and give it a shot. Think small items offered at checkout that don't add much to the bill but do add to your profit margin—for example, a wine opener with a bottle of fine wine. If it's a repeat customer, consider throwing one in the box for free and not even warning your customer about it. She will be delighted at the nice surprise.

OFFER SME CONSULTATIONS

We have talked about subject matter experts with regard to individuals answering forum questions, but one area in which to grow your business is

SME consultations. For instance, on my own site, you can buy time with me where I'll call you for an hour or half an hour and discuss any topic you want in my area of expertise. This service generates an extra 5 percent in sales each month. It is time-consuming, but since the topics are those I'm already passionate about, it is easy to do and actually quite fun. The SME consultations don't have to be done only by you, either. You can hire teams who are just as passionate about your product to take the calls.

CONSIDER A SALES TEAM

It sounds so counterintuitive: a sales team for an online business? Indeed, a sales team! Sales teams that specialize in either your product area or online business models can be of significant value in growing your business and expanding the types of people that frequent your online store. Many may not know about it, but a few dozen cold calls per day may increase awareness. Don't count this out until you've seriously considered what you can do. Commission-only salespeople (like college students) can be great, too, so you aren't paying if you don't see progress.

OFFER NEWSLETTERS THAT CAN BE FORWARDED

I love using newsletters, and every one of my websites has the ability for you to sign up to each of my newsletters right there on the homepage. Why? I send out one per month with great articles and advice, but I also advertise my products and services. One of the most important features of a newsletter system is automatic signup, and be sure it includes online spelling and format editors. Also be sure they track click-throughs on ads and graphics, and be sure that they can be forwarded without losing content. The one I prefer to use (after testing many) is at ymlp15.com, it is called Your Mailing List Provider. The costs are relatively inexpensive and you can embed images, have it host images, collect subscribers, comply with federal law requiring easy opt-outs that are promptly processed, customize newsletters, import subscribers, and perform mail merging and reporting. Most web designers would prefer that these are integrated with your Web 2.0 site, of course, so that is definitely something to consider.

GET YOUR SITE TO CLICK WITH YOUR AUDIENCE

Critical to advancing your business, regardless of your goals for how quickly you do it, is to get your site to click, no pun intended, with your audience. Check out some of the work and research that Jakob Nielsen, noted usability guru, has to say about usability. Interestingly enough, he's not a big fan of Web 2.0 because sometimes you have to give up usability, so he is in favor of a balance where there is more participation and collaboration. He likes the sense of belonging that Web 2.0 applications contribute to the experience, but not at the expense of usability. Nielsen, a former distinguished engineer at Sun Microsystems, is now a full-time consultant and speaker. He specifically points out sites that put marketing above usability, which is not a good thing. He remarks, in a *New York Times* article, about having to wait for a picture of a printer to load that showed nothing but a person standing beside a printer. So what *does* Nielsen like? Sites that perform any task the visitor might ask it to perform. If a site can't do that, he blames the designer. His favorite websites have been noted as Amazon, Yahoo!, Anchor Desk, and ZD Net (Richtel, 1998) He likes sites that attract the reader and take very little time to download, so the reader has information efficiently with underlines to relevant links and fresh information. He likes sites, as he noted in the quoted *New York Times* column, that help visitors find what they want, not what the marketing department wants to promote. If it's time for you to advance your website, you should look at his work and contributions to the usability world of the web, and take heed. His PhD in a field called user interface and many books on the subject of usability have been pared down to help companies, even small businesses, get real results. In Appendix A, I have listed several of his articles and links to his work that will help you as you work through the usability on your own site. Are you not sure where you fall? Get a small focus group together and ask. Go through your own site with family and friends, and ask, "What does my site offer my visitor? How is it consumer driven and consumer focused? Is my site too complex?"

USE PODCASTS

Podcasts are a quick way to get information out there that is more graphic, more engaging, more entertaining than pure text. If you want to grow your business, consider using podcasts to do it.

Podcasting Defined

Wikipedia, the online encyclopedia, defines podcasting as "a multimedia file distributed over the internet using syndication feeds, for playback on mobile devices and personal computers. Like 'radio,' it can mean both the content and the method of delivery; the latter may also be termed podcasting. If you believe that your clients won't want information from this medium you are mistaken; they already do and they are already getting it . . .

"The host or author of a podcast is often called a podcaster." The definition goes on to explain that "a podcast is distinguished from other digital audio formats by its ability to be downloaded automatically using software capable of reading feed formats such as RSS or Atom." (Wikipedia, 2006, as cited in Lazo and Babb, 2007)

Podcasting has changed the way many of us use the internet; it has changed the way we watch shows, get our news, and share our ideas. Even major television networks are making shows available via Podcast.

It is really up to you how far you want to take these powerful tools that can help you grow your business in a manner that you never imagined. You certainly cannot ignore this wave of technology as it builds momentum and heads toward you. It isn't as difficult as most believe to get started and really grasp the technology.

Who has not heard of the Apple iPod? Or YouTube? Some argue that these technologies have changed the way we do everything. This is true for at least two generations of people, if not more. The older the person is, the greater his tendency to use familiar, older technologies. Many strategists and bigwigs on Wall Street say Apple made its big comeback with the iPod, and the impact it has had on our society is unmistakable. There are ads or people working out at gyms, or walking down the street with their iPod. You've probably heard of the famous videos, cell phone video posted online, or perhaps the large Google buyout of the fascinating newsworthy site YouTube.

Note that you can host your own blog or podcast, and there is inexpensive (even free) software out there to do it. The software you'd be using and googling is generally referred to as open source blog software. This means that people can feel free to modify it and use it as they need. Usually in the interest of sharing, any useful and meaningful updates you make to the software itself are also shared in the online community. With the hosted version of podcasts and blogs, it does require that the user leave your site and go onto the hosted site, which isn't always a good thing. Hosting the podcast or blog yourself is definitely worth considering, and it isn't as hard as it sounds.

Know Your Podcasting

As with any technology, there are a lot of details you will need to understand about podcasting so that you can use it properly. The *New Oxford American Dictionary* declared podcasting the 2005 word of the year. Wikipedia further documents, "The content provider begins by making a file (for example, an MP3 audio file) available on the internet. You might create a small podcast that you post on YouTube explaining something you know that educates the public but sells your business at the same time.

"This is usually done by posting the file on a publicly available web server; however, BitTorrent trackers also have been used, and it is not technically necessary that the file be publicly accessible. The only requirement is that the file be accessible through some known URL (a general purpose internet address). This file is often referred to as one *episode* of a podcast."

In plain English, this means that the podcaster must post a file in readily readable format (such as MP3) to the internet (privately or publicly) for someone else to download. Some systems let individuals subscribe to the website to enable them to be notified or even autodownload new podcasts when they become available.

PodBlaze.com is one of the first websites to support podcasts, but there are many products out there today that let you create them.

MAKE SHOPPING A SNAP

One of the worst *faux pas* of commerce-driven websites is being unable to find what you want to buy. There is also such a thing as too much security—when you have so many hoops for the customer to jump through that she is turned off and leaves. Here is a bad scenario:

1. The buyer selects the product she wants by adding it to her shopping cart.
2. The buyer is prompted to continue shopping or check out now.
3. The buyer is so eager to buy that she goes ahead and clicks on Checkout, wondering how fast you'll get the product to her.
4. She enters her personal info (especially the phone number associated with the credit card), billing info, and credit card info and clicks on Submit.
5. The buyer is happy . . . but wait—the system is asking her to take a special code, and then a caller is going to call and ask for that code, so the buyer has to have it ready. This is extra "security" (or nuisance).
6. Your customer gets the phone call within seconds and then has to go through a series of verification processes, which includes leaving a voice signature.
7. When the customer is done, she enters the code she was originally given. (Are you thinking about now that this doesn't happen anywhere? Oh, it does!)
8. The verification process is complete and the website prompts the consumer to wait a moment while the order is processed.
9. The system finally verifies that the order is complete and the buyer gets an e-mail with the order information and specifics.

Yes, identity fraud won't be an issue here, but neither will longevity for your business because it won't have any! You have to balance security with usability. Many people, especially if they are in a hurry, are going to say forget it. Or, what if they use a K7 number (as previously discussed) as their billing number and there is no one to answer that phone? You are seriously inconveniencing your customers.

This is again part of profiling your customers. People want to feel your site is secure and safe, but they also want to know they can check out promptly. The bottom line is still how do you get them to come back, and how do you get them to buy more? Annoying them isn't the answer—understanding them is.

OPTIMIZE YOUR SITE

Although the concept of search engine optimization is highly debated among the internet community, one thing you'll need to do once your site is thoroughly tested is be sure you are ranking where you should be in Google and other search engines. After all, you want your site to be found, right?

Wikipedia (2008) defines search engine optimization as the "process of improving the volume and quality of traffic to a website from search engines via 'natural' search result for targeted keywords." The wiki writers go on to say that "usually, the earlier a site is presented in the search results or the higher it 'ranks,' the more searchers will visit that site. SEO can also target different kinds of search, including image search, local search, and industry-specific vertical search engines." I found that after people started posting photos to my site, my brand ranked higher in Google searches because I had images.

Another very serious consideration you need to make is how your pricing will come up in search engines that do nothing but price out products. Many of us have used sites like PriceGrabber to tell us who has the cheapest price, including shipping, handling, and tax, all at once—and if someone is buying by price, this is what he is going to look for.

How Does Optimization Work Exactly?

The keys to successful optimization are to set up your site for search engine crawling including meta tags; allow spiders into your site easily to crawl; include lots of content that can be searchable including graphics that are labeled; and use keywords for content! These will all make it easier for visitors to find your site. Good meta tags and good content are still the best way to get adequately indexed by search engine spiders so that when your target audience looks for what you sell or offer or do, they will find you first. Google remains one of the most popular search engines on the web and it generates most of its income from ads. Web spiders will read the web programming code starting with your header and then moving into the body of your web page. So if you have the relevant title, description, and keywords in your meta tags (which reside between your header tags in your web page code) this will help significantly. Including those same keywords in the body of your page is also imperative; good content writing is therefore vital because the content must align with your meta tag information and the category in which you hope the spider would include it at the respective search engine. Google will auto scan your site for tags.

Making your site search engine friendly means making menus and content management systems and shopping carts simple enough to search and make your site easy to find. There are tools that you can buy to help move up your search site ranking, but often using the right data and content on your site is sufficient. See Appendix A for a list of search engines far beyond Google.

Remember, even if you do get the traffic to your site, you need to have a very user-oriented site—one that makes people want to stay and want to *buy*. If your content is not perceived as well written, appropriate, engaging, and useful, there really won't be any reason for your visitors to try to dig deeper

SEO Code

Much like the secret Amazon book ranking code, not many people have truly "cracked" the SEO code, but we do know enough to help you get more traffic to your site. We do know that the ability for search engines to index and fully spider, or find all relevant links, is important. We also know that adding content to the site makes it easier to index and search by robots, which generally control the web's search work.

into the site, and thus you'll have no click-throughs and no sales. Be sure to use website analytical software to help you determine which parts of your site are most engaging to your site visitors and make the necessary amendments to the slow pages. Either remove them or spice them up. How? Ask your visitors what they want. Use surveys to get a good idea of what they want to see, read, do, get, buy, experience at your site, and give that to them. Give them something like coupons or discount codes or referral money toward your site if they complete the surveys. You want them engaged enough to keep coming back and to do some word-of-mouth (WOM) advertising for you.

RETHINK SOCIAL ADVERTISING

Another way to quickly advance your site is through social advertising. While I touched on this in Chapter 9, it bears a bit of repeating if you want to advance your business and haven't done this yet—but perhaps with a new light. Social media, sites like MySpace, Classmates.com, and Facebook, are reaching audiences very similar to that of television. Yes, think about that for a minute. You may not have started advertising in these areas, but they can be as far-reaching as *television*. The top 25 social media networks in February 2008 had more than 155 million unique visitors, and 70 percent of these were from three sites: Facebook, MySpace, and Classmates. If you add in YouTube and Flickr, you get another 60 million, with an estimated total of 215 million people watching social media monthly. On any given day, around 50 million viewers watch television, with the highest ratings being Super Bowl Sunday when about 100 million to 115 million people watch. Television is perhaps reaching a smaller audience in one month than five sites. Think about this for a minute. You also get a wide variety of individuals visiting your site. You can post commercials to sites. What would a 15-second commercial cost you on MSNBC compared with a free 15-second viral funny commercial or parody that will get more views? The audience reach is huge. This is also an extremely loyal group of individuals, because they use these sites for social reasons, and they network on these sites. This will ensure longevity long after the Super Bowl.

BE FLEXIBLE—THE WORLD IS ALWAYS CHANGING

According to the Australian website Business Victoria (2008), "Maintaining an awareness of the changes occurring in your business, market, and industry can help you to identify and take advantage of a range of opportunities. A strong understanding of your market will allow you to notice any gaps which could potentially be filled by a product or service you are able to develop and bring to market."

One of the site owners' primary notations is that developing new products or services or improving those already on the market can help you have what is referred to as a first-mover or first-player advantage in any market. Head starts are highly valuable to any new operation because you can be established as a market leader. However, one risk to this is that others will quickly copy you and get efficiencies you don't yet have.

The following examples, provided by Business Victoria (2008), outline two businesses that have been successful in their respective markets through innovative products and their identification of a need for such a product in the marketplace.

The first example they give is the business La Famiglia, started by Michael Clark in 1979. He used his experience in the small-goods industry to market chilled garlic bread and created a product that was sold at major grocery stores. He had first-mover advantage and now supplies many clients like Sizzler and Pizza Hut, and has gone international.

The second example cited by Business Victoria is Standfast. Cameron Baker created a product that would prevent people from falling from heights or boats and rocks. His company now producers harness systems that provide security for workers in all sorts of industries.

Your understanding of not only your target demographic but also the marketplace in general, and the ability to alter course, if needed, will exponentially increase your business's chances of success. It is vital that you take steps to research your market prior to making any big decisions about your product or service, whether you are contemplating adding products or services or altering a current product line or service menu.

STRIVE FOR CONSTANT PROGRESS

In May 2004, Entrepreneur Media Inc. published an article written by Karen Spaeder titled "10 Ways to Grow Your Business." Since the tenth idea discusses expanding into the internet (what this book is already about), I'll briefly outline the other nine suggestions. Choosing the option that is right for you will depend on various factors, such as what type of business you own, what resources are available to you, how much money you have available to invest in expansion, and more. If you have reached a point where you are ready to grow, read on.

Open a Physical Location

You decided to start an online business, but perhaps your first growth method will be to create an on-ground store! If you find customers not buying because they want to touch and feel the products, or find your business growing exceedingly rapidly, this might be a good option. It will take careful planning and number crunching. Be certain you already are meeting goals, and be sure to analyze trends and complete a new business plan with your updated information. Understand the impacts on your finances and choose a location that is best for your business; it may not be the cheapest place.

Become a Franchise or Business Opportunity

"Bette Fetter, founder and owner of Young Rembrandts, an Elgin, Illinois-based drawing program for children, waited ten years to begin franchising her concept

FRANCHISING MADE A BIT EASIER

It is often easier to franchise into local states before moving to others that aren't so close. Often franchising requires hands-on work, seminars, training, and so on. You may not have the income to do this on a national scale immediately . . . all in due time.

in 2001—but for Fetter and her husband, Bill, the timing was perfect. Raising four young children and keeping the business local was enough for the couple until their children grew older and they decided it was time to expand nationally." (Spaeder, 2004) This duo used franchising because they wanted something that would allow others to have an interest in their work. There are a lot of rules and regulations you must follow and it gets even more complicated when you have to do state-by-state research, so be careful when moving into this territory!

License Your Product

In her 2004 article, Spaeder says:

> "[Licensing] can be an effective, low-cost growth medium, particularly if you have a service product or branded product," notes Larry Bennett, director of the Larry Friedman International Center for Entrepreneurship at Johnson & Wales University in Providence, Rhode Island. "You can receive upfront monies and royalties from the continued sales or use of your software, name brand, etc.—if it's successful," he says. Licensing also minimizes your risk and is low cost in comparison to the price of starting your own company to produce and sell your brand or product.

To do this you need to find a partner to license with. I highly recommend working with a licensing expert or, at the very least, an attorney before embarking on this journey.

If your business idea, whether it is product or service based, is on the verge of being the next big thing, there is near unlimited potential for financial gain when expanding using this platform. If you are an Angels baseball fan, you are well aware of the thunder sticks. It is hard to go to any sporting event these days without seeing these noise-producing novelty items. It all started with one team, and one idea. Could your idea be the next market revolution?

Form Alliances

You can form strategic alliances or partnerships at any stage of the game, though I highly recommend forming at least some alliances before you even begin your business.

> Aligning yourself with a similar type of business can be a powerful way to expand quickly. Last spring, Jim Labadie purchased a CD seminar set from a fellow fitness professional, Ryan Lee, on how to make and sell fitness information products. It was a move that proved lucrative for Labadie, who at the time was running an upscale personal training firm he'd founded in 2001. "What I learned on [Lee's] CDs allowed me to develop my products and form alliances within the industry," says Labadie, who now teaches business skills to fitness professionals via a series of products he created and sells on his website, HowToGetMoreClients.com. (Spaeder, 2004)

Sometimes these alliances come by giving commissions or kickbacks for referrals. Isn't it better to build this into your profit margin and create more word-of-mouth marketing and keep partners happy than to risk having no business at all?

If you haven't already learned the lesson that it isn't always what you know, but whom you know, then now is a perfect time. The relationships you build and nurture may very well be the determining factor to the ultimate success of your new adventure. An alliance is nothing more than a mutually beneficial relationship, whether it is with another business, a vendor, supplier, and so on. Each and every time your business changes, whether because of a new product line or service, you should evaluate this option. With each new idea, the chances of associating yourself with another are presented. If your product, service, or idea is market changing, however, make sure you are protected (patents, copyrights, etc.) prior to spreading the word and testing the alliance waters.

Diversify Your Products or Services

There are lots of ways to diversify what you offer, whether you sell products or services. We discussed finding out what complementary goods are consistent with your product or service. Continue doing this. Teach courses if you need to on your products or services—even for free—particularly if they are complicated. A student once came to me with a solar idea, and I recommended to him that he offer free training classes because homeowners weren't going to believe it was as easy as he said. Speak regularly and often, and present as often as you can, even if it's for free. Sometimes you can do a presentation and have your travel costs covered, but if you offer to give your presentation for free, most organizations or clubs will allow you to market your work and materials, too.

Target Other Markets or Create Multiple Businesses

Even if your business is doing well, you might want to consider targeting other markets or even creating multiple businesses. Web architects often talk about malls and having numerous sites under one corporate name. Decide if there are additional segments of the population, too, that you haven't yet tapped into. If you've been focusing on the tween market, why not think of how your product, perhaps tweaked slightly, might help boomers too?

Advancing into Other Demographics

If you do decide to go into other demographics as an expansionary tool, be sure that you consider creating an entirely separate site for that new market. Sometimes what appeals to Gen Yers or tweens won't appeal to Boomers. Creating a site that will make everyone happy is tough, so you might be best served by multiple sites.

Even though you have already analyzed your market(s) prior to launch, as we've already discovered, markets change. Twenty years ago, the cellular phone market was strictly for business professionals, and even further limited to physicians (typically), but now cell phones are marketed even to children, with phones designed to go with any number of Disney character themes. A growing business is always evaluating where it stands in the market and where it can improve. Another section of data that you should constantly evaluate is where you expand. What haven't you been doing that you now can? What product haven't you been able to offer that you now can make available? Answer these questions, and you'll know where you can branch out!

Look into Government Contracts

We have discussed a bit the SBA's role in government contracts and helping small businesses score government contracts. "The best way for a small business to grow is to have the federal government as a customer," wrote Rep. Nydia M. Velazquez, ranking Democratic member of the House Small Business Committee, in August 2003. The U.S. Chamber of Commerce and the SBA also have a Business Matchmaking Program designed to match entrepreneurs with buyers.

Consider Mergers and Acquisitions

Sometimes even large companies have to merge and acquire other companies to grow. While some mergers are baffling (like Circuit City and Blockbuster), others are highly profitable and successful. Think of all the companies giant Google has purchased and how it has allowed them to expand product offerings far more quickly than if they were to redevelop those products on their own, and then perhaps most importantly and with most difficulty, compete against established brands. If you are in a good position to buy, do so. Try to retain the customers of your acquisition by not changing the site much, keep important and vital staff (particularly developers that will be highly recruited by other companies), and find ways for the technologies to work together. Don't wait for the accounting systems to work together though—get the business functioning and adopted into your strategy, and then quickly get financials integrated.

> Although there are some similarities in merging with or acquiring another business, there are some very distinct differences. This is a major undertaking and you should not move forward unless you are thoroughly aware of all of the intricacies involved. I recommend contacting a mergers and acquisition attorney.

Go Global!

There are many emerging markets that are changing the way we do business today. For instance, India and China now consume so much oil that they've pushed up the prices in the United States for gasoline. This increase in demand isn't just for oil; it is for goods and services, period. Having been to China, I can tell you that the desire for American products is very strong, and the youth there is very pro-democracy, pro-American, with few exceptions. Not marketing to this group is negligence to your business model. Going global can be as easy as shipping to anywhere and taking credit cards or as involved as going to other nations and working with local partners with whom you can cross-sell products.

Even though your business will be primarily internet based, this does not automatically equate to your business being internationally involved. If you are offering bookkeeping services to local small businesses, then why not expand to small businesses nationwide or worldwide? Change your website to let your visitors know you are now offering your services internationally. The possibilities are literally endless.

YourOnlineProfessor.com

The decision whether to work at home or work in an office is vital—not only for your sanity but for your profit margins and net income. Network with others and see how they made the decision—or when they changed their minds—at YourOnline Professor.com.

CHAPTER

12

AVOIDING PITFALLS

Eliminating Gotchas in the Online Business Place

Any business or business model has to avoid "gotcha's" to be successful, but online entrepreneurs have special pitfalls to be on the lookout for. I touched on many in Chapter 10, such as slipping into being a slacker or not maintaining your productivity, and balancing personal chores with business necessities or letting your competitive spirit slip into the night along with your sleep routines.

But there are bigger, broader pitfalls, too—not planning, not taking your business seriously enough, growing too slowly or too rapidly, not setting aside a work environment, and not maintaining connections with other individuals are among the many.

PLAN YOUR WORK AND DON'T RUSH

I admittedly rush into things myself; I get excited and just do it, all in one night. Then I find out from my wonderful friend and web designer (and expert book contributor), for example, that my haste has led to my shopping cart not working with the product I just bought. Oops . . . yes, I have learned many lessons, but this is the hardest one when you love what you do! Don't act in haste. Wait, don't rush. Plan and be diligent. Do your homework.

KEEP THE FOCUS

It is easy to lose focus—even to something that doesn't really need your attention. For instance, e-mail is a common distraction during the day when I am trying to build my brand. Try setting aside time for administrative tasks (like e-mail and phone calls) and separate time to focus on your core product. Keep the focus in your efforts, too; remember the ultimate goal. Whenever you are asked to do something else, ask yourself, "Does this get me closer to my ultimate goal?" If the answer is no, then refuse the assignment.

BE OPEN ABOUT ERRORS

When you make an error, fess up—and right away: you will maintain integrity and credibility. For instance, I recently shipped two people in my eBay store the wrong parts. I e-mailed them both immediately when one notified me he got the wrong part, and suggested they mail each other the parts and I would compensate them for postage and inconvenience—that way they both got their part faster and ultimately it cost me less (I would have had to pay double shipping). Both literally wrote back within two hours thanking me for being honest and even proactive. This enhanced my reputation, and instead of leaving negative feedback for me, they both left positive feedback and noted that I was proactive in resolving problems.

Errors are often aired in public in blogs. I have made incorrect calculations, unintentionally, on national television that were caught in blogs. I promptly found the blogs, corrected my mistake, and then even corrected any errors the next time I was on air. People respect this far more than just trying to cover it up.

MARKET TEST PRODUCTS OR SERVICES

You don't want to invest $10,000 in a product or service you have no idea will sell. Ask around; ask blog and forum members if they would be interested in your product and, if so, what the dollar value would be to them. Ask what they'd like in the service arena, too, and then be sure you provide it. Test your products, just like big companies would do with focus groups, but of course on a more manageable scale.

BE SPECIFIC

If you just sell everything, you are an expert in nothing. For an online mall that just makes residual income, this is fine, but if you want to build brand loyalty and a reputation in your field of expertise, you need to 1) know something about the field and 2) be a specialist. One way to showcase your expertise is to offer product reviews written by you or to encourage others that are specialists to post also. As people come for knowledge, they'll stop by your store.

MAKE SURE YOU HAVE ENOUGH MONEY

I have seen more businesses fail because the owner didn't create a plan and understand what kind of working money was needed than for almost any other reason. Be sure you budget and plan and stay within the budget. If you need expertise and advice, seek it out; don't just rely on yourself to find answers in online forums. Seek out experts whether they are financial planners or startup experts.

HEED THE WARNING SIGNS

If your sales are slumping do you blame it on gas prices? If customers are returning lots of product do you say they just didn't like the color? Don't ignore potential problems before they become disasters. Talk with your customers, find out what they were genuinely unhappy about. You can do this through an automated process or you can find out more information by googling yourself and your business and learning what others are saying about you. Whatever the warning sign, don't ignore it! Learning about it and addressing it could just save your company.

DON'T START OFF CHEESY

The very first site you put up is going to make a statement about you and your company. Do you want your image to say unprofessional and lacking in organization? Or do you want it to say professional, efficient, and knowledgeable? Build your site around the image you want it to portray to others. This means paying attention to the details, small and large, from spelling and grammar to spacing of icons and pictures. The more critical you are during this process—the closer to perfection you strive for—the more professional your site will appear, and subsequently the more professional and legitimate you and your business will be.

MAINTAIN RELATIONSHIPS

You have many relationships even in your online business: affiliate network companies, other business owners in a similar genre of product or service, your vendors, your fans, your naysayers, your suppliers, and your web developers. Everyone—especially your customers—has a special relationship with you. Promptly answer questions and be thorough with your response. Your response should be so thorough that rarely are follow-up questions needed. Treat business partners and customers with respect, integrity, and loyalty.

DON'T SELL YOUR LISTS

During the course of your business, you'll probably be solicited, particularly as you grow stronger, to sell your lists of individuals. If you didn't put a privacy policy on your site guaranteeing you'd never sell anyone's information, you do have a right to do it. But the question becomes should you? My answer is definitely no. There is a chance no one will find out where the information came from. But, chances are, people didn't read the fine print on your site that said you would sell their information to others—and you are violating ethics to do so, even if what you are doing isn't illegal. It is a way to make extra residual income, but not one that I recommend. Others have a different opinion, but my experience has told me to stay away from this entirely. Buy e-mail lists if you really need to, but I don't recommend selling them. Treat lists as precious noncommodities and take care of your lists and treat your customers with respect.

ADVERTISE

So many uninformed web business owners believe in the fantasy that was inspired by *Field of Dreams*—if you build it, they will come—and put up an internet store and wait for customers to come. They may, but they probably won't! You need to advertise. Using a well-planned budget, start with family's and friends' sites (reputable sites only!) that will swap banner ads with you. Then get on the blogs and forums and begin talking about your new company. Ask others to spread information by word of mouth; a mass e-mail to everyone you have ever met might drum up initial interest. Pay for advertising, but advertise and get out there immediately. Once you do, follow up with expert service immediately.

USE CHECKLISTS

You are juggling a lot on your plate. Using a checklist customized for you and your business model is imperative to success. Be sure that you are very clear on what you need to do, when you need to do it, and what the cost will be, and move forward very systematically. As a good friend keeps telling me, tread lightly and move with intention. You need to do the same in your business. A simple spreadsheet with everything you need to do (a starter is provided in Appendix B) is very helpful. You can find a copy of this list on my website at drdaniellebabb.com.

PRICE RIGHT

You may want to price 20 percent above others and say that your super service will make it worth it, but in the internet age everyone is looking for a deal. People use sites like PriceGrabber.com to literally find the cheapest company including shipping, and they just purely buy from that site regardless of service or reputation—just based on price. Consider where you want to position yourself in the market, and stick to it. Price right from the beginning; if you price high to start, you will run the risk of being called the high-price store that no one wants to visit, and by the time you lower your price, it will be too late.

DON'T HOLD INVENTORY

Inventory is expensive to maintain and to hold. Shipping from warehouses and directly from suppliers if you can is usually cheaper than having inventory. Consider this in your initial business plan and model.

DON'T EXTEND CREDIT TO B2B CUSTOMERS WITHOUT CHECKING THEIR CREDIT

B2B customers often expect you to offer net 30 terms immediately, but you need to run their credit. Would you rent to a tenant that hasn't paid her bills? I hope not! The same is true for your business. It is OK to expect cash on delivery for the first three to six months and extend credit after a period of time when you feel comfortable. It is ultimately your call, but this is one of those situations where discretion is advised.

WATCH YOUR CASH FLOW

You log into your checking account and notice—oops—you are in overdraft! Watch your cash flow very carefully by balancing your checkbook and keeping lots of receivables daily. Quickbooks is a great way to manage finances and one I've found useful and reliable for many years. You don't want to be late with vendor payments or unable to pay your hosting company.

One option to help you manage your finances and keep an eye on your bottom line, especially if you are often on the road or your Quickbooks files aren't readily available, is to set up "mobile alerts" through the financial institution that manages your business's funds. Note that not all financial institutions have this service available, but the large ones (Bank of America, Washington Mutual, etc.) either already do or have similar services planned. Bank of America, for example, has multiple ways to set up mobile alerts, which are alerts sent as text messages directly to your cell phone. I personally have my balance sent via text to me if it's falling below a particular limit. I have the option of having my available balance arrive as a text message every morning at the same time. These same alerts, through Bank of America, can also be set to arrive as e-mails, so even if your cell phone does not support text messages or you do not have unlimited text messaging service, your cell phone breaks, or your cell phone gets stolen, you can still have the information delivered to you and take advantage of this helpful service.

COVER YOUR BUSINESS'S BEHIND

Familiarize yourself with the rules of the game. There are rules that your business, meaning you, will need to follow, on a local, state, and federal level. The rules, laws, mandates, and regulations that affect you and your business will vary, depending on where you are (meaning where your headquarters is) and where you actually do business as well as where you expand to, if you choose to do that. Let's say, for example, you live in Bullhead City, Arizona, but you set up shop in Laughlin, Nevada. You will need to familiarize yourself with the laws and governing bodies in both locations. Which municipality's laws you follow will vary depending on the situation. If you do business in more than one state, things get a bit more complicated. You need to find out how and when you need to collect sales tax, too. Check with your tax accountant on this.

You need to make sure that you are following all the rules of the game, especially those set by the Internal Revenue Service (IRS), from day one. Not doing so can literally ruin your business, and if you are not protected by some level of incorporation, you might want to consider doing it—even if it's just a simple LLC. It is highly advised that prior to conducting business, you consult with not only a business attorney but also a licensed and qualified business accountant, to ensure that all legally required business documents are drafted properly and submitted correctly that all required IRS forms and documentation are processed and approved. You want to make sure that you have all your ducks in a row, from the very beginning. The same holds true for employment laws, which can put your business on the government's radar screen for a long time and equate to some very large fines, should you be found to have broken them, regardless of how good your intentions were.

Another priority is to structure your business immediately (after consulting a business attorney and/or a licensed and qualified business accountant). Structure in this sense means the legal establishment of your business. There are multitudes of structuring choices available, including sole proprietorship, partnership, limited partnership (commonly LP), limited liability company (LLC), corporation (for profit), corporation (not-for-profit), and cooperative. Each recognized structure carries with it its own benefits and drawbacks. Research each structure thoroughly to ensure that you choose the one that is best for your situation. Two great resources to start your education on this topic are the IRS's website (irs.gov/businesses/small/article/0,,id=98359,00.html) and FindLaw.com (smallbusiness.findlaw.com/business-structures/).

Question: Why structure your business? *Answer*: You don't want to be held personally liable for an aftermarket seat harness system you sold to racing enthusiasts in the event of a tragic accident. This is just one example of how establishing your business as its own legal entity can protect you, your family, and any outside investors. Again, it is highly advised that you consult with professionals when making this decision, as once a certain structure is established it can be very difficult to restructure. FindLaw.com (2008) lists the top ten reasons to contact an attorney before choosing a business form as:

- Contracts
- Registration, licensing, permits
- Determining who (and how) a business will be controlled
- Multi-state businesses and franchising
- Strict conformity to law
- Raising capital

INSURANCE

What types of insurance you carry will be widely dependant on your type of business, where you are based, if you are product or service oriented, if you have investors, what structure you chose, and more. Consult an attorney or a tax accountant that can help you assess what kind of risks your business carries and therefore the types of insurance that are advised for you to carry.

- Involving multiple entities
- Tax structures
- Limiting liability

DON'T BE AFRAID TO SAY NO

Some business partners aren't worth the trouble. For example, B2B buyers that return 50 percent of the product on which you charged a 2 percent margin, or eBayers with no usage history can quickly hurt you financially. Don't be afraid to say "no" to certain customers, suppliers, vendors, or anyone else that could cause more trouble than they are worth. This is often learned the hard way (trial and error) and over great lengths of time. Shorten this learning curve by doing your homework. It is not out of place or in any way disrespectful to request references or to research a potential customer, vendor, or supplier on the internet. After all, if they have nothing to hide, they should have no problem providing you with this information. The more facts you have, the better the chances are that your decision will yield a positive outcome.

BE SURE YOU ARE FULLY COMMITTED

Your business is going to have ups and downs. Being committed to it, sticking to budgets and working through to-do lists, is paramount to your success. If your family has to make sacrifices for this dream to come true, get them in on it early and often. Be sure you have fully committed all financial and time resources that you need, too, through budgets and sacrifice, if need be. This is also where the support of your family and friends comes into play: Do you have a weekly poker game that generally costs you $100 per week? Besides taking poker lessons, you may need to tell your friends you can join them only once per month because you need to stick to your budget. Do you take two family vacations per year? You may need to take one shortened vacation until you have enough working capital to expand again and live in more luxury.

Decide upon your plan and stick to it unless you have data to the contrary. Also realize that plans change, so you will still need to allow yourself to be flexible with regard to your tentative steps to success. You may want to expand an idea, or tighten your personal budget even more, or you may take on an investor. Having your plan set is vital to your success, as it is with any business, but the most successful entrepreneurs also realize that the ability to change and progress is just as important.

DON'T BE A SPAMMER

Spammers are purely hated in the internet age. You know all the jokes about solicitors calling at dinnertime? Spammers are considered worse! Be sure you are sending your marketing through affiliates, people who asked to join your newsletter, and people you write articles for, or through publicity, not through spam. E-mail only those people who have opted in. You can make people aware of the newsletter that you send out (not spam, but a newsletter with information that is valuable) through forums and blogs, but don't just randomly send e-mail to people. Not only can you get into trouble and risk your site and domain name being blocked from sending mail to internet service providers (ISPs), but you run the risk of giving your business a horrible reputation and alienating customers as well. Remember the old saying "Bad news spreads more quickly than good news." People love to have something to gripe about and if that gripe is about your product, service, marketing strategy, then you're going to lose customers and sales very quickly.

KNOW HOW YOU WILL BEGIN

If you don't know how you will begin, you'll have no way of knowing where you will end up, so you need to have a game plan together before you start your business. This is where your business plan comes in. It is often misconceived that only those entrepreneurs looking for business loans or multimillion-dollar investments need to come up with a business plan, but it is in your best interest to throw out that notion right here and now. You're probably thinking to yourself, "I'm just trying to sell cell phones on eBay; why do I need a business plan?" The answer is simple. Your business plan is your road map of where you are, where you want to go, how you are going to get there, and what others like you are doing. You should use it to perform self-checks in addition to having it available for the potential need to raise capital.

Let's break this down. You already know where you are, right? Maybe not. You see, you know generally where you are, but there are specifics that you may not be taking into consideration. Evaluate all of your previous employment history. What have you done in the past (even in the distant past) that has prepared you for this new business? What lessons from previous bosses and jobs have you learned? What upset you the most about terrible bosses or poorly run companies? What does your education lend to your goal and is it sufficient for your endeavor? What resources do you have currently available to you (family, friends, colleagues, etc.) that you will need when launching this new venture? Take some time to figure out these answers because they are not only the most difficult but the most influential to the rest of your plan. Don't overlook even the smallest of details.

OK, so you now know where you are starting from, including all of the experience and resources that you have at your disposal. Now it is time to consider where you want to go. This is a multipart task. You need to calculate where you want to be in the near future as well as the distant future. These projections could change, of course, over time, but you need to start somewhere. Think about where you want to be on the first day of business. Think about where you want to be after your first month, three months, one year, three years, even five years from the start of this adventure. Now write it all down. Also keep in mind that the grander the picture you draw for these time frames, the more involved will be the steps to accomplish them.

KNOW WHERE TO END UP

All right, you have determined where you are starting from and where you want to end up. Now you've reached the actual planning portion. This phase of your business plan is fairly self explanatory. No fancy business terms, no hidden messages. What are you going to do to succeed? What do you need to arrive at those moments in the future and ensure that you are meeting your self-set goals? What will you do to reach those milestones? Again, research, calculate, and write the steps down. Think about whom you will advertise to (who is your target demographic?), how you will advertise to them, what daily actions you will take to further your business, what annual actions you will take, what relationships you will build (vendors, suppliers, partners, affiliates, customers, the list goes on), what financial institution you will use (this should not necessarily be the same bank you do your personal banking with—do your homework; research and compare your options) and what types of accounts you will need, and more.

Be sure you have a clear strategy—everything from where you will operate to knowing when you will need to hire staff. It all needs to be documented so you are making logical decisions when the time comes to make them.

There are two reasons for creating a physical plan. The first is that you'll be able to review it as often as you need (and I advise you to do so as often as

Business Plans Again

This is why you need to have a physical business plan. If you just work off the cuff, then you are perhaps doomed for failure. You need to have an actual physical document that can be referenced and checked again and again to see if you're on target. Don't be afraid to revise it, either! Plans change.

possible) to help you stay on track. Another reason is it allows you to track your own progress. Although a business plan can be altered at any given moment on any given day, for the most part it should remain pretty constant, which allows you to check in on yourself from time to time. As an employee, you are often reviewed on an annual basis. So, too, should you review your own business and yourself.

The last step in your planning process is to figure out what is going on with the outside forces that will affect your business or idea. Essentially, figure out what works and what doesn't. You need to do this to ensure you are on the right track with both where you want to be and how you are going to get there. Research your competition. What are they already doing? What can you do better, faster, at less cost? What have they already tried and why did it fail (or succeed)? Can you capitalize on their mistakes and reattempt the same idea? Can you improve on something that they are already moving forward with? Knowing how the opposing teams operate and where their strengths and weaknesses are is one of the smartest steps you can take toward ensuring success. This also stands true for your target demographic. If you have no idea what makes your customers tick, how are you going to be able not only to provide them with the service or product you plan on but also anticipate their future needs as well?

If you can find a mentor that has already been there and done that, ask that person for advice. Having a support team and a coach throughout this process is great. Also be sure you are thoroughly trained in what you need to do; read as many books and articles as you can on the topic of running your own business, whether internet based or not. Be sure you are developing a strong brand from the day you start your business.

PROVIDE SUBSTANCE

Your site needs to have information as well as products. If you are selling monitors, provide customer reviews, exact dimensions, downloadable PDFs with product installation requirements–you name it. Offer substance over just products. Why, you ask? As the information age progresses, consumers are trending toward wanting to have more information available to allow them to make an informed purchase. Customers also use systems that use third-party ratings and reviews. No longer are the days of television commercials flashing "BUY NOW, NOW, NOW!!!"–it doesn't work that way with most markets. Now you find details on the product(s) or service(s), quality comparisons, price comparisons, awards earned, research conducted, expert recommendations, and more. Even in eBay businesses, the sales of those that just post pictures and "Top by J. Crew" will be drastically different from those that take the time to post measurements, tag information, purchase date, original purchase amount, and anything else they can think of.

DON'T WASTE MONEY

Many online business owners, myself included, have found themselves spending money on advertising that didn't work, promotional items no one cared about, and elaborate business cards and stationery that never got used. There is a well-known acronym that comes to mind: KISS. The gist of the KISS principle is keep it simple—really simple—especially in the beginning. It is great to advertise, but advertising right is greater! Be sure you are keeping tabs on your campaigns. For instance, don't pay for pop-up ads that you know aren't effective. Since we know text ads are most effective, go for those first. If your friends or affiliates offer to give you a banner ad for free, don't turn it down, even if you don't think it will reach what you would describe as your target market. People often waste money in advertising by not knowing where their ads will be placed, so be sure you're aware of this. Also, if you are told your ad is running on a certain web page, and every time you go to that web page your advertisement is nowhere to be found, chances are nobody else is seeing it either. Contact this company, get things straight, or demand your money back and cancel your ad. Whenever I buy ad space, I frequent the site to be sure my ad is visible and ask for click-through information weekly until I know the site is valid and really helping my business.

Another common area where people waste money is in copyrighting material. If you do a thorough Google search and go to government websites like that of the U.S. Patent and Trademark Office (USPTO.gov), you can learn all you ever wanted to know about copyrighting. There is no need for expensive copyright protection unless you have a highly sensitive project. Consult with an attorney if in doubt.

MAKE YOUR WEBSITE VIEWER FRIENDLY

People don't want to look at ugly storefronts and walk into dirty restaurants, and they don't want to click into discombobulated and disorganized websites. You need a clear message without distractions like flashing icons and style disasters. Focus on being a friendly site with great, organized information that is easy to find–including things you may not want to be easy, like returns. One section that is often overlooked is informing the visitor how to contact you and your customer service. This is one of the most crucial areas to your site and your business as a whole and adds legitimacy to your work.

KNOW YOUR RANK

You will want to know how you rank, if you are competing primarily (or even secondarily) on price. Another very serious consideration you need to make is how your pricing will come up in search engines that do nothing but price out products. Many of us have used sites like PriceGrabber to tell us who has the cheapest price, including shipping and handling and tax, all at once, and if someone is buying by price, this is what she is going to look for. Wiki lists these as the primary price search engines:

- Google Product Search (formerly Froogle)
- Kelkoo
- MSN Shopping
- MySimon
- NexTag
- PriceGrabber
- PriceRunner
- Shopping.com
- ShopWiki
- Shopzilla and BizRate
- TheFind.com

It is recommended you run your products (at least a few) through these price-comparison sites on occasion, particularly if offering a low price is what you are using as your primary marketing strategy.

AVOID COMMON WEB DEVELOPMENT HAZARDS

Be sure that you know the potential hazards of web development and ask your developer for updates. In an interview with a web developer for my book *Real Estate v2.0* (Babb and Lazo, 2007), I asked what the top five worst gotcha's are for web development from a designer's point of view. A summary of the interview follows.

Make Your Site Behave

The site can react and can actually *act* if it is designed to do so. Behavior also refers to how the website or web application interfaces with the server when it comes to loading or reloading site pages. It can also refer to interaction with the users, particularly how it responds to users, as if it is communicating with them.

Engage the User

Too much sophistication and technology can detract from the usability factor, which is important. Think of the highest-tech cell phone that makes it nearly impossible to dial numbers. It might look cool, but you'll prefer a phone that works. Websites must be easy to navigate, user-friendly, and useful, while still engaging the user. They should be intuitive, not too intimidating. Remember that even very savvy people may become intimidated by technology and want things simple—minus the bells and whistles.

Another thing to keep in mind is that the site should not be "heavy." This means that it needs to load quickly, and not be so inundated with items, graphics, and downloads, that it provides for a poor user experience. Web developers need to understand that only about half the U.S. population has high-speed internet. Websites can look amazing yet be built for the lowest common speed denominator.

Avoid Flash Multimedia

"Sites that use flash are a big problem. Flash and shockwave, both multimedia options, are ineffective uses of multimedia," wrote a web developer in her interview response. Find a way to directly involve users so that if they do not have a plug-in they can still use the site. Don't provide obstacles to getting to the site (such as a Flash introduction). Flash on the site itself may distract users from what you want them to focus on. What's better is a nice multimedia movie. You will get a lead when they fill out a form—either for a membership, a newsletter, feedback, or support—not from multimedia. You can generate interest in something but if there is no follow-through after the interest is piqued then it is pointless. In my opinion, the same rule applies to websites that have options for high speed, non-high speed, Flash, and non-Flash when you first visit. Not only are they annoying, but you should have technology that isn't dependent on a download—or a pop-up that may be blocked.

Make Your Sites Secure

Sometimes designers forget the value of securing transactions between the web server and the browser. For example, when people are filling out forms or providing any type of personal information, you need to be sure you offer a secure transaction and let people know that you are securing it by including a notation on the page(s) explaining that all information transmitted is done in a secure manner and where to find more information. For example: "We respect your privacy and have taken all steps to ensure your personal information is kept secure. Information you provide is encrypted and transmitted on a secure server. To find out more about the steps we take to protect you, click here." Make sure customers know you care about their privacy.

Some additional notes about security: Be sure you include a privacy statement that accurately reflects how and for what you'll use their information (or preferably that you won't use their info). Be sure you have an area detailing your security terms and conditions on your site (this is where the link noted earlier would lead). There are many standard ideas on just about any website, or you could go as far as to have an attorney write it up for you.

Ultimately, whatever you set as your terms, you must stand by. If you state that you won't share your customers' contact information with your affiliates, partners, and advertisers, and you do, then you are opening yourself up for a lawsuit and a lot of angry customers.

PROVIDE QUALITY CUSTOMER SERVICE

As I stated just a few sections back, you need to ensure that your customers know how to contact you and your customer service department. This means more than just an e-mail address that you check every now and then. The more information you can provide, the better off you'll be, as the more secure and confident your customers will be. Often, before I patronize a new online business, I first investigate their "About Us" and "Contact Us" sections to see how customer friendly they are and even try calling them to see if someone actually answers. If all I see is a random contact form and a short and superficial description of who they are, I move on—no questions asked. If I visit the customer service or contact section and I'm greeted with an abundance of contact options, return policies, common issues and troubleshooting guides, FAQs (frequently asked questions), RMA (return merchandise authorization) forms, and the like, then my comfort level goes up. I assure you, a person's comfort level has everything to do with whether she purchases your products or services. Don't underestimate the gut feeling of the customer. Even though you are a legitimate business, if you don't appear to be one from the outside looking in, then you will not be viewed as one by those who will be looking.

Expanding on the issue of having customer service thoroughly established and readily available, Jeff Cohen (Business.SolveYourProblem.com) states, "One of the quickest ways to kill your internet business, or any business for that matter, is to offer poor customer service. When people take the time to complain about some part of your product or service they will have been stewing away for a while before they decided to contact you. If they can't get hold of your or you don't respond to their communication, you'll end up with a very angry customer. When that angry customer has had enough and decides to let the world know about your terrible product they'll attract attention like bees to a honey pot." (2007)

The last thing anyone wants is bad press, whether about themselves or about their business. Remember the whole "bad news spreads more quickly" lesson?

Common Complaints

There are some more common issues and complaints that you want to be aware of–and avoid. Many are payment related, like double billing or being charged too much. Other people get upset if they feel you charged them more for shipping than it cost (even if you write shipping *and* handling on the website). Receiving the wrong item or a damaged item is very frustrating, as are technical problems (imagine getting a new camera with a Japanese manual that you cannot read), difficulty signing up for web services online, and so on. Be sure you have customer service set up to handle these issues. If you take a vacation, be sure you have someone covering for you! You want to handle these issues the same day or next day and immediately resolve them with your customer.

How to Contact an Upset Customer

I always recommend contacting the customer the same way he contacted you. If he called you, call him back. If he e-mailed you, e-mail him back. This is the best way to keep the customer's frustrations at a minimum.

FAQs Section

An FAQ (frequently asked questions), area can help customers troubleshoot on their own. One great idea is to create searchable FAQs and forums where users can help one another out. By posting there often, you will save phone calls and user frustration.

Remember, keeping your customers is a vital task in the daily operation of your business. Empowering your customers is a great way to start. By giving them the power to troubleshoot issues with products or get answers to common questions (regarding shipping, returns, you name it), you are contributing

SURVEY SAYS

In a survey of hundreds of online business owners, what were the most popular types of businesses?

- 28 percent had a web-only company
- 7 percent had a brick-and-mortar company that became a web-based company
- 55 percent worked in education online
- 19 percent were online writers
- 20 percent noted "other"

a high level of customer service. You also want to provide real self-service. I love Zappos as a model; online returns that are hassle free while combining "we are about you and your experience" feedback all into the return process in a no-nonsense fashion. Brilliant site!

Contact Section

You need to decide how you want customers to contact you. Do you want them to fill out a form with their order information and their name and contact information to ask a question to save time, or do you want them to just click on an e-mail link? Decide what is most efficient for you and least aggravating to the client. Why not provide both?

YourOnlineProfessor.com

There are pitfalls everywhere. Why make the same mistakes others have before you? Network in the forums at YourOnlineProfessor.com and jump in and share your stories, too. Make new lifelong friends and great business colleagues that you can mutually market with. This is key to growing in the online world!

PART

IV

EXPLORING OPPORTUNITIES

CHAPTER

13

20 ONLINE JOBS FOR EVERYONE

Get Started Today

This section is devoted to exploring specific jobs—things that you can do today to get started in your own online business. Haven't thought of something that taps into your passion yet and looking for ideas? Don't think you have any hard-driven passions and just want to get started somewhere? I'll outline some of the most in-demand jobs and what it takes to get them, and I'll reference some great resources for you to get started.

Now is the time to really take a very close look at Rat Race Rebellion at ratracerebellion.com. Rat Race offers thousands of prescreened, nonscam jobs for you to consider, most of which are online.

First, you will need to narrow down your interests—for instance, accounting and financial, artistic, or customer service. This will help you if you haven't already found your passion to begin working on a particular subject matter and getting started. Let's dive into the first category, accounting and financial.

ACCOUNTING AND FINANCIAL

What does the accounting and financial category encompass? Everything from balancing others' accounts to being an official certified public accountant (CPA) online to auditing others' books. If you enjoy math and running numbers, these jobs may be for you. Three sites recommended by Rat Race are

- *CPA Moms*: cpamoms.us
- *VT Audit*: vtaudit.com
- *Balance Your Books*: balanceyourbooks.com

ADMINISTRATIVE OR CLERICAL

So you type fast, like working as an assistant for others, have experience working with transcriptions, enjoy coding, or want to become a virtual assistant without starting your own site up? You have lots of Rat Race-reviewed options. Check out these for starters:

- *Mountain West Processing*: mountainwestprocessing.com
- *Net Transcripts*: nettranscripts.com
- *Affiliated Computer Services*: acs-inc.com
- *Team Double-Click*: teamdoubleclick.com

ARTISTIC

Do you have a knack for designing logos or helping others see the brilliance and beauty in photography? Do you want to be an art director, graphic designer, copyeditor, proofreader, photographer, web designer, presentation specialist, motion graphic artist, animator, coder, marketing manager, branding specialist, or some other creative, artistic individual? Check out these Rat Race-endorsed sites to get started today without creating your own business:

- *Metaphor Studio*: metaphorstudio.com
- *The Bradford Group*: thebradfordgroup.com/ct/chicagojobs/artistswanted bradford.jsp
- *Artisan for Hire*: artisantalent.com

CALL CENTER AND CUSTOMER SERVICE

Do you want to be the person who answers the phone when someone calls in response to an infomercial at 2 A.M. to order the best sticky goo in the world? Are you superfast and want to get paid by how fast you enter orders? Interested in working in tech support remotely? There are lots of options for call centers or customer service representatives for hire. Check out these sites, recommended by Rat Race, to get started right away without your own site:

- *LiveOps*: liveops.com
- *Arise*: arise.com
- *VIPdesk*: vipdesk.com
- *West at Home*: westathome.com

For a Rat Race Rebellion side-by-side comparison of call center and customer service hirers, go to ratracerebellion.com/CS_Comparison.html.

EDUCATION, TEACHING, AND TUTORING

Do you love educating others, tutoring, and teaching everyone from five-year-olds to doctoral students? My day job is an online teacher, and I know how rewarding this career can be! Check out drdaniellebabb.com for more information on becoming an online teacher, or use one of these Rat Race-reviewed sites to become a tutor or educator online.

- *Tutor.com*: tutor.com
- *Sylvan Online*: esylvan.com

- *SmartThinking.com*: smarthinking.com
- *Eduwizards*: eduwizards.com

HEALTHCARE AND MEDICAL

Do you love medicine and healthcare? Do you want to take calls from individuals panicked that their three-year-old's cough is more serious than they thought? Interested in reporting radiography results back to doctors or being a virtual nurse? Want to work in claims or recruiting in healthcare? Check out these three sites; there are many more on Rat Race's site.

- *Carenet*: callcarenet.net
- *UnitedHealth Group*: unitedhealthgroup.com/careers
- *Virtual Radiologic*: virtualrad.net

LEGAL

Are you a paralegal or attorney looking to work part time, add to your income, or leave your current day job? Do you want to be an on-call counsel or work for an attorney remotely? Check out these sites:

- *E.P. Dine*: epdine.com
- *Counsel on Call*: counseloncall.com

MEDICAL TRANSCRIPTION AND CODING

Do you have experience in medical transcription and coding? Do you want to continue this line of work but don't want to report into an office? Check out these four links with great jobs, approved by Rat Race:

- *MTJobs.com*: mtjobs.com/
- *Ascend Healthcare Systems*: ascendhealthcare.com
- *Spheris*: spheris.com
- *ExecuScribe*: execuscribe.com

NONPROFIT

Do you enjoy working in the nonprofit sector? Do you wish to do community service more than you want to make money? There are some great sites out there for individuals that want to do nonprofit work online. Here's one that Rat Race endorses:

- *Idealist.org*: idealist.org (Be sure to type in a keyword search for "telecommute.")

TECHNICAL AND WEB

Are you an amazing web designer, or a beginning developer who knows basic coding? Do you know how to fix computers, either sent into you or remotely via a help desk system? Do you want to be a coder but don't want to start your own site to get new work? Check out the following three sites endorsed by Rat Race. More and more U.S. web designers are moving to working with online coders, so this is a booming market.

- *devBISTRO*: devbistro.com
- *Rent A Coder*: rentacoder.com
- *Computerjobs.com*: computerjobs.com

TRANSLATION AND LINGUISTIC

Do you speak two languages and want to do online translation? Opportunities are endless for this profession—everything from book publishers who want translators to web designers who need to create sites or proofread sites for errors in communication in another language. Check out these Rat Race-endorsed sites.

- *Berlitz*: careerservices.berlitz.com
- *Lionbridge*: lionbridge.com
- *Butler Hill Group*: butlerhill.com

WRITING AND EDITING

Are you a writer by trade or passion? Do you enjoy journalism or writing press releases? Do you perhaps want to be a ghostwriter for a book? These opportunities and more await you at Rat Race Rebellion; for three ways to get started fast, check out these sites:

- *JournalismJobs.com*: journalismjobs.com
- *Mediabistro*: mediabistro.com
- *UC Berkley Journalism Jobs database*: journalism.berkeley.edu/jobs

PROJECT BIDDING SITES FOR FREELANCERS

Do you want to help other companies bid out jobs to outsourcers? Do you want to become an outsourced worker yourself? Do you want to be a freelance professional? Check out these sites, already previewed and endorsed by Rat Race, that will let you get started today. You could always start here and then work your way into your own business in the future.

- *oDesk*: odesk.com
- *Guru*: guru.com
- *iFreelance*: ifreelance.com

Here are some other ideas, too, not from Rat Race but independent research. Have you seen the iSold It companies for eBay? Why not become a trading assistant? Here is how eBay defines the role:

> Trading Assistants are experienced eBay sellers who have indicated their willingness to sell items for others for a fee. People who want to hire a Trading Assistant can search the Trading Assistant Directory to find someone to sell for them. All terms of how the services will work will be negotiated between Trading Assistants and their clients. You can become a Trading Assistant if you meet some basic requirements (1 past sale in the last 30 days and a feedback rating of at least 50 with fewer than 2 percent negative feedback points). The service will be free for qualifying sellers (though eBay does reserve the right to charge for it someday).

SOMETIMES THE BEST IDEAS ARE THE CRAZIEST ONES

There is a famous article circulating on the internet since 2007 called "The 20 Dumbest Business Ideas That Made Millions . . . or Not!" by Silicon Valley

Bloggers (go to thedigeratilife.com/blog/index.php/category/online-business/). The writer quotes John Deprice, slightly edited, on success stories. Here are some of the wackiest, most successful of the 20:

- *Million Dollar Homepage.* This was a web page with 1,000,000 pixels, and the owner charged $1 per pixel! Alex Tew, a 21-year-old who came up with the idea, is now a millionaire. Of course there are lots of copycats, but none like the original, found here: milliondollarhome page.com.
- *SantaMail.* Using a postal address in North Pole, Alaska, Byron Reese writes letters pretending he's Santa and charges parents $10 for each letter. Since the start of his business in 2001, he's a few million dollars richer. Check out his site at santamail.org.
- *Doggles.* Doggles is one of the most ridiculous ideas in my opinion, but it's very well known. Doggles sells pet goggles and jewelry online. Check it out at doggles.com.
- *LaserMonks.* Available online at lasermonks.com, LaserMonks is a for-profit subsidiary of the Cistercian Abbey of Our Lady of Spring Bank. Real monks refill ink cartridges, and had sales of $2.5 million in 2005.
- *AntennaBalls.* Jason Wall sold antenna balls online at this site, and it made him a millionaire. Want a custom antenna ball? He can do that, too. Visit antennaballs.com.
- *FitDeck.* This site sells decks of fitness cards that you can customize, created by a former Navy SEAL and fitness instructor with reported 2005 sales of $4.7 million. Talk about your passion paying off. Go to fitdeck.com.
- *Lucky Wishbone Co.* Yes, these are fake wishbones. The company produces about 30,000 wishbones daily for $3 each, and it had sales of about $1 million in 2006. Want to get one before you start your own site? Go to luckybreakwishbone.com.

The truth is, most crazy ideas don't get enough funding or take off enough to actually become anything popular or highly profitable. Some that didn't? From the same article: A google of graveyard registries; an in-flight magazine detailing all the noises heard during air travel, with explanations for each rattle; talking sneakers; and just about everything else you can think of, as well as plenty of ideas you would never think of.

FILLING YOUR OWN NEEDS

Sometimes the best ideas come from your own needs—like the stay-at-home mother who was unable to find attractive ways to carry unused diapers and created a diaper caddy, or the individual who wanted a particular DVD he couldn't find and started a site for trading. Want some more ideas? Check out a great article, cited throughout this chapter, at nichegeek.com/10_unconventional_but_successful_online_homebusiness_ideas.

FINAL QUOTES FROM THE TRENCHES

Survey participants were given the opportunity to offer some final thoughts—departing words, if you will—about online businesses. Here are some of their most interesting comments.

Cindy Hillsey, the owner of Virtual Partnering and Successful Pathways, said, "If you think being an online entrepreneur is for you take the time to check it out and make your dreams come true! Yes, there is hard work involved, but when you are doing the hard work for yourself it makes it all worthwhile." *Well said, Cindy.*

Bill Spearman in Huntsville, Alabama, said, "Starting an online job is a great part-time way to eventually free yourself from being in corporate bondage. If it works, you can submit your two-weeks notice, if it doesn't you can change strategies and keep trying until you reach the level of success to cut yourself free." *Amen, Bill.*

Mrs. Viki Gardner, "online instructor/mentor/course developer extraordinaire," said, "I have already mentioned the flexibility of working at home, and part of that is because I like the ability to take a break whenever I need one. For instance, I occasionally get excruciating migraines, and it is so nice to be able to take an Imitrex and lie down for a half hour or so, to recoup and refresh. This was a luxury I never had when teaching in public schools, and I would often go home in blinding pain, totally nonfunctional for the rest of the evening . . . My husband and I own a local vending business, and it is well-established, needing only a couple days' servicing and recordkeeping. I am now so busy online that my husband takes care of servicing the accounts without me. The rest of the time he is home with me, taking care of the recordkeeping, the house, the dogs, and me. This is my favorite part of being an online entrepreneur; being with my hubby 24/7! The perks of working at home are numerous; these are just a few of my personal favorites!" *Thanks, Viki!*

Another great quote, from Gloria Durham: "Working online has brought new meaning to my life in terms of extra cash flow. When I was offered my first online contract with teaching, I never realized there was a whole world of people working online and making great money as extra income. The flexibility that online work offers is invaluable. I can work as late or as early as I want and accept as many contracts as my time will allow. I can plan my time around family and personal events and travel whenever I choose. With my full time job, I am making over (6) figures. Working online is the best paid part time job I've ever had!" *Flexibility rocks, Gloria!*

Risa Garelick said, "Teaching online gives me the freedom to actually live my life as I wish, instead of living around the scheduled hours of a job. I feel fortunate to have the flexibility to spend more time with my child and doing the things that make me happy!" *I'm sure that Risa will never regret that time with her kids.*

"It is a complete joy each day and well worth the years and years of schooling, multiple degrees, and work experience that it took to get me to the place where I could achieve it," commented Mark D. Bowles, PhD, with bellehistory.com. *Congratulations, Dr. Bowles.*

Arnold Kinney says, "Being an online entrepreneur is extremely rewarding as it allows the flexibility to spend time with my family while providing substantial income. I started working online after working as a government contractor and as a consultant for several years. I have also run a 'brick and mortar' company. These netted me a six-figure income for several years. Working online allows me to make the same income, while being able to spend time with my family." *Who could ask for better than that?*

Chonta Clemons Flowers noted, "Being an online entrepreneur has made me want to look into other online opportunities as well. The flexibility it provides is unreal, especially if you like to travel. My husband is in law enforcement and he has to move according to the needs of his agency. Working online provides me the ability to move wherever we have to without disrupting our cash flow. I am also thinking ahead of expanding our family and it will allow me to be a very active parent in my child's life without giving up a viable income to help support us." *Excellent for you and your family, Chonta, congratulations!*

Great advice from Allyson Heisey: "Being an online entrepreneur can be rewarding when successful, but it requires dedication, determination and the willingness to take risks." *Oh so true.*

Dr. Lisa Kincaid said, "It has been one the best decisions of my life. Creating a work environment from home and be able to influence the lives of all of my students, while also making a living, and being home for my children–it is the perfect job!" *I hear that, Dr. Kincaid!*

"The ability to reach out and instill motivation, as well as inspiration, to a large dispersed class as you watch them progress through courses is a source of satisfaction to me," said Allen Thomas. *We share that satisfaction in common, Allen.*

My own web designer, Phillip Hollowell from PS Web Design Studios, said, "It was the hardest step to take (although I was a bit forced into it by being laid off from a standard job) but it has definitely been the most rewarding in the sense of flexibility and more time with family." *Good luck, Phil! Thanks for all you do! (For more information, visit pswebdesignstudio.com.*

Nicole Hickland said, "I love being an online entrepreneur, it allows me to make my own hours and essentially be my 'own boss.'" *Me, too, Nicole!*

"The sheer joy of waking up whenever I want, rolling out of bed, taking two steps to my computer and being at work! The gas money alone I save is worth it!" said Justin Pickering. *Indeed it is! Not to mention the savings on dry cleaning!*

YourOnlineProfessor.com

In this chapter we talked about businesses that many of you may decide to start if you aren't finding something of interest on your own. One of our partners, Rat Race Rebellion, has an excellent site at ratracerebellion.com. Be sure to join the conversation and links to great business ideas at YourOnlineProfessor.com.

CHAPTER

14

Another Option to Try Before You Buy

Following the Virtual Employee Trend

So you've read this far, and you love the concept of working online, but you aren't so keen on starting your own business—just yet. Maybe you want to test the waters and see what working from home is like before you embark on your own adventure. One way to do that is to become a virtual employee.

Virtual employees and virtual relationships in business are more accepted today than perhaps anytime in history and the

trend is still growing. Sometimes the skill sets, the products, or the services we need are best obtained out of our own area, particularly if we live outside of a big city. There are many opportunities for people who want to work online and become a contractor but don't necessarily want to start their own business to do so.

A trend has emerged in the market; one that finds a telecommuter as well compensated and part of the team as an on-site manager and one that provides incredible opportunity for the online entrepreneur. This chapter should help you recognize the opportunities in online businesses and the acceptance of online work worldwide. Even banks are now allowing you to include online business income to qualify for loans; a good bet that these jobs are reliable and stable.

Interestingly, 55 percent of survey respondents indicated that they work for someone else while working online, and the others worked purely for themselves. Many noted that it depends on the type of contract they are working on as to whether they have to ever report into the office.

ONLINE JOB HITS

When I conducted a basic Google search for "online jobs" in mid 2008, I got 45,500,000 results. Yes 45.5 million hits and counting. While Google hits aren't a reason to go into business, they are an idea of the market and interest in the business. Over 8 million hits came back when I submitted "doing business online" as my search criterion.

BURGEONING MONEY

According to a 2002 article in *BusinessWeek*, economist Jim Glassman found (while conducting a survey on behalf of PayPal) that sales over the internet (online sales) dramatically took off in 2006 in comparison with 2005. He estimated at the conclusion of the survey that online sales for 2006 would amount to more than $211 billion (up 20 percent from 2005). Over a longer period of time people will feel more comfortable purchasing large-ticket items, like cars and even houses, online. Many of us have bought and sold our cars through online auction sites like eBay, and sites like RealtyTrac let you bid online to buy a house.

During the study, Glassman found that when consumers log in to search out and purchase one item, they do often purchase more than they had planned. Much like product placement matters in retail stores and entices people to add to their purchase by the time they check out (if you don't believe me, visit the lines at the large cosmetics store Sephora, where tens of "small item" products are pitched to you as you're walking through the line), similar strategies work well for online stores. Many sites include enticing offers at checkout, like "Add this to your order for just . . ."; sites like VistaPrint let you supersize your purchase very easily, by adding magnets to those business card orders, for example.

So what does Glassman recommend to small online business owners? Offer something attractive and make customers feel special when they purchase. You may do this by sending a thank-you card with every purchase or a store coupon after the buy. Tie in other merchandise and services that are complementary, and create a safe, welcoming environment that offers high security and easy transactions.

eBAY SUCCESS

Of course one of the most famous online money makers in history is eBay. A study by eBay and Nielsen found that the average U.S. household has 52 unused items lying around worth an average of $3,100. (*Good Morning America*, 2008, abcnews.go.com/GMA/AsSeenOnGMA/story?id=4584928). Imagine if all the unused stuff lying around your house is worth this much, what an eBay business, where you actually find products for far less than you'll sell them for, could make in profit for you. One company, iSold It, has become a brick-and-mortar store selling for eBayers. What if you go garage-sale hunting and find items for sale and resell them online? How much could you make with other people's stuff?

What do we know about telework so far, besides that many giants like Amazon and eBay were started from very small ideas and grew into multibillion-dollar fortunes? That the number of teleworkers who work at home at least one day per month is now about 25 million. About 16 million of these individuals are self-employed and this number continually increases according to the American Interactive Consumer Study conducted by the Dieringer Research Group, 2006.

TOP TALENT

We also know that according to a compensation survey of 1,400 chief financial officers (CFOs) conducted by Robert Half International (Fisher, 2007), 46 percent said telecommuting is second only to salary as the best way to attract top talent. This means that CFOs are not worried about telecommuters, but they actually take it a step further and know it is a retention tool. Thirty-three percent said telecommuting was the top draw. CFOs were asked, "In your opinion, which one of the following incentives is most effective in attracting top accounting candidates?" Their responses:

- Offering higher starting salaries than competitors: 46 percent
- Allowing telecommuting and/or flexible work schedules: 33 percent
- Offering signing bonuses: 5 percent
- Offering extra vacation days: 3 percent
- Benefits/benefit package/insurance: 2 percent
- Other: 3 percent
- Don't know/no answer: 8 percent

Still not convinced corporate America has accepted telecommuting and it's a viable work alternative? Consider these facts from ivc.ca/studies/us/index.htm: In February 2008, the *Journal of Applied Psychology* published a study that identified positive results of telecommuting that included increased control, increased work-life balance, improved supervisor-staff relationships, reduced stress, increased job satisfaction, greater worker retention and improved productivity. In January 2008, IDC reported it expected the mobile work force to exceed 1 billion workers by 2010.

In November 2007, a Citrix survey found that 23 percent of U.S. workers regularly perform their jobs from somewhere other than their office and 62 percent that don't work off-site said they want to. In October 2007, a study by Computing Technology Association reported that 75 percent of North

American small businesses have at least one employee telecommuting on average, and 7 percent of their work force works from home one or more days per week.

In 2007, according to a WorldatWork and Dieringer Research Group Study, corporate America allowed 8 percent of its workers to telecommute. The Society for Human Resource Management (SHRM) in 2007 published a study that indicated telecommuting programs were up from 26 percent to 33 percent for part-timers; from 45 to 48 percent for ad hoc employees; and from 19 to 21 percent for full-timers. Corporate America is embracing the idea for all sorts of reasons, and even implementing technology to make it easier, cheaper, faster, and more efficient for the worker. Finally, a focus on the worker.

INCREASED PRODUCTIVITY

Don't think you'll be productive in a work-at-home environment? A study by Trends@Work from Future Step and Korn/Ferry International published in 2007 indicated that 78 percent say telecommuters are equally or more productive than office workers. And 46 percent preferred telecommuting to flexible hours. Seventy-three percent of workers rarely or never get work done during their commute, which equates to completely lost productivity. Why commute then? Why shouldn't your commute be to your home office? And if you follow that logic, why continue making someone else wealthy? In 2006, a report by Deloitte stated that by 2008, offshoring and remote working and virtual teams would hit 41 million corporate employees globally, and more than 100 million would work from home at least one day per month.

Is Your Boss Worried about Productivity?

You may think your boss is worried about your productivity while you stay at home and work, but chances are, your boss isn't. Instead, companies today are using flexible working hours and teleworking as retention tools when they cannot compete with salary.

A GROWING WORK FORCE

Want more fascinating information? The U.S. Census Bureau reported in 2004 that 4.2 million Americans, about 19 percent of the working population at that time, did some or all of their work from home—a 23 percent increase from 1990 to 2000. This was *twice* the growth rate of the work force overall. Folks working at home tend to be better educated and they work fewer hours. Do you think only large companies support this? Actually the greatest growth, according to an International Telework Association and Council (ITAC) survey, occurred in medium-size businesses of 100-999 employees (57 percent) and other data suggests that small and one-person businesses online are growing at a phenomenal rate. This is partly because of the availability of broadband access at home, allowing us to have virtual offices at our houses.

So what about companies that host services that allow you to have an online job, like eBay? At the end of the first quarter in 2008, eBay.com hosted approximately 547,000 stores worldwide, with approximately 46 percent of stores hosted on eBay's international sites. As noted at news.ebay.com/fast facts_ebay_marketplace.cfm, while eBay is well known for its auction format, users can also buy and sell in fixed-price formats, which accounted for 42 percent of total gross merchandise volume, or GMV (the total value of all successfully closed items on eBay Inc.'s trading platforms) during the first quarter of 2008.

Don't want to deal with nickel-and-dime sales and all that work to make just a few bucks? Consider this: the most expensive item sold on eBay to date is a private business jet for $4.9 million.

There are grant and proposal writers, graphics designers, logo designers, web designers, programmers, interior designers, architects, usability designers, tax accountants, lawyers, real estate agents, mortgage brokers, travel agents, economists, florists, nutritionists, and fitness trainers (and the list goes on) that also want to make residual income online. If you are one of them, how do you capitalize off the potential of doing business online? You can join forces with a big company online and promote your work through it, or you can start your own web business.

FIGURING OUT WHAT TO SELL ONLINE

What sells on eBay? According to the company's stats, the following are what categories are selling in terms of dollars: eBay Motors at $18 billion; consumer electronics at $5.8 billion; clothing and accessories at $5.3 billion; computers at $4.2 billion; home and garden at $4.2 billion; books/music/movies at $3.5 billion; sports at $2.9 billion; collectibles at $2.8 billion; business and industrial at $2.6 billion: toys at $2.4 billion; jewelry and watches at $2.3 billion; cameras and photo at $1.7 billion; antiques and art at $1.5 billion; tickets and travel at $1.5 billion; and coins and stamps at $1.4 billion.

There were 647 million new listings added to eBay.com worldwide in the first quarter of 2008. At any given time, there are approximately 115.3 million listings worldwide, and approximately 6.9 million listings are added per day. Users trade in more than 50,000 eBay categories. Users worldwide trade $2,040 worth of goods on the site every *second.* In the first quarter of 2008, GMV was $16 billion. According to the same page on eBay's site, the total value for the full year of 2007 was more than $59 billion.

The marketplace's net revenues totaled a record $1.48 billion in the first quarter of 2008, representing a year-over-year growth rate of 19 percent. Forty-five percent of business is from U.S. operations and 55 percent is from international businesses. The marketplace has approximately 83.9 million active users worldwide and eBay Inc. has a global presence in 39 markets, including the United States. If you wanted to start a quick online business, you could begin buying and selling, for profit, on eBay.

Obviously if you are fully supported by your employer in your efforts to work your day job from home, it is entirely possible and feasible to have your own small or midsize homebased or online business on the side. How many people in the United States work from home as their full-time jobs? In 2004, about 14 million; about 22 million today!

TELECOMMUTING FROM A HOME OFFICE

As a telecommuter, setting up a home office is not difficult and is quite affordable. It is therefore easy for you to come across as an established online entity; not too many people realize how important credibility is. It isn't uncommon for a potential online customer to first call you before deciding to make a purchase—sounds odd, right? It isn't, and it happens a lot. It's almost how they make sure that they're dealing with a legitimate business.

Identity theft is on the rise and people are so skeptical in some instances if they have to provide their credit card and person credentials. Be prepared to answer the phone as usual, employ the use of autoattendants to answer calls when you are unavailable, and return phone calls with a strong sense of urgency. There are places like RightVoice.com that will set up your autoattendant prompts for a nominal fee ($200) and companies like TalkSwitch.com ($699) that offer affordable mini PBX systems for the home office. Yes, you should get a separate phone for the home office that is dedicated only for your online business needs. A cheaper alternative would be to invest in voiceover internet protocol (VOIP) providers like Vonage.com ($14.95 to $24.99 a month), or MagicJack.com ($19.95 a year), but each of these is dependant on your internet service; in other words, if you have a power outage and no electricity indefinitely, you will have no phone service. Think carefully before cutting costs this way. A local telecommunications' provider would most likely continue to offer you telephone service in the case of a power outage.

It's important that as an online business owner you connect with your audience and get a feel for what their online business needs may ultimately demand of you. Besides, it may also be wise that you become a part of the same online culture that you venture to do business in, and this requires internet service from your local telecommunications providers. The price of high-speed internet service has significantly declined over the years so it would even be affordable for you to enjoy the internet experience as you probably do the cable and television experience.

BECOMING A VIRTUAL EMPLOYEE

This book is obviously geared toward the online entrepreneur, but in Chapter 13 I listed several jobs that you can start right away as a virtual employee working for someone else's company through Rat Race Rebellion, a great place to start. If you would prefer being a virtual employee in someone else's company rather than your own, you'll need to satisfy several requirements.

- You will need to be easily accessible by phone, both while at home and while on the road. As an internet business is a "We never close" business, it basically requires those who are handling the day-to-day operations of the business to never close either.
- You should be easily accessible at your home office, by phone, e-mail, online chat, and potentially even in person (depending on the business).
- You should be easily accessible while away from your home office—out of state, out of the country—again, by phone, e-mail, online chat, and still potentially in person.
- You must be able to check your e-mail and voice mail from anywhere—even from your car or while at the gym. A great method to ensure this is the use of a smartphone, personal digital assistant (PDA), or BlackBerry.
- If applicable, you must be able to close sales from anywhere (for efficiency and effectiveness, as well as higher productivity levels). This is where having good communication skills, both written and verbal, comes in.
- You must be able to participate in meetings, from anywhere. such as webinars and teleconferences.
- You must have flexibility in both your time and your resources.
- You must be efficient when working independently.

What were some of the most interesting businesses in the survey that was taken online by hundreds of participants regarding their online businesses? Jewelry, women's sports and fitness apparel, consulting services, residential and commercial cleaning, change management consulting, virtual assistants, and coaching and consulting.

If you don't have a passion yet that you want to follow up on, reread Chapter 13 and visit some of the sites listed there.

YourOnlineProfessor.com

You may not be ready to begin your own business just yet. Perhaps you read this book, and are working on discovering your passion, but you haven't yet decided what is right for you. That's OK! Virtual work can help you get the feel for what it's like working from home without the "day job" mentality. Check out YourOnlineProfessor.com for more resources.

CHAPTER

15

AVOIDING SCAMS

Identifying and Staying Away from Online Hornets' Nests

After my appearance on the *Today Show*, one of the top questions I received in more than 10,000 e-mails was "How do I know if a company or an online business model is a scam?"

In this chapter I will help you identify individuals and companies that are scams and teach you how to navigate the online world. Of course if you create your own online business, you aren't scamming yourself, but you may choose to begin by working for someone else's online business and building your client base.

In this chapter, I will sort out fact from fiction and set the record straight. I'll focus on who is legitimate and who isn't, and what the red flags are. There are thousands of legitimate jobs out there, and there are also thousands of illegitimate advertisers trying to take your dollars and turn them into, well, nothing but profit for them. You need to know how to recognize what is a good deal and what is bogus, and how to discriminate between business partners and business swindlers.

OPPORTUNITY SCAMS

Unfortunately, we all see lots of infomercials about getting rich quickly, and most of them, if not all, are bogus. Maybe two people each year made that $10,000 a month sitting by the pool, but chances are they made it from the 100,000 people that wasted $10. Don't be misled by testimonials: "I am a medical doctor, and I used this product, and it really worked!" or "If you aren't 100 percent satisfied with your profits, return it for a full refund!" Statistics show that if a product is cheap enough, people will throw it out rather than return it. Another way these types of companies prevent you from being able to return their product for a full refund is by ensuring you don't receive their product quickly enough to actually evaluate it within those first 30 days. You see, if you read the fine print, most of these scenarios truthfully do allow you 30 days to "try before you buy," but the trick is that those 30 days start the minute you place your order. They traditionally will offer you "expedited shipping" during the order process for an enormous additional cost (in addition to trying to sell you a conglomeration of other "related" products or services), which you probably won't take, and their standard shipping is nothing more than regular mail, at best. I have known some companies to actually mail parcel post, which can take weeks (as in more than three or four) to actually reach their destination. At this point, you have exceeded the allotted time allowing for a full refund, so you are now stuck with the product.

Going back to the "I'm a medical doctor" testimonial, again, if you listen carefully, rarely will they claim to be a "medical" doctor. More often than not, they will just say "doctor," which means that they could be an MD, but they could also be a PhD (doctor of philosophy–in who knows what area of expertise? It could be in automotive engineering). Other degrees that allow you to claim "doctor" include DO (doctor of osteopathic medicine) and DDS (otherwise known as a dentist), and the list goes on. Also note that the title of "doctor" carries different requirements, depending on the country. What qualifies you as a doctor here in the United States does not automatically qualify you as a doctor in Australia, but technically, if you did a commercial in Australia, you could claim your title of "doctor" (Australian law permitting).

In short, just because someone claims to be a doctor does not equate to meaning he is necessarily a real expert on whatever subject he is speaking on. So you see, things aren't always as they may appear on the surface.

Other companies try to show "documented proof" or use the phrase "enormous income potentials" and showcase people that made an extra $5,000 this month doing what they love. Be careful. Many did what they love, all right, and got paid to say that! Watch out for phrases like "work on your own schedule" and "make money in your spare time"—true online business ventures take work, time, and money. The Better Business Bureau offers some great information on avoiding scams, and the Federal Trade Commission (FTC) tracks scams, helps you avoid internet scams, and helps you lodge complaints if you find companies that aren't following through. The SBA also provides great resources for starting up your own business from scratch. If an agency is charging money for information on what is legit and what isn't, question that, too.

DOTCONS

The internet, as mature as it is today, is still a relatively new concept. Since so many people don't understand how it works and are inundated with media coverage of Google moguls that made $1 billion each last year in passive income, they are enticed and rightfully a bit entranced by the internet. If a company promises you a good life without much work, chances are it is a dotcon, what the FTC calls companies that offer you an incentive to recruit people or set you up with duplicate websites with products to sell. Really, dotcons are trying to get you to resell products for them. Since most states disallow them to profit off recruiting (such as in multilevel marketing schemes), they profit off you selling products for them. They sell and distribute tangible products, but what is really for sale is the redistribution over and over again. This is basically a multilevel marketing (MLM) or pyramid scheme on the internet! If you are paid to duplicate a site and then get others to duplicate sites for you or are paid each time the people you recruit sell products, run like the wind! This is a scam. Some of these companies go as far as to borrow the reputation of a well-known company by affiliating with it, making them look more legitimate. Then, you earn small commissions each time someone buys something from your site or the site of someone you referred into the network, but who really gets rich? Only the people at the top, just like with MLM schemes. One thing these sites often offer that is a red flag is free advertising for your site; of course they do—ultimately they profit more than you do for your sales. Small-business advisor Dr. Judith Kautz also notes something very important in an article she is quoted in on About.com: "There are countless stories of folks who have destroyed their social foundation through pressuring friends and family to buy their products." This is of course after you have tried to persuade everyone at church, and work, as well as relatives, neighbors, friends, and everyone else you can think of to buy your toilet paper instead of shopping at Ralph's with their club card. Also, the more people an individual brings into the network, the higher up the food chain she goes, which means she earns even more money for everything else that is sold.

Top Ten Dotcons

About.com has some great facts for consumers that are directly quoted from the Federal Trade Commission. You can download a PDF of this at job searchtech.about.com/gi/dynamic/offsite.htm?site=http://ftc.gov/bcp/conline/pubs/online/dotcons.htm. Here is a portion of what the FTC has to say about the most common consumer complaints:

> ***Internet Auctions***
>
> *The Bait*: Shop in a "virtual marketplace" that offers a huge selection of products at great deals.
>
> *The Catch*: After sending their money, consumers say they've received an item that is less valuable than promised or, worse yet, nothing at

all. [Author's note: I have received items like fake Gucci purses and fake Louis Vuitton handbags from eBay, too. While eBay is cracking down, these sellers are still out there.]

The Safety Net: When bidding through an internet auction, particularly for a valuable item, check out the seller and insist on paying with a credit card or using an escrow service. [Author's note: Always check out the feedback of the seller.]

Internet Access Services

The Bait: Free money, simply for cashing a check.

The Catch: Consumers say they've been "trapped" into long-term contracts for internet access or another web service, with big penalties for cancellation or early termination.

The Safety Net: If a check arrives at your home or business, read both sides carefully and look inside the envelope to find the conditions you're agreeing to if you cash the check. Read your phone bill carefully for unexpected or unauthorized charges.

Credit Card Fraud

The Bait: Surf the internet and view adult images online for free, just for sharing your credit card number to prove you're over 18.

The Catch: Consumers say that fraudulent promoters have used their credit card numbers to run up charges on their cards.

The Safety Net: Share credit card information only when buying from a company you trust. Dispute unauthorized charges on your credit card bill by complaining to the bank that issued the card. Federal law limits your liability to $50 in charges if your card is misused.

International Modem Dialing

The Bait: Get free access to adult material and pornography by downloading a "viewer" or "dialer" computer program.

The Catch: Consumers complained about exorbitant long-distance charges on their phone bill. Through the program, their modem is disconnected and then reconnected to the internet through an international long-distance number.

The Safety Net: Don't download any program to access a so-called "free" service without reading all the disclosures carefully for cost information. Just as important, read your phone bill carefully and challenge any charges you didn't authorize or don't understand.

Web Cramming

The Bait: Get a free custom-designed website for a 30-day trial period, with no obligation to continue.

The Catch: Consumers say they've been charged on their telephone bills or received a separate invoice, even if they never accepted the offer or agreed to continue the service after the trial period.

The Safety Net: Review your telephone bills and challenge any charges you don't recognize.

Multilevel Marketing Plans/Pyramids

The Bait: Make money through the products and services you sell as well as those sold by the people you recruit into the program.

The Catch: Consumers say that they've bought into plans and programs, but their customers are other distributors, not the general public. Some multi-level marketing programs are actually illegal pyramid schemes. When products or services are sold only to distributors like you, there's no way to make money.

The Safety Net: Avoid plans that require you to recruit distributors, buy expensive inventory, or commit to a minimum sales volume.

Travel and Vacation

The Bait: Get a luxurious trip with lots of "extras" at a bargain-basement price.

The Catch: Consumers say some companies deliver lower-quality accommodations and services than they've advertised or no trip at all. Others have been hit with hidden charges or additional requirements after they've paid.

The Safety Net: Get references on any travel company you're planning to do business with. Then, get details of the trip in writing, including the cancellation policy, before signing on.

Business Opportunities

The Bait: Be your own boss and earn big bucks.

The Catch: Taken in by promises about potential earnings, many consumers have invested in a "biz op" that turned out to be a "biz flop." There was no evidence to back up the earnings claims.

The Safety Net: Talk to other people who started businesses through the same company, get all the promises in writing, and study the proposed contract carefully before signing. Get an attorney or an accountant to take a look at it, too.

Investments

The Bait: Make an initial investment in a day trading system or service and you'll quickly realize huge returns.

The Catch: Big profits always mean big risk. Consumers have lost money to programs that claim to be able to predict the market with 100 percent accuracy.

The Safety Net: Check out the promoter with state and federal securities and commodities regulators, and talk to other people who invested through the program to find out what level of risk you're assuming.

Health Care Products/Services

The Bait: Items not sold through traditional suppliers are "proven" to cure serious and even fatal health problems.

The Catch: Claims for "miracle" products and treatments convince consumers that their health problems can be cured. But people with serious illnesses who put their hopes in these offers might delay getting the health care they need.

The Safety Net: Consult a health care professional before buying any "cure-all" that claims to treat a wide range of ailments or offers quick cures and easy solutions to serious illnesses.

Can you avoid getting caught by a scam artist working the web? Not always. But prudence pays.

According to About.com, the FTC offers these tips to help you avoid getting caught by an offer that just may not click:

> Be wary of extravagant claims about performance or earnings potential. Get all promises in writing and review them carefully before making a payment or signing a contract.
>
> Read the fine print and all relevant links. Fraudulent promoters sometimes bury the disclosures they're not anxious to share by putting them in teeny-tiny type or in a place where you're unlikely to see them. Look for a privacy policy. If you don't see one—or if you can't understand it—consider taking your business elsewhere. Be skeptical of any company that doesn't clearly state its name, street address, and telephone number. Check it out with the local Better Business Bureau, consumer protection office, or state Attorney General.
>
> Remember that the FTC works on behalf of consumers to prevent fraudulent, deceptive, and unfair business practices in the marketplace and to provide information to help consumers spot, stop, and avoid them. To file a complaint or to get free information visit ftc.gov, or call toll free at 1-877-FTC-HELP (1-877-382-4357); TTY: 1-866-653-4261. The FTC enters internet, telemarketing, identity theft, and other fraud-related complaints into Consumer Sentinel at consumer.gov, a secure online database available to hundreds of civil and criminal law enforcement agencies in the United States and abroad.

OTHER TYPES OF SCAMS

About.com offers an article by Judy Hedding that lists other types of scams as well. She specifically notes the notorious 809 scam, which requires that you call a phone number with an 809 area code. You may be calling to retrieve a prize you won or to settle money on an overdue account, but the 809 area code goes to the British Virgin Islands and can cost $25 per minute. The person answering tries to keep you on the phone as long as possible; this is equivalent to our 900 numbers for which you pay per call.

HOW TO PROTECT YOURSELF

People who prey on individuals desperately looking for money know what they are doing, and unfortunately individuals who consistently need quick money online also tend to do the same things! For instance, if you are desperately seeking a telecommuting position, you might decide to post to Craigslist something like "Mom desperately seeking a job that I can do online from home! I need flexible hours and a job, fast!" Who do you think is going to respond to this? The chances of it being a legitimate company wanting to hire you are slim to none. You need to use reputable sites and create a reputable company, and don't post on message boards out of desperation! This is one of many reasons I like Rat Race Rebellion's site, because there are no get-rich-quick schemes there—just legitimate, prescreened jobs (they don't control the ads, though, so just go for the job leads and ignore the ads).

Anyone who is a scammer and reads a post like the example in the last paragraph will be salivating at the opportunity to rip you off. So, rule number one: Don't leave messages on public boards! Don't talk about needing money or being available tomorrow or being out of time, or mention you were scammed already and need a legitimate job. Talk about setting yourself up for failure! If you want to test this theory, leave a message out there with a Hotmail address or Gmail address and see how many responses you get!

If you want to work for another business and sell products or services, or be a telecommuting employee with precreated jobs, you need to protect yourself from all sorts of scammers. Another way to protect yourself is to compare the person's response to your inquiries with those of a legitimate company. What would a real boss be asking you? What would a legitimate company be asking you? If you were having this discussion in person, would it go the same way?

Another common red flag is when the individual or business asks you for money to work! Would you ever go to a job interview and pay the interviewer $1,000 to "get started" in your new job? Heck no! So why would you do it online? This is a screaming crimson flag saying, "Stay away!" In fact, report the business to the FTC immediately. Don't let anyone know you are desperate, and be patient. The right job will come along, if that is your goal instead of starting your own business.

OTHER INTERNET FRAUD AND HOW TO AVOID COMPLAINTS IN YOUR BUSINESS

There are many other types of internet fraud schemes, and many can affect your business because people are skeptical about anything online these days. In a document released in 2008 by the FBI and in information released in the internet Crime Complaint Center (reports available at ic3.gov/media/annual reports.aspx), internet auction fraud was by far the most reported offense at 44.9 percent of referred complaints. Generally this was nondelivered merchandise, or payment issues, which made up 19 percent of those complaints. Check fraud made up 4.9 percent, and credit/debt card fraud, computer fraud, confidence fraud, and financial institution fraud round out the top seven categories of complaints in 2007. Be aware of what people are most skeptical of, and don't fall victim yourself. Don't buy from a supplier that has a terrible rating online or has complaints lodged against it. You are setting yourself up for failure. When you buy from suppliers, try to get a real address, not just a PO Box. Purchase goods from the company that actually holds the patent, trademark, or copyright, which you can quickly check out online. Remember that just because it appears that the company e-mailed you doesn't mean that it was that company really e-mailing you! It is very easy to spoof e-mail addresses.

Nigerian Letter Scam

Do you remember the Nigerian letter scam? Do you still get e-mails today trying to get you to send money to Nigeria? Do you need a refresher? Visit fbi.gov/majcases/fraud/fraudschemes.htm#nigerian. The following is a bit of information from the site. Why is this important to you? You need to be sure all communications coming from you, a business owner, are written in legitimate ways with legitimate business practices, and you need to be sure you don't fall prey to those trying to scam you out of your hard-earned money.

As quoted, from the FBI:

> Nigerian letter frauds combine the threat of impersonation fraud with a variation of an advance fee scheme in which a letter, mailed from Nigeria, offers the recipient the "opportunity" to share in a percentage of millions of dollars that the author, a self-proclaimed government official, is trying to transfer illegally out of Nigeria. The recipient is encouraged to send information to the author, such as blank letterhead stationery, bank name and account numbers, and other identifying information using a facsimile number provided in the letter. Some of these letters have also been received via e-mail through the internet. The scheme relies on convincing a willing victim, who has demonstrated a "'propensity for larceny" by responding to the invitation, to send money to the author of the letter in Nigeria in several installments of increasing amounts for a variety of reasons.
>
> Payment of taxes, bribes to government officials, and legal fees are often described in great detail with the promise that all expenses will be reimbursed as soon as the funds are spirited out of Nigeria. In actuality, the millions of dollars do not exist and the victim eventually ends up with nothing but loss. Once the victim stops sending money, the perpetrators have been known to use the personal information and checks that they received to impersonate the victim, draining bank accounts and credit card balances until the victim's assets are taken in their entirety. While such an invitation impresses most law-abiding citizens as a laughable hoax, millions of dollars in losses are caused by these schemes annually. Some victims have been lured to Nigeria, where they have been imprisoned against their will, in addition to losing large sums of money. The Nigerian government is not sympathetic to victims of these schemes, since the victim actually conspires to remove funds from Nigeria in a manner that is contrary to

Nigerian law. The schemes themselves violate section 419 of the Nigerian criminal code, hence the label "419 fraud."

Some Tips to Avoid Nigerian Letter or "419" Fraud

If you receive a letter from Nigeria asking you to send personal or banking information, do not reply in any manner. Send the letter to the U.S. Secret Service, your local FBI office, or the U.S. Postal Inspection Service. You can also register a complaint with the Federal Trade Commission's Consumer Sentinel. If you know someone who is corresponding in one of these schemes, encourage that person to contact the FBI or the U.S. Secret Service as soon as possible. Be skeptical of individuals representing themselves as Nigerian or foreign government officials asking for your help in placing large sums of money in overseas bank accounts. Do not believe the promise of large sums of money for your cooperation. Guard your account information carefully.

Impersonation or Identity Fraud

Impersonation fraud is when someone assumes your identity to perform a fraud or other criminal act. When you buy from merchants online and when you sell merchandise online, you need to do your very best to secure information and to protect credit card data given to you by customers so that criminals cannot hack into your database and then steal your customers' information (FBI, 2008).

As noted by the FBI (2008), "Criminals can get the information they need to assume your identity from a variety of sources, such as the theft of your wallet, your trash, or from credit or bank information. They may approach you in person, by telephone, or on the internet and ask you for the information. The sources of information about you are so numerous that you cannot prevent the theft of your identity. But you can minimize your risk of loss by following a few simple hints."

> Do you want to get rid of your entire customer base and shut down your business? Have credit card information stolen from your site and send each person an e-mail saying that they'll need to check her credit for the next year because you didn't encrypt your data—that is, *their* data.

The FBI provides some hints to avoid impersonation and identity fraud, and you need to report any potential breaches in privacy to the bureau right away.

From the FBI:

> Never throw away ATM receipts, credit statements, credit cards, or bank statements in a usable form. Never give your credit card number over the telephone unless you make the call. Reconcile your bank account monthly and notify your bank of discrepancies immediately. Keep a list of telephone numbers to call to report the loss or theft of your wallet, credit cards, etc. Report unauthorized financial transactions to your bank, credit card company, and the police as soon as you detect them. Review a copy of your credit report at least once each year. Notify the credit bureau in writing of any questionable entries and follow through until they are explained or removed. If your identity has been assumed, ask the credit bureau to print a statement to that effect in your credit report. If you know of anyone who receives mail from credit card companies or banks in the names of others, report it to local or federal law enforcement authorities.

Advance Fee Scheme

An advance fee scheme is when a victim pays money to someone in anticipation of receiving something of greater value, such as a loan, contract, investment, or gift, and then receives little or nothing in return. As noted by the FBI:

> The variety of advance fee schemes is limited only by the imagination of the con artists who offer them. They may involve the sale of products or services, the offering of investments, lottery winnings, "found money," or many other "opportunities." Clever con artists will offer to find financing arrangements for their clients who pay a '"finder's fee" in advance. They require their clients to sign contracts in which they agree to pay the fee when they are introduced to the financing source. Victims often learn that they are ineligible for financing only after they have paid the "finder" according to the

contract. Such agreements may be legal unless it can be shown that the "finder" never had the intention or the ability to provide financing for the victims.

When you are hunting for an online business, it is easy to latch onto business ideas that seem simpler than starting an entire website and selling a product, but resist them. They are probably schemes that will cause you to lose your shirt—or more.

The FBI notes some tips to avoid advanced fee schemes:

> If the offer of an "opportunity" appears too good to be true, it probably is. Follow common business practice. For example, legitimate business is rarely conducted in cash on a street corner. Know who you are dealing with. If you have not heard of a person or company that you intend to do business with, learn more about them. Depending on the amount of money that you intend to spend, you may want to visit the business location, check with the Better Business Bureau, or consult with your bank, an attorney, or the police. Make sure you fully understand any business agreement that you enter into. If the terms are complex, have them reviewed by a competent attorney. Be wary of businesses that operate out of post office boxes or mail drops and do not have a street address, or of dealing with persons who do not have a direct telephone line, who are never "in" when you call, but always return your call later.

> This is a great argument not just for using a K7 number but for having a business line that you actually answer. The more contactable you are, the more legitimate you will seem to the public.

The FBI continues,

> Be wary of business deals that require you to sign nondisclosure or noncircumvention agreements that are designed to prevent you from independently verifying the *bona fides* of the people with whom you intend to do business. Con artists often use noncircumvention agreements to threaten their victims with civil suit if they report their losses to law enforcement.

Common Health Insurance and Medical Equipment Frauds

Scams are of particular concern if you are selling medical equipment; be aware of what is out there so that you can be sure you use the exact opposite of the language used by the scammers–and of course a business model directly opposite theirs, too! You don't want to ever appear like a scammer, or you'll risk losing everything you worked for. As noted by the FBI:

> Equipment manufacturers offer "free" products to individuals. Insurers are then charged for products that were not needed and/or may not have been delivered. "Rolling Lab" Schemes are unnecessary and sometimes fake tests are given to individuals at health clubs, retirement homes, or shopping malls and billed to insurance companies or Medicare. Customers or providers bill insurers for services never rendered by changing bills or submitting fake ones. [Author's note: This happens online, too! Genetic screening, anyone?] Medicare fraud can take the form of any of the health insurance frauds described above. Senior citizens are frequent targets of Medicare schemes, especially by medical equipment manufacturers who offer seniors free medical products in exchange for their Medicare numbers. Because a physician has to sign a form certifying that equipment or testing is needed before Medicare pays for it, con artists fake signatures or bribe corrupt doctors to sign the forms. Once a signature is in place, the manufacturers bill Medicare for merchandise or service that was not needed or was not ordered.

The FBI also lists some tips to avoid health insurance fraud:

If you are contemplating offering whole foods or organic items or even health drinks or supplements online, you need to be aware of scams so you don't use any of the same methodologies and you can offer sound advice to your clients [a good idea for an FAQ section that makes you an expert, too].

> Never sign blank insurance claim forms. Never give blanket authorization to a medical provider to bill for services rendered. Ask your medical providers what they will charge and what you will be expected to

pay out-of-pocket. Carefully review your insurer's explanation of the benefits statement. Call your insurer and provider if you have questions. Do not do business with door-to-door or telephone salespeople who tell you that services or medical equipment are free. Give your insurance/Medicare identification only to those who have provided you with medical services. Keep accurate records of all health care appointments. Know if your physician ordered equipment for you.

Investment Scams

If one of your areas of interest is to create a site that helps people find investments, whether in real estate or the stock market, you should be aware of several scams in the investment area. I highly recommend that you educate your consumer base about the FBI's warnings and understand them yourself so you don't fall victim either. Starting with a letter-of-credit fraud, the FBI notes:

> Legitimate letters of credit are never sold or offered as investments. Legitimate letters of credit are issued by banks to ensure payment for goods shipped in connection with international trade. Payment on a letter of credit generally requires that the paying bank receive documentation certifying that the goods ordered have been shipped and are en route to their intended destination. Letters of credit frauds are often attempted against banks by providing false documentation to show that goods were shipped when, in fact, no goods or inferior goods were shipped. Other letter of credit frauds occur when con

LETTERS OF CREDIT

To get on net terms and be able to pay invoices in 30 days, some companies will want a letter of credit. It seems simple enough to buy one from company, but it is a scam. Don't do it; build your base over time by paying your bills cash on delivery, or COD, and eventually net terms will be extended to you.

artists offer a "letter of credit" or "bank guarantee" as an investment wherein the investor is promised huge interest rates on the order of 100 to 300 percent annually. Such investment "opportunities" simply do not exist.

If an "opportunity" appears too good to be true, it probably is. Do not invest in anything unless you understand the deal. Con artists rely on complex transactions and faulty logic to "explain" fraudulent investment schemes. Do not invest or attempt to "purchase" a "Letter of Credit."

The FBI continues:

Such investments simply do not exist. Be wary of any investment that offers the promise of extremely high yields. Independently verify the terms of any investment that you intend to make, including the parties involved and the nature of the investment.

[Another type of investment scam is the Prime Bank Note scam, where] international fraud artists have invented an investment scheme that offers extremely high yields in a relatively short period of time. In this scheme, they purport to have access to "bank guarantees" which they can buy at a discount and sell at a premium. By reselling the "bank guarantees" several times, they claim to be able to produce exceptional returns on investment. For example, if $10 million worth of "bank guarantees" can be sold at a two percent profit on ten separate occasions, or "traunches," the seller would receive a 20 percent profit. Such a scheme is often referred to as a "roll program." To make their schemes more enticing, con artists often refer to the "guarantees" as being issued by the world's "Prime Banks," hence the term "Prime Bank Guarantees." Other official sounding terms are also used such as "Prime Bank Notes" and "Prime Bank Debentures." Legal documents associated with such schemes often require the victim to enter into nondisclosure and noncircumvention agreements, offer returns on investment in a year and a day, and claim to use forms required by the International Chamber of Commerce (ICC). In fact, the ICC has issued a warning to all potential investors that no such investments

> exist. The purpose of these frauds is generally to encourage the victim to send money to a foreign bank where it is eventually transferred to an off-shore account that is in the control of the con artist. From there, the victim's money is used for the perpetrator's personal expenses or is laundered in an effort to make it disappear. While foreign banks use instruments called "bank guarantees" in the same manner that U.S. banks use letters of credit to insure payment for goods in international trade, such bank guarantees are never traded or sold on any kind of market.

The FBI offers many tips to avoid this type of fraud, and they apply to most types of internet business. Some to be aware of:

> Think before you invest in anything. Be wary of an investment in any scheme, referred to as a "roll program," that offers unusually high yields by buying and selling anything issued by "Prime Banks." As with any investment perform due diligence. Independently verify the identity of the people involved, the veracity of the deal, and the existence of the security in which you plan to invest. Be wary of business deals that require nondisclosure or noncircumvention agreements that are designed to prevent you from independently verifying information about the investment.

These seem like general business and security rules but when you get into your own business and are excited about a new opportunity, it's easy to overlook the obvious.

Ponzi Schemes

A Ponzi scheme is essentially an investment fraud wherein the operator promises high financial returns or dividends that are not available through traditional investments.

The FBI notes:

> Instead of investing victims' funds, the operator pays "dividends" to initial investors using the principle amounts "invested" by subsequent investors. The scheme generally falls apart when the operator flees with

all of the proceeds, or when a sufficient number of new investors cannot be found to allow the continued payment of "dividends."

This type of scheme is named after Charles Ponzi of Boston, Massachusetts, who operated an extremely attractive investment scheme in which he guaranteed investors a 50 percent return on their investment in postal coupons. Although he was able to pay his initial investors, the scheme dissolved when he was unable to pay investors who entered the scheme later.

Some Tips to Avoid Ponzi Schemes

As with all investments, exercise due diligence in selecting investments and the people with whom you invest. Make sure you fully understand the investment before you invest your money.

Pyramid Scheme

Pyramid schemes, (sometimes called franchise fraud, or chain referral schemes), are marketing and investment frauds where an individual is offered a franchise to market a particular product. The FBI notes:

> The real profit is earned, not by the sale of the product, but by the sale of new distributorships. Emphasis on selling franchises rather than the product eventually leads to a point where the supply of potential investors is exhausted and the pyramid collapses. At the heart of each pyramid scheme there is typically a representation that new participants can recoup their original investments by inducing two or more prospects to make the same investment. Promoters fail to tell prospective participants that this is mathematically impossible for everyone to do, since some participants drop out, while others recoup their original investments and then drop out.

Some Tips to Avoid Pyramid Schemes

Be wary of "opportunities" to invest your money in franchises or investments that require you to bring in subsequent investors to increase your profit or recoup your initial investment. Independently verify the legitimacy of any franchise or investment before you invest.

Better Business Bureau's Seal of Approval

Note that although seeing the Online BBB's (Better Business Bureau) seal of membership should mean quite a lot, and in most cases (I theorize) it does, its appearance on a website does *not* unequivocally mean that that site or company is a member. You see, most of the images you can view online, you can also copy, paste, and even save. So what does this mean? Anyone can copy the image of the Online BBB's (or any local BBB) seal and paste it into his website during the design process. People can also save the file and alter it, meaning they could add their name to the seal, alter dates, and so on.

> To contact your local BBB, visit BBB.org and search for your local chapter. To contact the BBB Online, visit BBBOnline.org.

"So how do I know if the seal I see means anything?" Easy—contact the BBB associated with the seal you see and ask if that particular company is a member. If it is not, do us all a favor and provide the BBB representative you speak with the company's contact information (including the URL at which the seal appears) so the BBB can investigate the situation and take appropriate action.

In short, the old adage stands true 99.9 percent of the time: If it sounds too good to be true, it probably is. If something just doesn't feel right, then investigate, or walk away.

> **YourOnlineProfessor.com**
>
> You want an online business, and who doesn't? The flexibility, the desire to be in charge of your own destiny—everything is there. However, you need to be aware of scams. Just like in any other business, there are people that will try to take advantage of you. Look out for anyone that wants money up front, or businesses that look like a pyramid scheme. Re-read through chapters in this book, and bounce the opportunities off other entrepreneurs at YourOnlineProfessor.com. See if they know about a company and its reputation before you get involved. Most people are honest and hard working, but we have to help each other and stay away from the bad eggs.

MOVING FORWARD

So we've reached the end of our journey together. You now have the foundation of knowledge to take your idea for a product, service, or business and run with it.

If you haven't already answered the question "Is this for me?" you need to make this a top priority. If the answer is "yes," then your next step should be to get your game plan out of your head and onto paper. Think about where you are, what your idea is, who it will affect, how you will make the idea a reality, what you need to materialize your dream, where you want your dream to ultimately lead, who has already tried this and who is doing it right now, how you will be different, how you will be better, what you will do if your idea doesn't take off right away, with whom you will advertise, whom you will partner up with, and more.

Once your ideas and aspirations have been put to paper, your next step, and by far your most vital step, is to move forward. Although a bit cliché, the Nike slogan comes to mind: "Just do it!"

What should happen if things don't go according to plan? Recall Chapter 13, and stay flexible. A close friend of mine came up with an idea one day to offer CPR classes online. He spent a fair amount of time over a week forming a plan and writing it all down, and even registered a domain name, only to find out that the American Heart Association was already doing this and was regulating it to the point of making it near impossible for anyone else to do the same. He is now trying to figure out how a partnership with the AHA could work, benefitting both parties but still allowing him to move forward with his idea. He didn't just give up and head back to his cubicle, he continues to brainstorm ideas to this day. Part of being an entrepreneur, above and beyond having the next greatest product or idea, comes down to being dedicated and persistent. It is these core qualities that will often make or break an idea or business.

My final hope for you is this: that you never give up. Take your dream and run with it. Nobody else can materialize your dreams like you can, so stop waiting for someone else to try. You've been given all of the information, now all you have to do is take that first step, and move forward. This book is incredibly unique in that you have a manual and the support of YourOnline Professor.com where you have access to other entrepreneurs just like you. You can join the conversation, talk with others in forums, chat with other business owners, and access many resources all designed to help you be successful.

I wish you infinite amounts of success. Please don't hesitate to write me and let me know how everything is going for you. Entrepreneurs are the lifeblood and heart of the American economy and spirit. Enjoy.

APPENDICES

APPENDIX

A

RESOURCES FOR THE ONLINE BUSINESS

MARKETING

Following are two sources for information on marketing and advertising your business, both have been reviewed and recommended by the author.

1. *MarketMe.com*. A great source for marketing online. Check out their articles and resources.
2. *HubSpot*. I covered blogging in Chapter 9, but here is a great resource that will help you get started with blogs right away: blog.hubspot.com. This site specifically talks about marketing and blogging for your business.

BUSINESS PLANNING RESOURCES

When you get started, you need solid company checklists and company creation information. You also need solid business planning advice and you need as many free tools as you can get your hands on to keep your costs low. Below are some resources on checklists and information on how to create your company to get you started.

Small-Business Checklist

The IRS publishes its own small-business checklist to help you make sure your bases are covered. There are great resources here (believe it or not) that can help you get started. Check them out at irs.gov/businesses/small.

Doing Business on the Internet

This is a great site for local governments on business reference services and how to do business on the internet: loc.gov/rr/business/ecommerce/.

Online Business Planning

Not only can business plans take an incredible amount of time, but often finding a template means paying $200 or more for something solid. Not at MyOwnBusiness.org; this site offers lots of great information at no cost. Check out its online business plan with numerous sections at myownbusiness.org/plans/doc/all.doc.

PRESS RELEASES AND MEDIA INQUIRIES

There will be times you want to respond to media inquiries (or have requests for interviews in your area of expertise sent automatically to your e-mail) or times you will want to send out a press release. You can do all this through one great site, at profnet.prnewswire.com. Memberships are relatively inexpensive for the service and direct customization of alerts that you can receive.

SOCIAL NETWORKING SITES

In Chapters 8 and 9, I touched quite a bit on the three main sites: MySpace, LinkedIn, and Facebook. Here are the URLs: myspace.com, linkedin.com, and facebook.com.

MONITORING YOUR CLICK-THROUGH RATES

I also discussed in Chapter 8 how critical it is to monitor which campaigns are successful when you advertise. Two great sites to check out are click-tracks.com and onestat.com, both of which offer great third-party information. It isn't free, but it is extremely accurate. If you have a feeling your affiliates aren't quite being honest or measuring data in the way that is considered acceptable by business practices, this can help you validate or invalidate their findings.

WEB MARKETING TODAY RESOURCE ROOM

Web Marketing Today is a great site on online marketing in general, and includes information on what developing countries are using to process payments so you can be sure you are one step ahead of globalization in developing and third world nations. The site also provides reviews on the top payment-processing companies and the pros and cons of each. Access all this at wilson web.com/research/.

FREE ADVERTISING NETWORK AND TEXT LINK EXCHANGE

If you want to use free advertising companies and exchange text links (remember, we know they have higher click-throughs than graphics), check out adgridwork.com. This site is 100 percent free, no payments required, ever. Thousands of sites are on the network and they offer text links in addition to graphics. They promote to targeted audiences because you define the sites on which you want your information to appear (this also helps you control credibility). They also offer free metric tools that let you see how well your ads are doing out there in cyberspace.

BANNER EXCHANGE SITES

One thing discussed in advertising is banner advertising. But you might not have the capital to buy ads outright. Banner exchange sites let you place banners through credits on other sites by offering their links on yours; for each click-through you earn a credit that buys you the appearance of your ad on other sites. Check out home.free-banners.com/tour.htm for more information.

GOOGLE ADWORDS GUIDE

I discussed Google AdSense and AdWords in Chapter 8, but here is a great guide to Google AdWords online: googleguide.com/adwords.html.

AFFILIATE NETWORKING

There are lots of resources for affiliate networking, but if you want to learn how it works from reputable agencies and organizations, check out these sources:

- *My Affiliate Program at myaffiliateprogram.com*. This site offers solutions like tracking and networking.
- *Commission Junction at cj.com*. This is a great higher-end affiliate provider company from which you can download ads for extra revenue or with which you can become a partner.
- *ClickBank at clickbank.com*. This is an affiliate company for digital products only. Take a look at its ability to accept credit cards at take-payments-online.com/Clickbank.html.

CHECKING THE VALIDITY OF SITES

The Better Business Bureau at bbb.org is a great resource for checking the validity of websites, as is the Federal Trade Commission at ftc.gov.

REPORTING INTERNET CRIMES

To report an internet crime, use the following tool from the FBI: ic3.gov/.

USABILITY

The guru Jakob Nielsen has numerous web sites and write-ups to help you with usability in your own site. Check out these links with some great information:

- *The New York Times* at nytimes.com/library/tech/98/07/cyber/articles/13usability.html#1
- UseIt.com on Jakob Nielsen, with links to lots of his articles, publications, and columns at useit.com/jakob/
- 25 Years in Usability at useit.com/alertbox/25-years-usability.html. This link provides all sorts of great information including a historical perspective going back to 1983 on web design and mainframe systems and the role of usability.
- Link Guidelines on different colors that are best to use for web sites based on research at useit.com/alertbox/link-list-color.html
- A column on right-hand column justified navigation menus and how they impede "scannability," with a before and after comparison at useit.com/alertbox/navigation-menu-alignment.html
- Two great articles on just how little users actually read and fundamental guidelines for web usability. Both are at useit.com/alertbox/per cent-text-read.html and nngroup.com/events/tutorials/usability.html, including information collected in 2008 at useit.com/alertbox/user-skills.html on user skill, the gullibility of Google, guidelines to live by, improving web site profitability (at useit.com/alertbox/roi.html, analyzing return on investment), e-mail newsletters, podcasts, news feeds, and RSS, splash screens, breadcrumbs, you name it! All at useit.com/alertbox/user-skills.html. There are also some great examples of some poor sites on here that you must see. Nielsen also has analyzed what usability issues have remained over time and what has remained a constant nemesis to users, at useit.com/alertbox/guidelines-

change.html–and of course, most importantly perhaps, how to learn from history.

SEARCH ENGINE SITES

Search engines are critical because in many cases, you can manually request for your site to be searched and crawled by crawlers and robots, increasing your page hits and ranking by various search criteria. Here is a more comprehensive list from Wikipedia on search engines used, based on the type of field. This is accessible at en.wikipedia.org/wiki/List_of_search_engines. In the general category, Wikipedia lists:

- Alexa Internet
- Ask.com (formerly Ask Jeeves)
- Baidu (Chinese)
- Exalead (French)
- Gigablast
- Google
- Live Search (formerly MSN Search)
- Sogou (Chinese)
- Sohu (Chinese)
- Wikia Search
- Yahoo! Search

It lists many more that are geographically limited in scope. To check these out by country, visit en.wikipedia.org/wiki/List_of_search_engines#Geographical_limited_scope. From Russia to Japan, you can learn the top search engines in those countries, which is very relevant if you accept overseas transactions.

For business searching, Wikipedia lists three sites: Business.com, Nexis (Lexis Nexis), and Thomasnet. It lists many more for the enterprise category, but these are not as commonly used. You can access that comprehensive list at en.wikipedia.org/wiki/List_of_search_engines#Enterprise.

If you are running a job search site you will want to know what the main job search engines are. Following are those listed at Wikipedia:

- Bixee.com (India)
- CareerBuilder.com (USA)
- Craigslist (by city)
- Eluta.ca (Canada)
- HotJobs.com (USA)
- Incruit (Korea)
- Indeed.com (USA)
- Monster.com (USA)
- Naukri.com (India)
- Recruit.net (International)
- SimplyHired.com (USA)
- TheLadders.com (USA)

For medical search engines, check out Wikipedia's list at en.wikipedia.org/wiki/List_of_search_engines#Medical.

News is also becoming a top priority; Wikipedia lists Google News, MagPortal, NewsLookup, Nexis (Lexis Nexis), Topix.net, and Yahoo!

GREAT PLACES TO BUY COMPUTERS

If you don't want to pay an arm and a leg for a computer that is tough to upgrade and has a case that's hard to crack (open up and see what's wrong), take a look at these sites for PCs: PCMall.com, TheNerds.net, TigerDirect.com; they are all strong sites. I don't recommend buying from big resellers like Comp USA. They are adding a markup in an industry that today, online, has very little markup.

APPENDIX

B

ONLINE BUSINESS CHECKLISTS AND TIPS

There are many things that you need to get started in your online business. The following checklist is meant to help you mentally, emotionally, and financially plan and prepare for your business.

FILL IN WHEN COMPLETE	BUSINESS PLANNING
	I have decided on an LLC/sole proprietorship/corporation/ partnership,etc.
	I have filed a Fictitious Business Name Statement.
	I have decided on a company name.
	I have my tax requirements in order and/or have talked with a tax advisor/planner.
	I know what my core business products or services will be.
	I know if my business is going to be homebased or will require an office.
	I have analyzed my competition.
	I have insurance, if required.
	I have a business license, if required.
	I am passionate about the product or service and know it well.
	I have secured products or services and have the business process streamlined.
	I have secured any needed permits (see later in this section).
	FINANCIAL PLANNING
	I have the startup capital needed or have a plan to get startup capital.
	I have a list of items I will need to start my business.
	I have a one- to two-year cash flow projection that I can live with.

Checklist for Success

FILL IN WHEN COMPLETE	WEB SITE INITIAL SETUP
	I know if I'm using a web developer or designer.
	I know if I'm creating my own site or having a designer do it.
	I know if I'm going to secure my own hosting or leave it to my developer.
	My content, graphics, logos, and so on are ready to be handed off to the web designer.
	I know what type of integration I want on my site. I know what I intend to offer (blogs, chats, forums, FAQs, etc.).
	I have my business policies,; return policies, etc. written down for the web developer.
	I have the domain name and hosting services secured.
	TECHNOLOGY SETUP
	I know what technology I will need.
	I have a computer.
	I know if I need server space and what type of server I will need to rent/lease/buy.
	I have e-mail set up.
	I have high-speed internet access.
	I have a business line.
	I have faxing capabilities.

CHECKLIST FOR SUCCESS, CONTINUED

FILL IN WHEN COMPLETE	ADVANCED E-COMMERCE
	I have a merchant account and business checking set up and in place.
	I have the capability to process online transactions.
	I have created a solid shopping cart.
	I have sophisticated security implemented on my website.
	I have a solid backup system in place.
	ADVANCED BUSINESS PLANNING
	I will be able to recognize if I need to hire employees.
	People are beginning to know my name or my business's name in my area of expertise.
	I am using social networking sites to help build my brand.
	I am networking myself well online and participating in areas where potential clients are.
	I have an advertising campaign; I sell ads and/or buy ad space.
	I am becoming highly networked in my business area.

CHECKLIST FOR SUCCESS, CONTINUED

OCCUPATIONS REQUIRING STATE LICENSES

There are many careers that require state licenses. These are some common jobs requiring licensing that may take some time and effort to get:

- Contractors (of nearly any type)
- Mortgage brokers/insurance agents/bankers
- Doctors
- Accountants/tax advisors
- Real estate agents or brokers
- Cosmetologists (even for online advice)
- Auctioneers
- Security (of any type—investigations, guarding online activity, etc.)

PRODUCTS REQUIRING PERMITS

Many products you might want to sell online require permits. If you intend to sell any of these, be sure you get the appropriate license:

- Guns or any type of firearm
- Lottery tickets
- Liquor

SALES TAX PERMITS

If you need to collect sales tax (generally if you are shipping to a state that has a sales tax or you are conducting your business in a state with a sales tax, you must charge sales tax and therefore report sales tax), you need a sales tax permit. You can get a reseller's permit for your own state. Visit the site for your state's board of equalization; most have forms online.

GOVERNMENT AGENCIES FOR CERTAIN CAREERS

There are certain careers that require you to have special federal permits that go beyond the state licensing discussed earlier. Some of these (with their associated federal web site) are

- *Investment advice*: Securities and Exchange Commission at sec.gov
- *Online pharmacies*: Federal Drug Administration at fda.gov
- *Transportation of goods*: Department of Transportation at dot.gov
- *Selling any type of alcohol, firearm, tobacco, or anything related* (double-check): The Department of Alcohol, Tobacco and Firearms at atf.gov
- *Selling meat or other products*: Federal Drug Administration at fda.gov

TEN TIPS FOR BLOGS AND PODCASTS (FAQ)

I am sure by now you have a list of questions that need to be addressed. Here are my top ten tips for podcasts and blogs and an FAQ section for both, adapted from a book by Babb and Lazo.

1. *Update your podcasts often.* If you want people to keep coming back, your content has to remain original.
2. *Be consistent.* Pretty soon, you'll have an entire series of podcasts and blogs. You should have a consistent theme throughout with regard to the look and feel. This will serve as your own trademark.
3. *Be timely and timeless.* Your content has to be timely in terms of the issues that are most appealing to people at that particular time and needs to maintain its freshness.
4. *Sacrifice some speed for quality.* In my opinion, it is preferable to have a presentation-quality podcast that takes a while to load than it is to have a low-quality one that loads right away. The initial extra wait is well worth it.
5. *Preparation is key, but scripting is not.* When recording your podcast, you certainly need to be prepared for the content that you'll be providing. However, don't script it, because scripting can sound stiff and impersonal.
6. *Conduct interviews.* Don't assume that you know exactly what people are going to want to see in your blogs and podcasts. Why go through the trouble of creating content only to have to revise it significantly later? Find out up front and minimize the rework.
7. *Don't take personal attacks personally.* Not everyone subscribes to the adage "If you don't have anything nice to say, don't say anything at all." If you

do receive some negative feedback on your blog or podcast, look at it constructively and definitely don't allow it to discourage you.

8. *Get your own domain name if you don't already have one.* Although there are plenty of platforms out there for blogs and podcasts, using one is impersonal because it just makes you appear as one in a sea of many. Therefore, make a small investment at the outset and secure your own domain name that will come to be closely associated with you in time.
9. *Come up with a hooking strategy.* Very often, attracting new users and hooking users require two different strategies. Ask yourself the following two questions and hopefully some aspects of each answer will be different: "What do I need to do to get people to visit my blog and/or view my podcast?" "What do I need to do to create enough interest in people's minds to have them keep returning to my blog and view my podcast?"
10. *Comment on other blogs.* A great way to spread the word about your own blog is to post on other people's blogs, especially if those blogs are popular. Make sure your posts are interesting enough to generate interest in your own blog, but definitely don't simply advertise your blog without adding value.

Frequently Asked Questions

- *Do I need to buy an iPod to create a podcast?* You absolutely and most certainly *do not* need an iPod.
- *OK, so if I don't need an iPod, why do they call it podcasting?* Well, the name actually does originate from the word *iPod.* It's basically a combination of *iPod* and *broadcasting.* I wish that I had enough influence to change the name because it is confusing!
- *How do I know if my podcast is successful?* You'll have to define first what success means to you. If it's in terms of number of downloads, a third-party hosting service can provide these numbers for you. However, if it's in terms of your bottom line, then it's up to you to determine how much your business has increased as a result of your podcast.
- *Can I legally add copyrighted music to my podcast?* In short, no. Many people do without realizing that it's illegal. However, there are many

up-and-coming musicians who are willing to provide "podsafe" music.

- *Is it expensive to create a blog? Expensive* is a relative term, but the answer is probably "no" by most people's definition. In fact, Blogger.com allows you to do it for free!
- *How do I advertise my blog?* Of course you can use methods like emailing and your existing advertising; however, actual content will go a long way towards spreading the word.
- *What should I include in my blog?* Look at other blogs for ideas, but certainly don't copy them. A great way to start is to interview your existing clients!
- *Are there directories of blogs to which I can add my blog?* Absolutely. Check out BlogWise.com and BlogStreet.com. There are many others as well.
- *What is RSS?* It stands for *rich site summary* (Web 1.0) or *really simple syndication* (Web 2.0). It's basically a way for blog sites to share headlines, much as syndication works in newspapers.

APPENDIX

C

IMPORTANT TERMS

If you are interested in learning more about any of these terms and definitions, I recommend that you type the word along with "definition" into Google. There are several great resources that will help you explore each of these definitions more fully and give you an understanding of how to implement the various products and technologies! Some great can't-miss sites are HowStuffWorks.com, WhatIs.com, and Wikipedia.com.

Atom

Atom is a pair of standards. Atom syndication format is XML that is used for web feeds. Atom publishing protocol is a very simple set of rules (language) used for web resources. A web feed can be downloaded by websites or by users that subscribe to a feed to view its content.

Blog

A blog is a user-generated website often used in Web 2.0. Notations or entries are created in what looks like an online journal or notepad. They are often embedded within web pages to create a community or forum. A blog often has numerous components, including text, links, other web pages, graphics, and notes and news.

Blogcast

A blogcast is the combination of a blog and a podcast on one website. The site can be found by search engines, making the podcast searchable.

Blogger

A blogger is someone who has her own blog. A blogger can be anyone; the blogger need not be a professional who blogs for a living nor a member of the media.

Blogosphere

The blogosphere is all the blogs out there on the internet as a community. The interactive and community nature of blogs means that many bloggers link to one another, which creates a big interconnected network of blogs. You will want to be sure to post on others' blogs as well as your own. By becoming a member of the blogosphere, you will increase name recognition, and you will attract others to your blog, too. Be sure you link other blogs to yours and offer enough content to make other bloggers want to do the same.

Domain Name

A domain name is the name that you type into a web browser to get to a website. For instance, if you type in "entrepreneur.com," you will go to

Entrepreneur's website. The domain name is important, because your business is often known by its name. Sometimes people choose to buy domain names that are not synonymous with or the same as their business's name. You might also have two names, a main site and one that directs visitors to the main site. This is known as URL forwarding. You can also *grip* a URL, which means that if you are hosting your site on your own internet space through your internet service provider, your service provider will show only that domain name (not the actual, often convoluted name) in the web browser. These powerful tools will help you maintain the integrity and consistency of your site.

Dynamic Web Page

Dynamic web pages are pages that are not static; that is, they change based on the user, the user's preferences, or the instructions on the user's computer. This creates interactivity that standard web pages do not provide. User experts often recommend we always build dynamic sites. The features allow users to feel as though the site was custom designed just for them and encourage users to come back often.

Electronic Commerce (e-Commerce)

E-commerce is the internet marketplace. Any site that is used to sell or buy products or services is an e-commerce site. For instance, Amazon and eBay are e-commerce sites. Even if you are using your site only to provide information on your services, it would still be considered an e-commerce site.

Homepage

The homepage is the URL that is loaded automatically when you go to a page. For example, if you type in "google.com," you may really be taken to *google.com/index.html*. Although you will be unaware of this, technically the *index.html* file is the homepage. When you click Home on a site, the site takes you to the homepage. You want your homepage to be inviting and encouraging to visitors. Sites are usually known by their homepage, so this is a critical element that sets the tone for your work and your visitors' expectations.

HTML

HTML stands for "hypertext markup language." It is the most commonly used language on the internet. If you go to your web browser and go to View and then Source, you can see the HTML code that is used to generate the page you are viewing. HTML code is what programmers write to make your web page accessible and viewable by a web browser.

HTTP

Hypertext transfer protocol (HTTP) transfers information on the internet onto your computer screen when you are surfing the web. It facilitates requests by the user or server, then responds to the user or server. HTTP, although unseen, is required to make the web work. When you look in your web browser, before the domain name is the *http://* notation. This indicates to the web browser that the protocol it should be communicating with is hypertext transfer protocol and not another that your browser supports, like file transfer protocol (FTP). On the other hand, if you decide to design your own site from a template and you upload information, you will type *ftp://* into your web browser or into an FTP utility.

Internet

The internet is the term encompassing the entire network of all computers that make up not only the web but e-mail, file transfer protocol, and all of the other sites and computers on the public network. The internet is a network of networks that was originated by universities and the government. Today, it is used for everything from e-mail to chat to phone calls. What we commonly call the internet is really the web; that is, anything you see in a web browser on your PC, your handheld device, and so on.

iPod

The iPod was created and launched by Apple in 2001. It has become a bit of a phenomenon and, some say, has restored Apple's success in the marketplace. Apple's iPod uses iTunes software to communicate. A common misunderstanding is that you must have an iPod to listen to a podcast. In fact, you can download Apple's iShare software from apple.com without having an iPod. Some iPod models let you watch video, read books, and listen to audio. The iPod has spun off numerous other technologies from Apple and other companies.

Meta Tags

Meta tags are important in your website, because they define the data about your website's contents and identify how your site will be retrieved in search engines. Search engines will crawl your site for meta tags, using them as the search criteria. Make sure your web designer knows the essential keywords you want used for the site and includes them. It is easier to include them at the beginning of the site development rather than going back and adding them later. Adding them later can cause confusing and conflicting information in search engines, and because the engines have already crawled your site, they may not go back to look for updates. However, you can force search engines to look for updates or use specific keywords through tools available on each of the search engine sites and through third-party applications.

Moblog

Moblog is a combination of a *web blog* and *mobility applications* (such as cell phones). The moblog first emerged in Japan, where camera phones were of high quality and had a lot of bandwidth.

MySpace.com

MySpace is a social networking website offering an interactive environment that relies on relationships. Individuals create their site (so do products and businesses, by the way), and users who want to be identified by their "friends" add those particular products or companies to their network.

Open Source

Open source is a strategy as much as it is a technology. Open source is a method of distributing software that lets individuals modify code and post it for others to use and benefit by. Linux is an example of open source software that is in direct competition with nonopen source software, such as Microsoft Windows. With the high cost of proprietary software and the difficulty of obtaining support at times, many companies and individuals have turned to open source software for solutions.

PayPal

PayPal is a company now owned by eBay that facilitates online payments. First used primarily to handle eBay transactions, it is now used for all sorts of things. Because of its ease of use and security, I recommend it as a way to handle online payments without having to pay credit card merchant fees. I use it in my own sites regularly. It allows people to send you secure payments, and as a buyer, you have the ability to dispute transactions and follow up. Paypal also has dividend accounts and credit and debit cards that let you access the cash in your account quickly.

Photoblog

A photoblog or photolog is a way to share photos on a blog. Usually the focus isn't so much on text, as at traditional blogs, but on the photos themselves. YouTube in its current form is more of a video blog, as individuals upload videos, but in still format, it would be a photoblog. Interestingly enough, photoblogs have become more common because people have cell phone cameras and therefore fast access to a camera whenever something interesting happens.

Podcast

A podcast is media that is sent over the internet and is downloaded through feeds, mobile devices, RSS, or computers. *Podcasting* is the act of casting your podcast—that is, of submitting your podcast to the public domain on the internet or the private domain on your intranet.

RSS

RSS is a web feed that updates content in blogs, news feeds, or podcasts. Feed readers are fed by information to which a particular user subscribes. You will want to get your podcast or blog out to RSS feeds so that individuals can subscribe to it and you can build your online reputation.

TypePad

TypePad, made by Six Apart Ltd., is one of many blogging services. Check it out at typepad.com.You may want to use it as your method of submitting blogs.

Uniform Resource Locator (URL)

A URL is what you type into a web browser to get to a particular site. For instance, *drdaniellebabb.com* is the URL of my website.

Video Blog

A video blog, or vlog, is an entry into a blog that has video or video and text. YouTube became a popular vlog site as individuals from all over the world used their cell phones with cameras to upload video. Everyone became an instant journalist! You can use sites like this to create virtual tours apart from the Multiple Listing Service or MLS.

Vodcast or Video Podcast

Video podcasts came about recently as a way to capture podcasts that incorporated video. This is yet another great way to incorporate visual details on your business, your tips, or even your properties.

Web 2.0

Web 2.0 is an ill-defined term that essentially means "the second version of the web." This second version of the web is based on collaboration and interconnectivity, on community and interactivity, and depends on a community to generate content. It isn't just a push technology; it is a social networking term that collectively describes all of the websites where users have a say in the content.

Web Browser

A web browser is the software that you use to access the web. For instance, Internet Explorer and FireFox are web browsers you may use to access the internet. Internet Explorer has the largest market share, with Netscape and FireFox behind it. Internet Explorer is integrated into the Windows operating system, which comes on most PCs. The version of the web browser you use will dictate what you can and cannot see on a web page, as not all web programming code displays the same way on all browsers.

Web Server

A web server is the computer or server that takes in HTTP requests from all of its users and then processes them. It may forward a request to another server, it may handle the request itself, or it may queue the request for later processing. Usually, web servers work in conjunction with database servers and email servers and do not stand alone to provide web services, though they can. You will need to buy space on a web server or have your own web server (not recommended) to host your site.

Webcast

The word webcast is part web and part broadcast. It means the sending and receiving of video live over the internet. It is different from a weblog, which can be viewed at any time, or a podcast, which is downloaded later. A webcast is inherently live. Companies use these to deliver annual reports and let their shareholders take part in meetings, for instance.

Webinar

A webinar is a seminar that is sent over the internet; essentially, it is a web conference. While a webcast is unidirectional—the data is pushed onto the client—a webinar is interactive and synchronous, meaning that the audience participates in real time. Webinars are powerful tools for educating your audience.

Website

Website is a term that means the entire set of web pages that make up a domain. For example, all of the web pages on kaplan.com together encompass Kaplan's website.

World Wide Web

The World Wide Web (WWW or web) is the entire collection of all the hyperlinked sites on the internet. The WWW excludes e-mail and chat systems; it is everything accessible via your web browser.

World Wide Web Consortium (W3C)

The World Wide Web Consortium (W3C) is an international standards organization that encompasses numerous organizations that work together to develop standards for the web. It publishes a set of standards that any web development effort should meet.

YouTube

YouTube is a free video-sharing website that lets users upload, review, and share video clips with one another. It has become immensely popular; even major news outlets use video published to it on a regular basis. It was created by three former employees of PayPal and uses Flash to display videos that are uploaded to the site. It was recently purchased by Google and is considered a powerhouse in the world of online entertainment.

APPENDIX

D

FAST FORMS

Regardless of whether you have a brick-and-mortar business or an online business, you still have to follow business protocol in setting up your business structure and documenting your business appropriately. The first set of forms listed in this section are applications and documents you will need from articles of incorporation to employment applications. The second set of tools are spreadsheets—including examples for your use and the

original source site that you can use to download incredibly powerful tools to help you with your analysis! There are many great free forms online as well as those from sources like LegalZoom.com for a fee. I have done my best to compile some great forms here for you to use, but first, a legal disclaimer:

> Forms and requirements from the IRS and the government change all the time. Courts change rules all the time through decisions that they make, leaving companies vulnerable if they use older forms. These forms should be used not as complete templates, but as guides of what to expect as you fill out your forms and required paperwork to create your new business. Most forms, regardless of where you acquire them, must also be highly modified to suit your purpose and business.
>
> The first set of forms found here is from LectLaw.com. You should visit this site because it has excellent forms, advice, and referrals. As Jeff Liebling, president of the company, said in an e-mail to me, "Lectric Law Library is the best thing in the entire Universe—be it animal, vegetable, or mineral." He also offers an important caution and warning, noted below, which goes for all forms in this book, too, although below, I am quoting LectLaw, sarcasm and all!
>
>> Although we try to ensure the Library's holdings are accurate and virus-free, we only guarantee that it contains no intentional mistakes or defects and has no fraudulent, unlawful, or improper purpose.
>>
>> Otherwise there is no guarantee made or implied about the accuracy, currency, usefulness, functionality, safety, toxicity, or anything else regarding the Library or anything in it, near it, related to it, or connected with it in any way. Use it at your own risk!
>>
>> This means that if you use the Library's material for whatever purpose and, due to our completely negligent and idiotic error, you are embarrassed, imprisoned, bankrupted, flunked, deported, divorced, molested, castigated, outcast, crucified, sickened,

beaten, drowned, excommunicated, ridiculed, or elected to high public office–don't [complain] to us about it. (From Ralf's Library Tour)

NOTE TO LEGAL PROFESSIONALS: You can skip this part. If you don't already follow its advice you are (or will soon be): fired; disbarred; in jail; being sued; hiding from clients; under investigation; all of the above, or; serving on the Supreme Court.

Important Hints for Students, Pro Ses, and Other Lay People

1. Be careful in using any of our material. While we try to ensure the Library's holdings are accurate and current there is no guarantee we've always succeeded. Before using it in a real-life situation check it against a current "official" copy at your local law library or elsewhere. And this is good advice for all legal info, no matter the source. It's even rumored that the government can screw things up.
2. The laws and rules are always changing. Don't rely on your memory or old books. Remember what our Head Librarian Ralf claims to have told Aristotle, or Plato . . . or Pluto: *"There's nothing more dangerous than an outdated lawbook–except maybe a pissed-off judge."*
3. Even if something is accurate–in context–it may not be as applied to your specific situation. For example, a form, procedure, or other information may be entirely accurate as it applies to Alabama but if you use it in Wyoming you'll be immediately burned at the stake. So please contact an appropriate professional or go to the law library.
4. Be aware that much legal information can only be a static snapshot of a constantly changing, growing, evolving concept. Also, with many subjects (e.g., many court procedural rules), even if you completely understand them, You Don't. For an approximation of what is really required in practice you can start at a real law library. However, with that said, you should also realize that certain–*some say all*–legal questions (e.g., to

whom and what do RICO—*racketeering*—laws apply) have no firm, unchanging answer. This is one of the main reasons judges exist.

5. Despite what some may say, a normally intelligent person can figure out the answer to most legal questions—if they spend enough time and effort. But, do you want to spend six weeks learning and researching how to deal with a legal issue when a legal professional might only charge a small amount to do it?
6. Advice for lay people who will be appearing in court: Unless you're a masochist or trying to lay a foundation for an insanity defense when addressing a judge you should refer to him/her as "Your Honor"—NOT "Your Highness," "Your Holiness," "Buddy," "Sweetie," etc., and, no matter how attractive he/she is, DON'T hit on the Judge while court's in session. This may be one of the few times you should watch what the lawyers do and act like them. *Just be careful you don't make it a habit!* Finally, read some of the Library's transcripts, especially the ones in our News Room from the Freeman proceedings, and do the exact opposite.
7. A last bit of advice for now: If you're not sure what you're supposed to do in a given legal situation don't just wing it. Check the laws, rules, commentaries, etc.—and if you're still not sure, Get Advice From Someone Who Knows. For procedural matters a judge's or court's clerk may be able to help, while on matters of law—*understanding the difference between the two is about as easy as nailing Jell-O® to the wall*—contact a knowledgeable legal professional." (Liebling, 2008)

That said, we can move onto some of the most important documents you'll need to start and run your business. You can find them online at lectlaw.com.

DOCUMENTS AND APPLICATIONS

SPREADSHEETS

By far some of the best spreadsheets out there are available on the web at exinfm.com. One particular spreadsheet at exinfm.com/excelpercent20files/Workbook1-2.xls has numerous workbooks at the bottom that include everything from balance sheets to income statements, from horizontal analyses to key financials.

Figure 24. Sample Balance Sheet

Figure 25. Sample Income Statement

Figure 26. Sample Cash-Flow Statement

Figure 27. Sample Balance Sheet

Figure 28. Ratio Analysis

Figure 29. Final Budgets

APPENDIX

E

REFERENCES

About.com (2008). "Job Search Tech on Online Scams" as cited on the FTC's web site. Retrieved from jobsearchtech.about.com/gi/dynamic/offsite.htm?site=http://ftc.gov/bcp/conline/pubs/online/dotcons.htm.

Babb, Dani, and Lazo, Alex. *Real Estate v2.0.* (New York: Kaplan, 2007).

Business Victoria. (2008). "Identifying Business Opportunities." Retrieved May 24, 2008, from business.vic.gov.au/BUSVIC/STANDARD//pc=PC_50032.html.

Census Bureau Reports. (2004). "Stay at Home Parents Tops 5 Million." Retrieved from census.gov/Press-Release/www/releases/archives/families_house holds/003118.html.

Cohen, J. (2007). "Poor Customer Service Will Ruin Your Business." Retrieved from business.solveyourproblem.com/niche-marketing/improve_customer _service.shtml.

DeGaetano, G. (2008) "Attention Span: A Fundamental Human Requirement." Retrieved from the Parent Coaching Institute's website: thepci.com/articles /degaetano_AttentionSpan.htm.

Federal Bureau of Investigations. (2008). "Fraud Schemes." Retrieved from fbi.gov/majcases/fraud/fraudschemes.htm#nigerian.

FindLaw. (2008). "Top Ten Reasons to Contact an Attorney Before Choosing a Business Form." Retrieved May 25, 2008, from FindLaw for Small Business website: smallbusiness.findlaw.com/business-structures/business -structures-overview/business-structures-overview-attorney.html.

Fisher, A. (2007). "Commute to Work in 30 Seconds." *Fortune.* Retrieved from money.cnn.com/2007/08/06/news/economy/work.from.home.fortune/in dex.htm.

Innovisions Canada. (2003). "U.S. Telework Scene–Stats and Facts." Retrieved from ivc.ca/studies/us/index.htm.

Little, S. (2005). "Using 'Weak Signals' to Identify Opportunities." *Small Business Trends.* Retrieved May 24, 2008, from smallbiztrends.com /2005/05/using-weak-signals-to-identify.html.

Mays, R. (2008.) "Don't Blame the Scammers: The Real Deal on Telecommuting." Retrieved from homeparents.about.com/library/weekly/ucros2.htm.

Paulino, T. (2008). "8 Worst Company Domain Names Ever Created." Retrieved from marketme.com/2008/03/20/8-worst-company-domain-names-ever-created.html#more-105.

Prescott, R. (2006). "Don't Let Poor Customer Service Kill Your Business." Retrieved May 26, 2008, from promotethebusiness.com/Poor_Customer _Service_Your_Business.html.

Richtel, M. (1998). "Making Web Sites More Usable Is Former Sun Engineers Goal." *The New York Times* on the web. Retrieved from nytimes.com /library/tech /98/07/cyber/articles/13usability.html#1.

Sloan Consortium. (2007). "Five Years of Growth in Online Learning." Retrieved from sloan-c.org/publications/survey/index.asp.

Small Business Administration. (2008). "Opening Small Business Opportunities: Federal Government Contracting." Retrieved from sba.gov/services/contracting opportunities/index.html.

Spaeder, K. (2004). "Ten Ways to Grow Your Business: Looking to Take Your Business to the Next Level?" *Entrepreneur.com.* Retrieved May 24, 2008, from entrepreneur.com/management/growingyourbusiness/article70660.html.

Telecommute Connecticut! (2006). "National Survey Finds 11 Percent of Employees Telecommute." Retrieved from telecommutect.com/employers /employers_research1.php.

U.S. Department of Labor, Bureau of Labor Statistics. (2004). "Work at Home Statistics." Retrieved from bls.gov/news.release/homey.toc.htm.

U.S. Department of Labor, Bureau of Labor Statistics. (2007). "Bookkeeping, Accounting, and Auditing Clerks." Retrieved from bls.gov/oco/ocos144.htm.

BUSINESS AND FINANCIAL TERMS

There are many great glossaries online and many books that have nothing but glossaries for business owners. Here is a good list of terms specifically for business and financial planning for you to use as you work through your business plan and ultimately grow your business! Although this book focuses on the online business, financial and business terms are relevant to you, too.

More importantly, though, there is an outstanding glossary available to you online, with additional small-business resources to help you in your journey. The Small Business Taxes and Management website, at smbiz.com, provides lots of great information for business owners including practical tips, highlights on legislation, and lots of great tools for taxes and managing your business. I highly recommend you check it out.

The glossary information below is reprinted, with permission, from that site. The glossary is available at smbiz.com/sbgl001.html and smbiz.com/sbg l002.html—two more great pages on a fantastic site worth spending some time on! It includes many tax and financial terms as well that are often the most complicated for new or small-business owners to understand. Much thanks to Steve Hopfenmuller for his graciousness and for allowing our readers to benefit from his great work.

Another great resource is the Small Business Administration, which has its glossary at: sba.gov/smallbusinessplanner/plan/getready/serv_sbplanner_gready_glossory.html.

Accountant's opinion. If an independent certified public accountant is requested to audit a company's books, he will issue an opinion as to the condition of the financial statements. There are several degrees of opinion from clean to adverse. A clean opinion doesn't mean that every number is correct, only that the financials fairly represent the position of the company. An adverse opinion means the financials don't represent the position of the company. A disclaimer means the auditor can't (for any number of reasons) express an opinion on the statements.

Accounting controls. Methods and procedures intended to safeguard assets, authorize transactions, and ensure the accuracy of financial records.

Accounting equation. Simply stated, assets are equal to liabilities plus owner's equity.

Accounting method. Any number of approaches for calculating the income of an entity. Usually applied to the general means of recognizing income and expenses, e.g., cash or accrual. But it can also apply to the method of keeping inventories, etc.

Accounting procedure. Similar to accounting method, but applied to more routine issues. For example, the method of computing depreciation, handling small capital expenditures.

Accounting rate of return. A method of computing the profitability where the total cash inflow over the life of the project is reduced by expenses. This amount is divided by the estimated life of the project to arrive at an annual return. That's divided by the investment's cost. The result is an average rate of return. See *Discounted cash flow*.

Accounts payable. A liability arising when a vendor provides goods or services that are not immediately paid for and where the liability is not formalized in writing but backed by the reputation and credit worthiness of the debtor. When a business using the accrual basis of accounting purchases goods or services the company reports an expense and an account payable. When payment is made the account payable is reduced.

Accounts receivable. For accrual-basis businesses, transactions not paid in cash create an account receivable, an unsecured promise to pay in the future. The accounting entry is a debit to accounts receivable and a credit to sales. On payment, the account receivable is credited and cash is debited.

Accounts receivable financing. Financing where the company's accounts receivable are used as collateral. This type of financing is usually short-term in nature.

Accounts receivable turnover. Ratio obtained by dividing total credit sales by accounts receivable. The result indicates how many times the receivables have been collected during the period covered by the sales. It's a measure of how well the company is collecting its accounts receivable.

Accrual accounting. Under this method of accounting, income is recognized when earned, whether or not collected, and expenses are recognized when events have occurred that determine that a liability exists and the amount of the liability can be ascertained with reasonable accuracy. For example, on December 31 you ship a customer 100 widgets. You have to record the income in that year, even though you won't get paid until the following year. If you were buying the widgets, you could accrue the expense in the tax year you ordered them. There are some special rules for tax purposes and there can be a significant divergence between recognition of income and expenses for tax and financial accounting purposes.

Accrue. To record an item in the accounting books when using the accrual method of accounting. For example, you accrue income when the customer signs a contract, even though you won't receive any cash at that time. When you accrue an item of income or expense can depend on a number of factors, including the entity's procedures. IRS requirements here frequently diverge from accounting rules.

Accrued expense. An expense that has been incurred, but not yet paid in cash. Similar to accounts payable, but usually associated with non-trade vendors. For example, an electric bill.

Activity. For the passive activity rules, it's the integral economic unit for measuring a taxpayer's level of participation in a trade or business. One location can have more than one business activity. For example, you might have an S corporation that sells computers at retail and does typesetting out of the same location. The two may be separate activities. On the other hand, two or more related businesses can also be combined into one activity.

Additional paid-in capital. Equity contributions to a corporation in excess of the amount of capital stock. See *owner's equity*.

Add-on interest. Interest charged on the original principal of a loan, despite a reduction in principal by repayments. Also called *add-on rate*.

Adjusted basis. Used for determining depreciation and gain or loss on the disposition of an asset. Your adjusted basis in an asset is your beginning basis (see *Basis*), decreased by depreciation, depletion, or any Sec. 179 expense taken or increased by capital additions. For example, you purchase a machine for $10,000 (your basis) and take a Sec. 179 expense deduction of $1,000 and depreciation of $2,000 in the first year. At the end of the year your adjusted basis is $7,000. Note: Even professionals often say basis when they really mean adjusted basis.

Adjusted gross income. Also known as AGI, it's your individual income before personal exemptions or standard or itemized deductions. It's the total of wages, interest, dividends, capital gains (or up to $3,000 in losses), profit or loss from real estate or pass-through entities (e.g., S corporation), pension income and certain other items less contributions to an IRA or Keogh plan, one-half of any self-employment income, and health insurance for self-employed individuals, and certain other deductions.

Adjusted trial balance. A list of all the ledger accounts with their adjustments and the adjusted balances.

Adjusting entry. An entry made at the end of the period to assign expenses to the period for which they were incurred and revenue to the period in which it was earned. It is are also used to correct entries that could not be accurately made before the end of the year.

Administrative dissolution. The dissolution of a corporation by the secretary of state or similar state authority as a result of the corporation's failure to file corporate tax returns, file an annual report, maintain a registered agent, etc.

Administrative expense. Sometimes part of general expense, it's an expense that isn't directly associated with selling, manufacturing, distributing, etc. but part of overall management such as accounting, general management, etc.

Administrative services only. Where one party provides only administrative or clerical services to an employee benefit plan. (Typically the employer is the administrator.) Another party acts as the trustee.

Administrator. A person appointed by a court to settle the estate of a person who has died without a will (intestate). The term is *administratrix* if the person is a female. An administrator serves the same function as an executor.

Adverse opinion. Instead of an unqualified opinion, it's an opinion by a CPA that the financial statements do not represent fairly the results of the operations of the company and/or are not in conformity with generally accepted accounting principles (GAAP).

Affirmative covenant. A covenant on a bond, loan, or mortgage that requires the debtor to perform certain actions.

After-acquired clause. A clause in a mortgage or similar loan document that provides that any mortgageable property acquired after the mortgage is signed will be considered additional security for the loan.

After-tax real rate of return. A rate of return on an investment on an after-tax basis and adjusted for inflation.

Agency. A relationship between a principal and an agent who acts on behalf of the principal in a transaction with a third party.

Agent. A person or entity authorized to act on behalf of another party. While a person can act on his own, a corporation can only act through its agents.

Aggregation. The combination of several business operations into a larger unit. Primarily used to combine passive trade or business undertakings into one or more activities in order to determine whether a taxpayer is a material participant.

Aging of accounts receivable. A way to estimate bad debts by analyzing individual accounts receivable according to the length of time they have been outstanding. For example, outstanding accounts may be split into those 30 days or less outstanding, 60 days or less outstanding, etc. The analysis includes arriving at the balance for all the accounts in a group. (Also known as *aging schedule.* The result is referred to as *aged accounts receivable.*)

Allocation base. An approach for assigning a given cost to two or more departments of a business.

Allowance for doubtful accounts. An offset, or contra account, to accounts receivable to reflect the estimated collection losses on outstanding accounts receivable. The allowance reduces revenue. Such an allowance is generally not allowed for tax purposes. Also known as an allowance for bad debts and allowance for uncollectible accounts.

Annual percentage rate (APR). The effective interest rate required to be disclosed under the Truth in Lending Act.

Annuity. The dictionary definition is a contract issued by an insurance company that pays an annuitant an amount periodically for a certain time for the remainder of his life. Common usage has expanded that definition to the point where you must dig deeper to understand the meaning. Variations include a deferred annuity where you make payments into a fund over a period of years, known as a deferred annuity (where tax on the fund's income is deferred), an immediate annuity (the original definition), or many other plans where a series of payments, either into or out of the fund, are involved.

Appropriation of retained earnings. Restriction of retained earnings that is recorded by a formal journal entry. The restriction may be made voluntarily by the board of directors to show the earnings are being accumulated for a particular purpose or the restriction may be the result of a covenant in a loan agreement.

Articles of incorporation. Document to be filed in most states with the secretary of state or similar authority of a state by the founders of the corporation specifying such items as the name, location, nature of the business, capital investment, etc. The document is also known as a Certificate of Incorporation. The corporation only comes into existence when the filing is approved by the state.

Articles of organization. Similar to Articles of Incorporation, but the document filed with the secretary of state or similar authority of a state by the founders of a limited liability company (LLC). It is also known as *articles of formation*.

Assessments. The right to secure additional payments from partners or coventurers in a project.

Asset activity ratios. Ratios used to determine how effectively the business is managing the assets. Examples include inventory turnover and receivables turnover.

Asset-backed security. A security collateralized by assets such as receivables, inventory, installment contracts, loans (in the case of a lender), etc.

Asset-based financing. Loans or other financings where the creditors and any equity investors base their lending/investment decisions on the cash flow from the project or asset.

Average cost method. Inventory costing method based on the average cost of inventory during the period. Average cost is determined by dividing the cost of goods in inventory by the number of units of the same type in inventory at any point in time.

Bad debt expense. Generally, the cost of uncollectible accounts receivable, which occurs when customers to whom a business has extended credit fail to pay. It can also refer to any debt owed you which is uncollectible.

Balance sheet. Listing of the assets, liabilities, and owner's equity at a spcific point in time.

Basis. Used in determining depreciation or gain or loss on the sale of property. In the simplest situation, your basis in property you purchase is the cost. For example, you pay $1,000 for a machine–that's your basis. How you acquire the property determines your basis. For example, if you inherited the machine, your basis would be the fair market value at the decedent's death. In a simple tradein, your basis is equal to your adjusted basis in the equipment traded in plus any cash paid. If you contributed the property to a corporation, the corporation's basis would be the basis of the property in your hands. Your basis in the stock in an S corporation is your cost plus profits taxed to you less losses passed through and distributions. There are a number of other ways of arriving at basis. See *Adjusted basis.*

Basis point. A way of quoting the yield on a bond, note, or other debt instrument. One basis point is equal to 0.01 percent. Thus, a 50 basis point yield increase in a bond would be equal to 0.5 percent.

Beneficiary. A person entitled to the benefits of a trust, will, insurance policy, pension plan, etc. For example, if you name your daughter as the sole beneficiary of a life insurance policy, only she is entitled to the proceeds.

Blind pool. A partnership or syndication where the investments to be purchased are not specified at the time the investments are sold.

Book value of an asset. The asset's cost less accumulated depreciation.

Book value of stock. The book value of the assets of a company less the liabilities. Can be translated into book value per share by dividing by the number of shares outstanding.

Break-even point. The dollar amount or unit amount of sales where total revenue equals total expenses.

Business interruption insurance. A policy that pays a stipulated amount when the business cannot operate because of some insured peril. For example, a policy will pay a certain percentage of the business's earnings lost because of a fire.

Businessowner's program. An insurance policy designed for small offices or stores, covering the building and contents for full replacement cost as well as liability insurance.

Buy-sell agreement. An agreement between owners (shareholders or partners) of a business providing that surviving co-owners of the business will purchase the shares of a co-owner who dies. The agreement provides a formula for valuing the business on the date of death of the co-owner.

Bylaws. The rules governing the operation of an organization. In the case of a corporation, the bylaws are drawn up at the time, or shortly after incorporation. (Most stationery stores have standard forms which can be modified.)

Cancellable contract. A contract that may be cancelled at any time without penalty. Usually requires a certain amount of days' notice by the party cancelling before the contract is terminated.

Capital. Sometimes used as a synonym for the owner's equity in a business.

Capital budgeting. A formal plan for making investments in plant, equipment, other fixed assets, advertising projects, etc. Items included in the capital budget have lives in excess of one year and often require long-range planning.

Capital expenditure. The purchase of or outlay for an asset with a life of more than a year, or one that increases the capacity or efficiency of an asset or extends its useful life. Generally, such expenditures cannot be deducted currently for tax purposes (or expensed for financial accounting purposes). Instead, they must be depreciated or amortized over their useful life.

Capital gain (or loss). A category of gain or loss under the tax law resulting from the sale or other disposition of specified property such as stock or bond investments, real estate, etc. It does not include property used in a trade or business. However, special rules apply in such situations that can result in similar treatment for business property.

Capitalization rate. The rate of interest used to discount the future income from a property to arrive at a present value.

Cash balance plan. A cash balance plan is an employer-sponsored retirement plan that has some characteristics of both defined benefit and defined contribution (DC) plans. The employer credits each employee with a specific percentage of pay each year and applies interest to these amounts at a rate of interest that the employer chooses. The benefit is therefore defined as an "account balance," as in a DC plan. A cash balance plan differs from a DC plan, however, in that the employer retains control of the funds held by the plan and chooses how to invest these funds. The account balance in a cash balance plan is merely an accounting of the employee's accrued benefit under the plan. It is not an individual account owned by the employee. Because the employee is required to receive a benefit that is no less than the amount of pay credits and interest credits that have been applied to his or her "account," cash balance plans are legally defined benefit plans and are insured by the Pension Benefit Guaranty Corporation.

Cash-on-cash return. Usually reserved for real estate income properties, it's the annual cash flow from the property divided by your cash investment. Sometimes called *return on equity* or *equity dividend rate*. It's a quick and dirty way to evaluate an investment.

Claims-occurrence basis. With this type of insurance policy the insurer is responsible for claims from events that occurred during the time the policy was in force. It makes no difference when the claim is filed.

Example–A customer slips on a wet floor in your store in March 1997. You're covered by Madison Insurance. The customer doesn't file a claim until a year later when you're covered under a new company, Chatham. Under a claims-occurrence basis policy you'd report the claim to Madison, the insurer at the time the accident occurred. Under a claims-made basis you'd report the claim to Chatham, the insurer at the time the claim is filed.

Closely-held corporation. A corporation with five or fewer shareholders who own more than 50 percent in value of the stock at any one time during the year. Note, this is the IRS definition. In common usage the definition can be broader.

CLUE report. The full term is Comprehensive Loss Underwriting Exchange report. It contains any insurance claims on real property, the insurance company involved, the type of claim, whether or not it was related to a catastrophe, the cause of the loss, and the amount paid for the previous five years. The report is often consulted by insurance companies before issuing a policy. The report can only be requested by the owner or an insurer. However, a buyer should ask the owner for a copy before going to contract.

Collateralization. To pledge mortgages, bonds, accounts receivable, or other marketable properties as security for a loan.

Coinsurance amount limit. A requirement under burglary insurance that a minimum amount of insurance be maintained, based on the type and amount of merchandise.

Coinsurance clause. In the case of a partial loss where the property is not insured for the indicated percentage of its cash value at the time of the loss, the recovery from the company is based on a percentage.

Example–Your insurance policy contains a coinsurance clause of 80 percent. Your building sustained $100,000 in damages. The actual cash value of the property at the time of the loss was $500,000, but you only carried $300,000 of insurance. Based on the coinsurance clause, you should have had coverage of $400,000 (80 percent of $500,000). You can't recover the full $100,000 in damages. Instead, your recovery is limited by the percentage of your coverage ($300,000/$400,000) times the loss, or $75,000. If you had coverage of $400,000, your insurance would have reimbursed you for the full $100,000 loss.

Commercial paper. Short-term (generally 2 to 270 days) obligations (notes) issued by banks and corporations with high credit ratings. These notes are usually unsecured and usually issued at a discount.

Common control. In tax parlance, the situation where a group of five or fewer persons own more than 50 percent of an undertaking and therefore have the ability (whether or not it is exercised) to direct operations.

Consequential losses. Indirect losses from an event.

Constructive total loss. A partial loss where the cost of repairing the damage is greater than the value of the property after restoration.

Contingent business interruption insurance. An insurance policy that provides benefits if your earnings are reduced because of damages to another business on which yours is dependent.

Convertible term. Term life insurance which is convertible into whole life without showing insurability.

Conversion costs. The costs required to convert raw materials into finished product, including direct labor and overhead.

Cost method. An appraisal method that values a property based on the cost to reproduce it today. That amount is usually adjusted for depreciation.

Example—Madison owns a 15-year-old factory building. The cost to reproduce the building today would be $900,000. The appraiser adjusts that figure downward for wear and tear and, possibly, the cost to upgrade electric service.

Covenants. Promises included in an agreement to perform or not to perform certain acts. For example, a loan may contain a covenant that the borrower's debt-to-equity ratio cannot exceed 2 to 1.

Credit enhancements. Using third-party guarantees such as a cosigner, the pledging of assets, an insurance company bond, or a letter of credit to provide additional security for a loan.

Debt instrument. A generic term representing any written promise to repay the debt.

Debt service. The cash required to pay the interest and principal due (usually during one year) on outstanding debt.

Debt-to-equity ratio. Total liabilities divided by total shareholders' equity. This is a measure of the cushion available to creditors should the firm be forced to liquidate. The ratio is sometimes calculated by dividing total long-term debt by shareholders' equity.

Default. The failure of a debtor to comply with a provision of a bond indenture or loan agreement (commonly known as a technical default) or to make timely payment of interest or principal when due.

Defeasance. In corporate finance it is generally the discharge of old, low-rate debt without repayment prior to maturity. The corporation replaces it with newly issued securities with a lower face value by paying higher interest or having a higher market value. The technique can result in tax and balance sheet advantages.

Deferred charge. An expenditure carried as an asset until the amount represents a true expense for the period. For example, if a one-year insurance premium is paid three months before the end of the fiscal year, three months of the premium would be an expense in the year paid, nine months would be an expense of the following year. Thus, 9/12 of the premium would be a deferred charge. In this case it would be represented by an account called prepaid insurance. Deferred income is the opposite situation. For example, six months' rent received in advance. Any amount not properly credited to the current period would represent a liability.

Deferred interest bond. A bond where interest payments are not made currently, but at a later date. Similar to a zero coupon bond, which pays "interest" and principal at maturity. The interest, in effect, is compounded and paid at maturity. Market prices for such bonds are much more volatile than bonds which pay interest currently.

Defined benefit plan. A defined benefit (DB) plan is an employer-sponsored retirement plan in which employee benefits are based on factors such as length of service and average salary. Benefits in a DB plan are prefunded and pension assets are held in a trust fund under the control of the employer. By law, DB plans must offer benefits in the form of an annuity, although they also may offer optional forms of payment, such as a lump-sum distribution. In a DB plan, the employer bears the investment risk. If the pension trust is not adequately funded to pay the benefits promised, the employer may be required to contribute more money to the plan. Defined benefit plans are insured by the Pension Benefit Guaranty Corporation.

Defined contribution plan. A defined contribution (DC) plan is an employer-sponsored retirement plan in which the employer contributes a specific dollar amount or percentage of pay into a retirement account for the employee. In some DC plans, such as Sec. 401(k) plans, the employee also defers some of his or her salary into the account. In participant-directed plans, the employee controls how the money in the retirement account is invested. In a DC plan, the employee bears the investment risk. The benefit under the plan is whatever amount is held in the retirement account, which depends on the amounts contributed and investment gains and losses. Defined contribution plans are not insured by the Pension Benefit Guaranty Corporation.

Demand deposit. The technical name for a checking account or any other type of account where the funds can be withdrawn without prior notice.

Demand loan. A loan with no set maturity date. The loan is payable whenever the lender chooses to call it.

Direct costing. Also known as variable costing, a method of calculating costs that involves only raw materials, direct labor, and variable overhead.

Direct costs. Costs directly related to conversion of raw materials into product. Includes raw materials, direct labor, and variable overhead.

Direct overhead. Costs directly associated with the manufacture of goods. That could include factory lighting, rent, insurance. Indirect overhead could include office expenses, R&D, lighting, etc.

Direct placement. Also known as a private placement, the sale of securities directly to one or more professional investors or institutions, frequently insurance companies. The sale of securities in this fashion avoids many of the fees typically associated with public offerings.

Disappearing deductible. An insurance policy where losses below a certain amount are excluded. Those above a certain amount are paid in full and those in between are paid at a multiple of the loss.

Discontinued investigation. For IRS purposes, a subject investigation that resulted in a determination that there was no prosecution potential.

Discount. This term can have a number of meanings, depending on the context. When used in connection with a loan, it's where the bank deducts its interest payment before giving the loan proceeds to the borrower. For example, where $100 is borrowed at 10 percent for one year, the borrower receives only $90. For bonds, it's the difference between the current market price and the face amount of the bond.

Discounted cash flow. The application of a factor, based on the cost of the firm's capital or prevailing interest rates (with a possible adjustment for risk), to the cash inflows and outflows from a project or investment. Also called net present value analysis.

Disintermediation. When individuals (or other entities) take money out of savings accounts and put the funds in money market accounts.

Distress termination. The sponsor of a defined benefit plan that does not have enough money to pay the full benefits it owes to participants and beneficiaries may terminate the plan if the sponsor is financially distressed and unable to fund the plan. The PBGC will then take over the plan as trustee and use its own assets and any remaining assets in the plan to pay pension benefits to current and future retirees within the legal limits.

Dividend exclusion. Regular (not S) corporations can exclude from income 70 percent of dividends received. If the corporation owns 20 percent or more of the stock of the other corporation, it can exclude 80 percent. A 100 percent exclusion is provided for 80 percent plus owned corporations.

Dividend payout ratio. The ratio of the annual dividend to the earnings of a company. Stable, mature companies (such as utilities) typically have a high payout ratio.

Due diligence. The thorough investigation of a potential acquisition candidate, real estate investment, etc. Often used to refer to the investigation of a company for an initial public offering.

Due-on-sale. A clause in a mortgage that stipulates any balance remaining on a mortgage is due when the underlying property is sold.

Earnings form. Business interruption insurance where the payment is a specified amount only when the loss is caused by an insured peril.

Electronic crimes program. An IRS program established to provide guidance and resources in securing, documenting, processing, maintaining, and presenting digital evidence in support of IRS criminal investigations.

Electronic fraud detection system. The primary computer system used by the IRS that enhances its ability to identify and stop fraudulent filings.

Embezzlement. Theft or use of money or property by an individual in whose care the money or property had been entrusted.

Endangered status. Under the Pension Protection Act, a multiemployer plan is considered to be endangered if it is less than 80 percent funded or if the plan is projected to have a funding deficiency within seven years. A plan that is less than 80 percent funded and is projected to have a funding deficiency within seven years is considered to be seriously endangered.

Endorsement. A written agreement modifying a standard insurance policy to meet certain conditions or to complete a policy.

Entity. A partnership, corporation, LLC, S corporation, trust, estate, or joint venture of any kind recognized for tax purposes.

Excess liability insurance. A policy that covers losses that exceed those covered under another policy. For example, your regular policy covers losses up to $300,000. You purchase an excess liability policy that covers losses from $300,000 to $2,000,000. In effect, an excess liability policy is one with a very high deductible. Also known as an *umbrella policy.*

Extra risk. An insured that does not fall within the standard risk range. Insurance can only be obtained for a higher than normal premium or with less coverage.

Fair market value. The price at which an item can be sold by a willing seller to a willing buyer, neither of which is under any pressure to buy or sell. Furthermore, it's assumed that both parties are dealing rationally, have knowledge of relevant facts, and are not related.

Fixed costs. Costs that do not vary with the number of units produced. For example, depreciation. In the long run all costs are variable and some costs have both a fixed and variable component.

Fixed price contract. A contract which provides for a firm price.

Flow-through entity. An entity where the income, losses, and certain other items of income and deduction are passed through to the owners. For example, partnerships, trusts, and S corporations.

Forward supply contract. A contract for future supply of definite quantities of goods or services over a fixed period.

Free and clear. In real estate the term is used to indicate that the investment analysis has ignored any debt on the property. (Debt can distort the analysis by increasing the return if the interest rate is lower than the rate of return on property and vice versa if the interest rate is higher.)

Full absorption costing. Method of computing costs that starts with direct costs (materials, direct labor, variable overhead) but adds non-variable overhead.

Full costs. All costs including direct costs and general and administrative expenses as well as selling expenses.

Garage liability insurance. A policy for businesses that work with autos. The policies provide coverage for operations in progress and completed operations as well as the premises.

General crime exclusions. Refers to perils in an insurance policy that are excluded because they are usually covered under another type of policy.

Gross lease. As opposed to a *net lease*, a gross lease is one where the tenant is responsible for either none of the increase in operating expenses of the building, or only the amount above a stop. If a *base* or *stop* is involved, the lease is sometimes known as a *modified gross lease.*

Hard costs. The direct costs of acquiring a business (such as the purchase price), constructing a building (brick and mortar), etc., as opposed to legal, accounting, consulting, and financing costs, which are called *soft costs.*

Hedged position. A hedged position occurs if you own a second asset that should move in the opposite way the first asset would react to changes in the market. For example, you own a stock and a put option and/or a call on the stock.

Hold harmless. An agreement where one party agrees to release another party from any legal liability that may occur as the result of a specific event.

Holdback. The portion of a loan not paid out to the borrower until a certain requirement is completed. For example, a lender may release 10 percent of the total amount of a loan on completion of the foundation, an additional 15 percent when rough plumbing is in, etc.

Illegal source financial crimes. Crimes involving illegally earned income, such as money laundering.

Immediate notice. In insurance parlance, a clause requiring the insured to provide notice to the insurer (or a representative) as soon as reasonably possible following a loss.

Implied warranty. A warranty that is assumed to be part of a contract despite the fact that it is not expressly stated.

Imprest funds. Funds set aside as a cash reserve for expenditures expressly designated. Also, a petty cash fund.

In-the-money. For options, if exercising the option will result in a gain, the option is in-the-money. For a call option, it is in-the-money if the market price of the stock is greater than the exercise price. A put option is in-the-money if the market price of the stock is less than the exercise price.

Indirect costs. Costs that can't be directly related to the cost objective or a product.

Intangible asset. An asset that is a right and nonphysical, as opposed to equipment, buildings, etc., which are tangible assets. Examples include copyrights, patents, trademarks, goodwill, capitalized advertising costs, computer software, leases, licenses, etc.

Intangible costs. Expenditures incurred to create an intangible asset. For example, legal fees to negotiate a lease, the cost to acquire a license, etc.

Integrated operations. Two or more business operations which are conducted as though they were one single economic unit.

Interest-only loan. A loan where the borrower pays only interest and not principal during the course of the loan. Some loans have an interest-only period, then require payment of interest and principal. The total amount borrowed is payable as a balloon payment at maturity. Sometimes referred to as a *bullet loan*.

Interim financing. Short-term financing that's conditional upon securing intermediate or long-term financing. Also known as a *bridge loan*.

Interim statement. A financial report that covers only a part of the company's year. Often used to refer to a quarterly financial statement.

Joint-and-last survivor annuity. A type of annuity where income is payable during the lifetimes of two or more annuitants and continues until the death of the last survivor.

Joint-and-last-survivorship option. When paying out the proceeds of an insurance policy, payments continue until the death of the last survivor of two persons.

K-1. The information form from a partnership, S corporation, trust, or estate, which provides the flow-through income and losses to be reported on an investor's individual return.

Kicker. An additional benefit a lender or investor receives as an inducement to make the loan or investment. For example, a lender may receive an equity kicker allowing him to receive a share of the income from the property if it exceeds a specified amount or giving the lender warrants to purchase shares of stock in the investment at a price below market value.

Latent defect. A defect which could not be discovered by ordinary and reasonable inspection.

Legal source tax crimes. Crimes involving legal industries and occupations and legally earned income.

Lessee. A party who rents property from another under a lease.

Lessor. A party who owns property and leases it to a tenant.

Level premium plan. Premiums due on an insurance policy that remain level throughout the term, regardless of any dividends that may be paid.

Leverage. 1) Financial leverage is the act of increasing the return on an investment by borrowing some of the funds at an interest rate less than your return on the project. 2) Operating leverage has the same objective, but you increase your return by increasing cheaper fixed costs. Leverage can be positive or negative. If the return on an investment is greater than the cost of borrowing, leverage is positive. If the return is less, leverage is negative.

Lien. A type of encumbrance that makes designated property security for a debt or for an obligation. For example, a mortgage or a tax judgment.

Life income period-certain annuity. The annuitant is guaranteed payments for the rest of his life, but should he die before a certain time, there is a payout based on a minimum number of payments.

Limited liability company. An entity created under state law that is taxed like a partnership (i.e., income and losses are passed through to the partners), but where the liability of the owners is limited to their investment in the company. That is, they can't be held personally liable for the debts of the company.

Limit of liability. When an insured is covered by more than one policy for a loss, each insurer pays according to a predetermined formula.

Limited partner. An investor in a partnership whose personal liability is limited. Such investors are generally considered passive for income tax purposes.

Limited-pay life. Premiums on a life insurance policy that are payable for a stated period or until the insured reaches a certain age.

Liquidated damages. A specific sum of money, set as part of a contract, to be paid by one party to the other if the first should default on the contract.

Liquidity premium. The part of an interest rate or other return that is intended to cover the fact that the investment is illiquid.

Liquidity risk. The risk that a party will not have enough cash to meet its obligations as they come due.

Loan commitment. An agreement by a lender to make a loan in the future if all the conditions in the agreement are satisfied.

Loan-to-value ratio. The percentage a lending institution will loan to the appraised value of a property. For example, if the property is appraised for $100,000 and a bank will loan only $70,000, the loan-to-value ratio is 70 percent.

Long bond. A bond that matures in more than ten years.

Long position. In stocks, bonds, etc. it means you own the stock, bond, option, etc. Often just referred to as simply *long*.

Lost instrument bond. A bond that guarantees that the owner of a lost stock, bond, etc. certificate or other financial instrument will hold the firm harmless against loss if it will issue a replacement certificate.

Lowest responsible bidder. The bidder who is awarded a contract because his bid is lower than any of the other bidders whose reputation, past performance, and business and financial capabilities are acceptable.

Lump sum. A price for a group of goods or services where there is no breakdown of price for the various items.

Manufacturer's output policy. An insurance policy that covers the loss of property owned by a manufacturer but located off the premises.

Manufacturing costs. All costs necessary to manufacture the product.

Market-value clause. A clause in an insurance policy that allows for the settlement of a claim based on the market value rather than the actual cash value.

Material participation. Regular, substantial, and continuous involvement in a business on the part of either the taxpayer and/or spouse. Allows losses from trades or businesses to be deducted without limitation under the passive loss rules. Applies to S corporations and partnerships.

Maturity date. The date on which a loan, mortgage, bond, etc. is due and any outstanding principal must be paid.

Mechanic's lien. A claim in favor of mechanics, contractors, laborers, or material suppliers against a building or other structure. The lien can only be filed by persons who worked on the building or supplied materials.

Modified adjusted gross income. Your AGI (adjusted gross income) computed without considering any passive activity loss, IRA or SEP plans, taxable social security, or the deduction for one-half of the self-employment tax.

Multiemployer plan. A multiemployer plan is a collectively bargained plan maintained by more than one employer, usually within the same or related industries, and a labor union. These plans also are sometimes referred to as *Taft-Hartley plans,* after the Taft-Hartley Act of 1947 (P.L. 80-101).

Named nonowner. A policy designed to protect nonowners who drive an uninsured vehicle.

Name schedule bond. A fidelity bond that covers only the persons listed.

Negative amortization. A situation where the outstanding principal on a loan increases because debt service payments are insufficient to cover even all the interest, and the unpaid interest is added to the principal amount.

Negative assurance. A report by a CPA stating, based on certain limited procedures, that nothing has come to the attention of the accountant that would indicate the financial information in certain statements is not presented fairly.

Net assets. Simply the excess of assets over liabilities of an entity.

Net capitalized cost. In leasing, it's the price of the vehicle after deducting manufacturer's discounts, dealer participation allowances, and cap cost reduction (down payment) from the manufacturer's suggested retail price.

Net lease property. Property where the tenant or lessee pays most, if not all, of the expenses. The tenant may pay the expenses directly, or reimburse the landlord. If the tenant is responsible for all the expenses, the lease is often called *triple net* or *NNN.* For tax purposes, a net lease is where the deductions allowed solely by reason of IRC Sec. 162 (general business expenses) are less than 15 percent of gross rents from that property *or* property where the lessor is either guaranteed a specific return or is protected in whole or part against loss of income. Deductions allowed solely by reason of Sec. 162 are deductions other than interest, taxes, and depreciation.

Net operating income. In real estate parlance, it's gross income less operating expenses but before items such as debt service, brokerage commissions, tenant improvements, and other *capital* items.

Net sales. Sales based on the gross invoice amount less returns, allowances, discounts, and any other adjustments.

Nonpassive activity. A trade or business in which the taxpayer materially participates, that is, on a regular, continuous, and substantial basis. Losses can be deducted without limitation as to the passive loss rules. Income cannot be offset by passive losses, except those passive losses remaining after disposition of a passive activity.

Nonprobate property. Property owned by a decedent or in which the decedent had an interest on the date of his or her death which passes to an heir by provisions other than a will or the laws of intestacy. That can include assets held jointly or by a trust, life insurance not payable to the estate, etc.

Nonqualified retirement plan. Nonqualified plans are designed to provide benefits to company owners, executives, and highly compensated employees. Unlike qualified plans, nonqualified plans are not required to cover rank-and-file employees, and neither the amount that can be contributed to the plan nor the amount of benefits that they can pay are limited by law. Because nonqualified plans are not required to meet the standards set in law for qualified plans, they do not receive the preferential tax treatment that is accorded to qualified plans. Moreover, any assets that are set aside to pre-fund benefits under a nonqualified plan are subject to the claims of the plan sponsor's creditors in the event that the plan sponsor enters bankruptcy.

Office personal property form. An insurance policy that covers all risks related to occupancy of an office for physical damage.

Open-end contract. A contract in which the quantity and/or duration is not specified.

Open-end lease. A lease in which the lessee assumes the risk for depreciation at the end of the lease. That is, if the equipment is worth less at the end of the lease than the residual value set at the beginning of the lease, the lessee must pay the difference.

Opportunity cost. The cost of not doing something. For example, if your business has excess cash and uses it to purchase an item of equipment, the opportunity cost is the interest you would have earned had that money been earning interest in say, a money market account.

Option. The right to buy (or sell) or lease a property at a certain price for a limited period of time. For example, you pay $2,000 for a option to purchase 20 acres of land for $200,000. The option expires in one year. Depending on the terms, you may or may not be able to sell the option.

Option premium. The amount paid for an option.

Out-of-the-money. In options, it means the current exercise of the option would produce a loss. Thus, a call option is out-of-the-money if the current price of the asset is less than the exercise price; a put option is out-of-the-money if the current price of the asset is more than the exercise price.

Overhead costs. Costs related to manufacturing that are not direct costs (i.e., materials, direct labor, and variable overhead). Overhead costs include fixed, variable, and semivariable costs.

Owner's equity. The amount of an owner's interest in an entity that is at-risk should the company become bankrupt. In the case of a corporation, it consists of capital stock, additional paid-in capital, and retained earnings. Capital stock may be par value or no par value. If par value, the total capital stock is equal to the number of shares outstanding times the par value. Additional paid-in capital is additional amounts paid for the stock over and above the par value. Retained earnings come from the net profits of the corporation. Profits increase retained earnings; losses and distributions decrease them.

Example—Madison Inc. issues 200 shares of its common stock to Fred Flood for $60 per share, for a total of $12,000. Madison's common stock has a par value of $0.50. On the balance sheet the transaction would be recorded as capital stock of $100 (200 shares times $0.50 par value), and additional paid-in capital of $11,900 (the difference between the amount received for the stock and the par value).

Assume further that Susan Newly buys 200 shares the following week for $70 per share ($14,000 total). The capital stock amount is the same ($100), but now the paid-in capital amount is increased by $13,900.

Participation. Where two or more lenders share in a mortgage loan. Often used on large loans to spread the risk.

Passive income. Income from a passive activity. In other words, income from rentals or businesses in which you do not materially participate.

Passive loss. Loss from a passive activity, that is, rental or trade or business in which you do not materially participate.

Payback period. The length of time it will take for an investor to recoup his cash outlay. Often used as a quick way to analyze an investment, usually in personal property. For example, a new machine will cost you $10,000. It will generate income before depreciation of $3,000 the first year; $4,000 the second year; and $3,000 the third year. The payback period is 3 years.

Period costs. Expenses related to a particular accounting period.

Performance bond. A contract of guarantee by a successful bidder to protect the buyer from loss due to the bidder's inability to complete the contract as agreed.

Personal property replacement cost endorsement. A provision in an insurance policy that changes the recovery from an actual cash value basis to a replacement cost basis.

Placed in service. Strictly a tax term. You can only start depreciating property (or take a Sec. 179 expense election) when the property is "placed in service." That means when the property is available for use in its assigned function. For example, you purchase a machine in 2006 and it's not delivered until 2007. Even though you may have paid for the machine in 2006, you can't begin depreciation until 2007. Similarly, if the machine is delivered in 2006, but the technicians didn't arrive to install and test the machine until 2007, you can't begin depreciation until 2007.

Prepayment privilege. The right to prepay a mortgage without penalty.

Price at the time of delivery. A term used in sales contracts when market prices are so volatile that a vendor will not give a firm price or use an escalator clause but will only agree to charge the price charged other customers for similar purchases on the day he ships or delivers the goods.

Price protection. An agreement by a vendor with a purchaser to grant the purchaser any reduction in price which the seller may establish prior to, or within a certain time after, shipping of the purchaser's order.

Prime costs. Direct labor and material costs.

Private letter ruling. These are written pronouncements from the IRS interpreting the Internal Revenue Code with respect to a specific set of facts and circumstances. Letter rulings arise from a taxpayer's request to interpret the law, usually before engaging in a transaction. For example, when two corporations decide to merge, they typically request a letter ruling to insure the transaction will be tax free. The ruling applies only to the taxpayer requesting it and cannot be cited as precedent. However, letter rulings often give important insight into the way the IRS would rule under similar circumstances. Despite the filing fee and legal costs involved in obtaining a ruling, if the tax consequences are substantial, a ruling is often advisable.

Private limited partnership. A partnership that does not have to be registered with the SEC, but can have no more than 35 accredited partners.

Private placement. Also known as a *private offering,* the sale of an investment or business to a small group of accredited investors that conforms to certain exemptions from registration with the SEC.

Pro forma. Generally, financial information that reflects a hypothetical or projected transaction. For example, reconstructing a balance sheet or income statement to reflect the effects of a loan. (The loan will increase assets and liabilities and interest expense.) Also used to describe projected financial statements in general.

Pro rata liability clause. When more than one insurance company covers a property, the clause provides a formula for sharing liability among the companies.

Publicly traded partnership. A partnership whose interests are traded on an established securities market or are readily tradable on a secondary market.

Quick assets. Consists of cash and assets that are readily convertible into cash. That includes marketable securities, accounts receivable, etc. Another definition is current assets less inventory.

Quick ratio. Also called the acid-test ratio, it's equal to the sum of cash, short-term investments and net current receivables divided by current liabilities. It's a measure of whether or not the business could pay all its current liabilities if they came due immediately.

Rate of return on assets. In real estate parlance, the net operating income from a property divided by the price of the property.

Recharacterization rules. Generally, rules which reclassify passive income as non-passive. This type of income should not be reported on Form 8582 and cannot be offset by passive activity losses except those passive losses remaining after disposition of a passive activity.

Reformation. The act of changing the terms of a contract to meet the original intentions of the parties.

Release price. The amount that must be repaid on a development loan when a property under a blanket mortgage is sold.

Renewable and convertible term. Term life insurance that is both renewable for an additional period without evidence of insurability and convertible into a permanent or whole life policy. A policy may contain one or both clauses.

Replacement cost. The cost of replacing a property with one having similar amenities and functionality, but not identical improvements.

Reproduction cost. The cost of reproducing the improvements on a property so as to duplicate the original property.

Residual value. The value at the end of a term. In leasing, it's the value, either fair market value or some stated value, at the end of the lease. In finance and accounting, it's the fair market value at the end of the equipment's design or economic life or life in the business.

Revenue ruling. This is an official IRS interpretation of the Internal Revenue Code or Regulations on a specific issue. The ruling may have been prompted by a Technical Advice Memorandum, taxpayer request, court decision, etc. As opposed to a private letter ruling, a revenue ruling usually has broader implications and can be cited by the IRS or taxpayers as precedent. Revenue rulings carry less weight than IRS regulations.

Revocable beneficiary. In the case of an insurance policy, the policyholder, in the case of a trust, the grantor; has the right to change the beneficiary at any time.

Risk transfer. The shifting of risk from one party to another. The purchase of insurance is one example of transferring risk. Since there is an opportunity for tax evasion in risk transfer, the IRS may scrutinize such transactions.

Roll down. The act of moving from one option position to one with a lower exercise price.

Roll forward. The act of moving from one option position to one with a later expiration date.

Roll up. The act of moving from one option position to one with a higher exercise price.

Round trip trade. The purchase and sale of a stock, commodity, etc. in a very short period of time.

Rule of 72. Formula for determining the time it will take for your money to double for a certain compound interest rate. Divide 72 by the interest rate in percent; the result is the number of years. For example, 72 divided by 10 percent equals 7.2. The actual number of years it will take your money to double at 10 percent is about 7.28 years.

S corporation. A corporation that is not taxed as a separate entity. Instead, the income, losses, credits, etc. are passed through to the shareholders.

Sale-leaseback. A transaction where the owner of a property sells it to another party but retains occupancy by immediately leasing it back from the buyer. Frequently a way of raising cash or getting rid of an unwanted property.

Sandwich lease. Where a tenant subleases part or all of his space to other tenants.

Seed money. The initial contribution by a venture capitalist or angel for financing a start-up business. It can be equity capital, but is usually a loan or convertible debt.

Segment margin. The profitability of a specific portion of the business rather than the business as a whole. The segment can be a product line, division, geographic area, group of stores, etc. The accuracy of the measure depends importantly on how operating expenses are traced to that segment.

Segregation of duties. The concept of separating the duties and responsibilities of employees so as to ensure no individual can both perpetrate and hide irregularities. For example, the same person who posts receipts should not be in control of depositing funds; a person who has control over writing checks should not be assigned to reconciling the checkbook.

Self-directed IRA. An IRA account that is actively managed by the owner. The owner designates a custodian to consummate the transactions.

Semivariable costs. Expenses that have both a fixed and variable component.

Senior refunding. The substitution of a loan maturing in 5 to 12 years with a loan maturing in 15 or more years. Often used to consolidate multiple loans or to extend the maturity date.

Sensitivity analysis. An approach to taking into account risk by calculating the changes in potential returns if the original assumptions change. For example, by using your best estimates for costs and revenue you compute that a new machine will provide you with 18 percent return. If revenues are 10 percent lower, the return will be 14 percent.

Settlement options. Different ways of taking the proceeds from a life insurance policy. For example, rather than receiving the proceeds in a lump sum, the beneficiary can request the insurer to pay the amount out over several years. Interest is added to the principal to reflect the delayed payout.

Short. An investor is said to be short if he has sold stock that he does not own, that is, he has sold stock he borrowed from his broker. In the case of an option, the seller or writer has a short position if he has sold the option short.

Significant participation activity. A business in which you participate more than 100 hours without materially participating. If the total hours of participation in your significant participation activities (SPA) exceed 500, the total net income from SPAs is treated as nonpassive.

Simple interest. Interest that is computed solely on the principal balance, ignoring previously accrued interest not paid.

Soft money loan. Financing, often by the seller of a property, where only credit, not cash, is provided.

Specific coverage. An insurance policy or endorsement where coverage is limited to the property specified in the contract.

Specific performance. An action to compel a party to carry out the terms of the contract. In real estate transactions that usually requires the seller to deliver the property since land is considered unique and no other remedy would sufficiently compensate the buyer.

Specified perils contract. An insurance policy on real or personal property where only coverage is limited to the enumerated perils. For example, flood insurance covers only floods, no other peril.

Spendthrift clause. A clause in a trust, insurance policy, etc. that guards the assets against unwise use by the beneficiary. In some cases the assets cannot be attached by creditors. Often used by parents to provide for children who might otherwise waste the assets or pledge them.

Standby loan. A commitment by a lender to make a loan on specified terms. Generally, neither the potential borrower nor lender anticipates the loan will be taken down. Instead, it's anticipated it will be replaced by a permanent loan.

Straddle. Any of a number of possible investment positions where the investor owns both a put and a call or protection from a drop in the market and a rise in the market. The put and call would have both the same exercise price and the same expiration date. An investor is long in a straddle if he buys a put and a call; he is short a straddle if he writes a put and a call.

Straight deductible. In an insurance contract, a constant amount or percentage of value which the insured bears on every loss.

Straight-line depreciation. Depreciation (also applies to amortization) where the amount for each period is equal. For example, annual depreciation on a $12,000 asset with a ten-year life would be $1,200 per year.

Subordination clause. In real estate lending, a clause in a mortgage that allows it to become junior to subsequent liens.

Substantial part of an activity. An identifiable piece or unit of a larger activity, such as a separate division or branch, or a separate product line of a business with several lines or divisions. Generally used in connection with the passive activity loss rules.

Subvented lease. A special lease provided by vehicle or equipment manufacturers that make it more attractive than a lease offered through regular sources. In essence, the lease is subsidized by the manufacturer.

Suspended losses. Passive losses that are carried forward indefinitely until the taxpayer has passive income or there is an entire disposition of the activity. Also called carryover or carryforward losses.

Tangible asset. A physical asset such as equipment, buildings, etc. rather than an *intangible asset.*

Target normal cost. Under the Pension Protection Act, a defined benefit plan's target normal cost for a year is the present value of benefits expected to be accrued in the current year, including benefits that are attributable to increases in compensation.

Tax deferred. A term that indicates no tax is currently due on the transaction or income received. Instead, tax is due at a later date when the transaction is closed. Earnings in an IRA account are tax deferred until you retire and the income is distributed to you. A tradein is a tax-deferred transaction. You report no gain until you sell the property received in the tradein.

Technical advice memorandum. This is written advice issued by the IRS national office at the request of an IRS district office or Appeals Office on a technical or procedural question, usually arising during the audit of a taxpayer's return or a claim for refund. Like private letter rulings these are reported to the public, but are not official IRS pronouncements. Thus, they cannot be cited as precedent.

Tenancy at will. The occupancy of property at the will of the owner. The agreement may be written or oral, but the tenant may leave at any time without liability and the owner can evict the tenant at any time.

Term. The life of a contract, agreement, loan, etc.

Term contracting. A technique in which a source of supply is established for a specified period of time. The contract often has an estimated or minimum quantity.

Term insurance. Life insurance that is issued for one or more years specified in the contract. As opposed to whole life, the policy does not build any cash value.

Tiered entities. Partnerships or trusts or S corporations invested in other partnerships or trusts or S corporations.

Treasury inflation protection securities (TIPS). These are treasury bonds where the principal is indexed to the CPI. The total yield is made up of current interest payments and semi-annual CPI adjustments to principal. While only the interest is paid, both portions are taxable. Because of the CPI adjustment, the interest rate is relatively low.

Trial balance. A list of all the ledger accounts with their balances at any point in time.

Vacancy and collection loss. The reduction in potential gross income from vacancies and bad debts in real property. For example, a building has 50,000 square feet of space that should rent for $10 per square foot. The gross potential rent is $500,000 per year. However, vacancy and collection losses are projected to reduce that by $40,000 to $460,000 annually.

Valuable papers insurance. Insurance that provides coverage for the destruction or loss of papers that have intrinsic value.

Value-added tax. A tax imposed on each step in the production process. The measure of the tax is the difference between the cost of the item to the taxpayer and the price at which the item is transferred to the buyer. For example, you purchase raw materials for $100. After machine work and assembly, you sell the item for $150. The tax is levied on the $50.

Value date. In banking parlance, the date on which the funds become available to the depositor.

Vanishing point. The point at which premiums on a cash value life insurance policy will end. See *Vanishing premium*.

Vanishing premium. A provision in many cash value life insurance policies where the premium, after a certain point in time, will end with the policy remaining in force. That time is usually estimated based on the premium and the assumed rate of return.

Variable costs. Costs that change in direct proportion to the amount of product manufactured. For example, the cost of direct materials depends on the number of units produced. See *Fixed costs.*

Variance. In cost accounting, it's the difference between the actual cost and the standard cost of the cost components. In financial accounting, it's the difference between actual income and expenses and budgeted amounts, or between comparative statements (e.g., prior year to current year).

Vendor's lien. Collateral for a note or credit advanced by the seller of the property.

Vertical integration. The IRS definition is a relationship between two businesses where one supplies more than 50 percent of its property or services to another, or where one receives more than 50 percent of its property or services from the other.

Voidable. A transaction that can be annulled if one of the parties asserts a claim to do so.

Unsecured creditor. A creditor who does not have any security (collateral) for the debt he holds.

Waive. To voluntarily relinquish a right or privilege.

Waiver. In insurance terminology, a provision in the policy releasing the insurance company from liability to pay for specified losses that would normally be covered under the policy.

Waiver of mistake or informality. The act of disregarding errors or technical nonconformities in a bid that do not affect the substance of the bid and will not adversely affect the competition between bidders.

Waiver of premium provision. A provision available in many disability income and life insurance policies that allows the policy to stay in force without the payment of premiums if the insured has been disabled for a specific period of time (typically six months on life insurance policies).

Warehouse receipt. A document showing ownership of goods stored in a warehouse. The receipt can be used to transfer ownership of the goods without having to ship the actual goods to the buyer.

Wash sale. A tax term describing the sale of stock or securities and the purchase of identical securities within 30 days before or after the sale. For tax purposes, any losses on the transaction are disregarded.

Watered stock. Generally, stock that is overvalued because of accounting gimmicks or where unauthorized shares have been issued.

Waybill. Document prepared by a common carrier that provides the details of the route shipped goods are to follow.

White goods. A term used in retailing and economic measurement for large household appliances such as stoves, washers, dryers, refrigerators, etc.

Winding up. The processing of liquidating a company. Includes paying off creditors, selling and/or distributing assets to owners, etc.

Window dressing. Sprucing up a balance sheet, financial statement, etc. for a monthly, quarterly, or annual report. Examples include trying to collect receivables just before the end of a quarter; booking sales at the very end of the period; in the case of a mutual fund, selling less desirable or investments with losses and replacing them with higher-quality issues before the statement date.

Wire transfer. The transfer of money between two banks using a wire transfer system or the Federal Reserve's transfer system. Banks usually charge an extra fee for this service, but the transfer to your account is done faster, hence the funds wired from another party are available quicker than if you received the check and your bank waited for the funds to clear.

Withdrawal plan. In the case of mutual funds, a plan that allows shareholders to receive regular payments of income or capital gains.

Without prejudice. A legal term indicating that an action is made without any admission or waivers. For example, where a party offers to settle a legal dispute without admitting liability.

Without recourse. Where a creditor's only recourse in the case of default is to sell any pledged property. Also applies to the factoring of receivables, loans or notes, etc.

Work in process. Jobs currently being processed. Usually refers to manufactured goods where some work has been performed on the raw materials, but the goods are not yet ready for sale.

Workers' compensation benefits. Life and health insurance coverage for employees only while they are on the job. Medical expenses, disability income, dismemberment, and death benefits are provided under the policies.

Working capital. Amounts invested in cash, accounts receivable, inventory, and other current assets. Unless otherwise indicated, it refers to net working capital; that is, current assets less current liabilities.

Workweek. The normal number of days and hours employees are scheduled to work for a week. In economic statistics, a measure of the economy. The longer the workweek, the more employees in general are working–a reflection of whether employers are hiring new employees or just extending the hours of current employees.

Write off. To reduce the value of an asset on a company's books to the fair market value, or fair market value less the cost of disposal. For example, a computer purchased for $5,000 and depreciated down to $3,000 is now found to be worth no more than $500. You write off $2,500 to show the asset at the current market value. Also known as *write down*. This procedure is generally not allowed for tax accounting purposes.

Write up. Generally, the reverse of *write off*, above. Usually not allowed for accounting purposes.

Yearly renewable term. A term policy covering one year that is renewable each year without having to show insurability.

Yield equivalence. The interest rate at which a tax-exempt bond and a taxable one have the same after-tax return. The theory assumes that both bonds are of similar quality. To find the equivalent taxable yield of a tax-exempt bond, divide the tax-exempt yield by 1 minus your marginal tax rate.

Example—A tax-exempt bond is yielding 6 percent; your marginal tax rate is 31 percent. One minus .31 is .69. Divide that into .06; the result is .08695, or 8.7 percent. Thus, a 6 percent tax-exempt yield is equivalent to an 8.7 percent fully taxable yield.

Yield spread. The difference in yields among bonds of the same maturity that's caused by differences in the quality of the bonds.

Yield to call. Similar to *yield to maturity* but the call price and earlier call date are substituted for maturity date when calculating the yield. For example, Madison Inc. issues a bond for $1,000 at 10 percent. The bond matures 15 years later, but is callable at the end of 7 years at 105 ($1,050). The higher call price and the shorter term is used to compute the yield.

Zero balance account. A checking account designed to have a zero balance. The bank transfers enough funds from an interest bearing account each day to pay all checks presented to the bank for payment.

Zero-base budgeting. A technique where each budget starts from zero, rather than starting with the prior budget and increasing or decreasing it. Theoretically, under zero-base budgeting, every expense has to be justified. It should foster a closer look at all expenditures.

INDEX